Patterns
of Antislavery
among
American Unitarians,
1831–1860

Also by DOUGLAS STANGE

Radicalism for Humanity:
A Study of Lutheran Abolitionism

Patterns of Antislavery among American Unitarians, 1831–1860

Douglas C. Stange

Rutherford • Madison • Teaneck
Fairleigh Dickinson University Press
London: Associated University Presses

© 1977 by Associated University Presses, Inc.
Associated University Presses, Inc.
Cranbury, New Jersey 08512

Associated University Presses
Magdalen House
136-148 Tooley Street
London SE1 2TT, England

Library of Congress Cataloging in Publication Data

Stange, Douglas C
    Patterns of antislavery among American Unitarians, 1831-1860.

    A revision of the author's thesis, Harvard University.
    Bibliography: p.
    Includes index.
    1. Slavery in the United States—Anti-slavery movements. 2. Slavery and the church—Unitarian churches. 3. Abolitionists—United States. I. Title.
E449.S898   261.8'34'4930973   75-18245
ISBN 0-8386-1797-2

PRINTED IN THE UNITED STATES OF AMERICA

For
Jutta Eva Blaesing Stange
helpmate in love and freedom

Contents

Prologue

This is the story of the Unitarian denomination and the antislavery crisis, spanning the years 1831 to 1860. Within the chronological history of the story, an attempt has been made to stress a typological approach. With a primary focus on antislavery, the Unitarian advocates of that reform movement are characterized. This study concentrates on the activity of individual Unitarian ministers and laymen as antislavery reformers.

This book is a more comprehensive and deeper study of the denomination's role in the antislavery crisis than previous material has provided. It attempts to include the ideas and contributions of Unitarian laymen as well as ministers and, perhaps more important, of Unitarian laywomen, for the contributions of women as opponents of slavery often exceeded those of men. Information on black Unitarians prior to 1860 is provided wherever historical materials have made possible its inclusion.

In Part I an introductory chapter outlines the general history of the patterns and achievement of the antislavery movement in the United States, thereby serving as a chronological foundation for the remaining chapters. Under the heading *Patterns and People Defined*, the next three chapters delineate a typology of antislavery, namely, Antislavery as Religion (as it was to the radicals, the Garrisonian abolitionists), Antislavery as Philosophy (as it was to some moderates), and Antislavery as Politics (as it was to other moderates, usually called *political abolitionists*). In Part II chapters 5 and 6, under the heading *Patterns Merge,* show how gradually the different antislavery types become less and less clearly defined. In Part III chapter 7, under the heading *Patterns Framed,* tells the story of the fierce struggle by antislavery reformers to move the Unitarian body toward denominational antislavery activity.

Three conclusions may be drawn from this story. First, there was a general lack of enthusiasm for the emancipation of American slaves on the part of the denomination as a body—enthusiasm that one would properly expect from a church that held central the theological affirmation of the brotherhood of man, that throve in the geographical center of reform activity, and the leadership of which possessed an educational and cultural attainment of the highest level. Second, as a result of the antislavery crisis the Unitarian denomination experienced the stresses and strains similar to those of other denominations, and for all practical purposes underwent a fragmentation that was less evident than that of other denominations only because of the loose congregational polity of the Unitarians. Third, the dedication and persistence of a small group of individual reformers succeeded in wearing away the opposition of their denomination toward political preaching and toward participation in antislavery reform. That they needed a generation in time to bring this about should be the lament not only of Unitarians, but of all Christians.

Acknowledgments

This study began as a doctoral dissertation at Harvard University under the tutelage of Dr. Conrad Wright. All errors in opinion and interpretation are entirely my own. Indubitably they were corrected at one point or another by Dr. Wright, but like the radical Garrisonians, my own insistence on infallibity persisted to the end. That a son of Luther could happily complete under a son of Channing a critical study of the Unitarians points to the determination of the former and the liberality of the latter. It also acknowledges Dr. Wright's accomplished role as mentor rather than master.

Three magnificent women helped to see this study completed. For their sagacious criticism, professional assistance, and gentle prodding, I thank Dr. Maria Grossmann, Head of Collection Development, the Harvard College Library; Elisabeth Jupp, historian and teacher in Middlesex, England; and Lenore Dickinson, Head Librarian of the Arnold Arboretum and of the Library of the Harvard University Herbarium.

Many librarians patiently and diligently helped to secure materials for me, and their contribution is gratefully acknowledged. They are the guardians and purveyors of a researcher's treasures and their work is greatly appreciated. I acknowledge the friendly, efficient, and sometimes long-suffering assistance of the following— apologizing warmly for any names inadvertently ommitted: Peter Oliver, Charles Woodbury, and Alan Seaburg of the Harvard Divinity School Library; Carolyn Jakeman and Rodney G. Dennis of the Houghton Library, Harvard University; Harley P. Holden and the late Clifford K. Shipton of the Harvard University Archives; Patricia Miller King of the Schlesinger Library on the History of Women, Radcliffe College; H. L. Short and Anne K. Swift of the Manchester College Library, Oxford; Kenneth Twinn of Dr. Williams's Library, London; Stephen T. Riley of the Massachusetts Historical Society; Dorothy M. Potter of the James Duncan Phillips Library of the Essex Institute; William A. Deiss of the Olin Library, Washington University; Mary B. Prior of the South Carolina Historical Society; Howard H. Peckman of the William L. Clements Library, University of Michigan; and James Lawton and his staff at the Boston Public Library. I also thank librarians Sheila Hart, Neil R. Jordahl, Christine D. Hathaway, Lee Major, Frances Forman, Jean T. Reed, Roy P. Basler, E. L. Inabinett, Sara S. Fuller, Joseph G. Gambone, Philip T. Mooney, Carolyn A. Davis, Carolyn A. Wallace, Dorothy Harris, B. B. Lacy, Ann Hyde, M. Stone Miller, Jr., Margaret Anne Fisher, William Joyce, Robert L. Volz, Nathaniel N. Shipton, Sybil M. Fielder, Eleanor L. Nicholes, and Joan N. Harris.

In addition to Dr. Wright, three other scholars gave of their precious time and kind criticism: Professors Frank Friedel and William Hutchison of Harvard University and Professor Sydney Ahlstrom of Yale University. For offprints, suggestions, letters of advice and encouragement, I thank George H. Gibson, Charles Richard Denton, Elizabeth M. Geffen, Jean Holloway, William H. Pease, Harold Schwartz, Abe C. Ravitz, and the late Richard H. Shryock.

I am also indebted to Edwin F. Williams, editor of the *Harvard Library Bulletin,* for permission to reproduce part of the material dealing with the Follens that appeared in my article in January 1976 entitled, "The Making of an Abolitionist Martyr: Harvard Professor Charles Theodore Christian Follen (1796–1840)."

No person, of course, provided as much help, encouragement, patience, love, and understanding, as did my beloved wife, Jutta.

Patterns
of Antislavery
among
American Unitarians,
1831–1860

PART I

The Patterns and People Defined

1

The Patterns and Achievement of the Antislavery Movement in the United States—1820-1865

A. PROLEGOMENA

THE abolition, the removal, the complete destruction of a significant aspect of society, as in the case of the institution of slavery in the United States, can rarely be accomplished without shaking the foundations of institutions and greatly altering individual lives. Before the abolition of slavery had been achieved, American society divided into factions, and during the long antislavery controversy the beliefs of these conflicting factions sometimes changed, coincided, or sometimes became fixed. It was the most bitter controversy of its time and the final pattern of attitudes only slowly became definite. The leading attitudes in the antislavery drive that had extremely

important representatives within American Unitarianism
may be usefully categorized as follows:

1) Antislavery as Religion (as it was to the radicals, the
   Garrisonian abolitionists).
2) Antislavery as Philosophy (as it was to some moderates).
3) Antislavery as Politics (as it was to other moderates,
   usually called "political abolitionists").

These leading attitudes will be elaborated as they appear
chronologically in the narrative of this first chapter.

The drive to achieve an end to slavery in America would
sooner or later have to confront the Constitution of the
United States. For it was in the compromises of the
Constitution that slavery became subtly but clearly imbed-
ded in the laws of the nation. The issue of slavery had not
been the paramount question at the constitutional convention, but through the discussion and bargaining that took
place, the advocates of slavery gained in three clauses
recognition of their "peculiar institution": 1) Representatives and direct taxes were to be apportioned according to
the number of free persons in each state and "three-fifths of
all other Persons"—i.e., slaves; 2) the prohibition of the
"migration or importation of such Persons as any of the
States now existing shall think proper to admit"—i.e., the
slave trade—shall not be prohibited by Congress prior to
1808; 3) "No Person held to Service or Labour in one State
. . . escaping to another"—i.e., a fugitive slave—could be
freed in that state, but must be returned. Without using the
words *slave* or *slavery*, the institution was nevertheless
referred to three times.[1]

With these constitutional provisions in the background
no sparks would fly as long as each state acted on its own.
The revolutionary generation, true believers in the liberty
they had just obtained from England, influenced by the
Enlightenment and Locke, prodded by Quakers and the

small emancipation societies of Benjamin Franklin, John Jay, Alexander Hamilton, and others, saw to the emancipation of Negro slaves in Vermont (1777), Massachusetts (including Maine, 1780), and New Hampshire (1784), with gradual abolition begun by Pennsylvania (1780), Rhode Island and Connecticut (1784), New York (1799), and New Jersey (1804). The Northwest Ordinance of 1787 abolished slavery in the area from which were carved Ohio, Indiana, Illinois, Michigan, Wisconsin, and part of Minnesota.[2]

In New England antislavery fervor blazed like a fire, burned less brightly in the middle states, and flickered out in reaching the Mason and Dixon Line and the Ohio River. Maryland's legislature received memorials to abolish slavery in the state in 1826, 1827, and 1829 with no result. Tennessee citizens in 1821 unsuccessfully petitioned the legislation for gradual emancipation. A bill to emancipate all the slaves in Kentucky was introduced in the state's House of Representatives, but shelved after its first reading by a vote of 18 to 11.[3] The well-known Virginia debates over emancipation took place in December 1831, urging legislation that would emancipate and colonize the state's slaves. The antislavery forces at first appeared to make progress, but in the end a conservative reaction snuffed out any hope of success.[4] Emancipation was not seriously considered by any other southern state.[5]

The advocates of emancipation in the Virginia legislature were committed to a colonization program that would get rid of freed Negroes altogether. They shuddered at the idea of having a large free black population in the state.[6] Their abhorrence was shared by most Northerners, who, like their Southern brethren, believed that the African race was inferior and could not be integrated politically and socially into the superior white civilization. Negro disfranchisement, separate schools, living areas, hospitals, prisons, cemeteries, and Negro pews were prevalent throughout the North, even in Massachusetts, "the cradle of Liberty."[7] But the program for colonization received impetus from Virginia's desire to have neither an integrated nor segregated society, but an exclusively white society. In 1816 the Virginia legislature petitioned the governor to persuade the President of the United States to acquire a territory in Africa, or elsewhere outside the boundaries of the United States, to which freed Negroes might be sent. A short time later several prominent Southerners met in Washington, D.C., to discuss the matter. They founded, in 1817, the American Society for Colonizing the Free People of Color of the United States, or, as it was popularly known, the American Colonization Society.

Judge Bushrod Washington, a slaveholder and nephew of George Washington, became the Society's first president. Henry Clay, John Randolph of Roanoke, Thomas Jefferson, James Madison, and John Marshall gave it their blessing. Congress gave it $100,000. The auxiliaries of the Society spread to every state except South Carolina. Its colonies did not grow fast. The first settlement of eighty-eight colonists at Sherbo Island failed dismally in 1820, but the Society persevered and in 1822 founded Liberia. In the following decade, a mere 796 emigrants were sent there, and even by 1865 only twelve thousand colonists had been settled.[8]

The ideal of the Society was, of course, to remove Negroes from the prejudice and oppression existing in the United States to a hypothetical freedom, equality, and opportunity in Western Africa; to provide the way for the Southern slaveholders to free their slaves (since so many states required deportation from the state or the country to follow any acts of emancipation); to provide Africa with Christian pilgrims to civilize and evangelize the continent; and to make a first step toward the ultimate aim of ending the African slave trade. In actuality, the Society presented its program in the South as a safeguard for slavery through the removal of a potentially dangerous element, the free Negroes—all possible conspirators and insurrectionists. Slavery would thereby be more secure and stable.[9]

B. RELIGIOUS ANTISLAVERY

In the 1830s there was a great exodus of supporters from the Society. This was primarily a result of the massive attack upon the Society by the young firebrand William Lloyd Garrison, in 1832, in his *Thoughts on African Colonization*. He had shocked Boston the previous year with the appearance of his newspaper the *Liberator*, which proclaimed a "harsh as truth" editorial policy and began with an arrogant, perhaps messianic, salvo: "I WILL BE HEARD!"[10] The *Liberator* advocated immediate abolition and improvement of the condition of free Negroes. The great success of the movement for immediate abolition in Great Britain, where at that time it had strong evangelical support, convinced Garrison that a similar movement could succeed in the United States. His message earned him Negro support— 400 of the *Liberator's* first 450 subscribers were Negroes— and Garrison later proudly considered it their paper.[11] But the message and the intense and colorful language in which it was expressed brought him the hatred of both Southern and Northern conservatives. When the Nat Turner insurrection occurred in Virginia in August 1831, Southerners, without any evidence, immediately blamed the *Liberator*. They banned it in many parts of the South and the Georgia Legislature placed a price on Garrison's head. Garrison tried to insure the continued publication of the *Liberator* and to form an organization to procure immediate abolition by helping to found the New England Antislavery Society. In the constitution of the Society, Garrison and his fellow apostles extolled "immediate freedom" and sought to "improve the character and condition of the free people of color . . . and obtain for them equal civil and political rights and privileges with whites." To further these aims the Philadelphia blacks and other members of the Negro community convinced Garrison of the need to denounce the colonization program. He had himself abandoned his early naive support of colonization (as several other abolitionists did later), and now in the face of the endorsement of colonization by influential ministers and men of "wealth and elevated station," Garrison revealed his *Thoughts*.[12]

"The colonization scheme [is] inadequate in its design, injurious in its operation, and contrary to sound principle," wrote Garrison. He declared his "conviction of its sinfulness." He made his case by exhibiting the Society's own statements, giving extensive evidence from the *African Repository*, annual reports, and other publications of the American Colonization Society and its auxiliaries. Furthermore, he made a damning catalogue of the Society's beliefs: 1) The Society is pledged not to oppose the slave system, 2) apologizes for slavery and slaveholders, 3) recognizes slaves as property, 4) strengthens and secures the slave system and increases the value of slaves, 5) is enemy of immediate abolition, 6) is nourished by fear and selfishness, 7) seeks the utter expulsion of the blacks, 8) disparages the free blacks, 9) prevents the elevation of the American Negro, and finally, 10) deceives and misleads the nation.[13] Although Garrison in pressing his case twisted the testimony of some witnesses and hacked and truncated the evidence of others, his presentation still can rightly be praised as a "major contribution to the theory of racial democracy." No effective rebuttal came from the defense.[14] The verdict was quickly returned: Guilty. An antislavery advocate who continued to defend the Society became a "rarity."[15]

If Garrison had succeeded in "reducing colonization to irrelevance,"[16] he offered antislavery advocates the substitute of a program of immediate abolitionism; if he helped weaken the American Colonization Society irremediably, he desired the formation of a national antislavery society to take its place.[17] Garrison rapidly achieved these goals. His *Thoughts* influenced several antislavery leaders: Elizur Wright, Jr., and Beriah Green on the Western Reserve; the Evangelical merchant millionaires of New York City, Arthur and Lewis Tappan (Arthur purchased 100 copies of *Thoughts*); and Theodore Weld and the students at Lane Theological Seminary in Cincinnati. In April 1833 Negroes raised almost $400 to send Garrison to England, to solicit funds there for a Negro manual labor school. Garrison, however, used the opportunity to smear colonization and to inflate his own image as *the* American abolitionist. At the time of his visit the English Parliament was enacting an emancipation plan for the British West Indies. Capitalizing on this auspicious coincidence, Garrison debunked the American Colonization Society and its chief fund-raiser in England, Elliot Cresson, and garnered praise for himself. As for soliciting money, Garrison failed miserably and had to borrow $200 for his passage home from a Negro Baptist minister, Nathaniel Paul.[18]

Garrison returned on the crest of the wave of excitement over the good news of the English emancipation act. Arthur Tappan was just breaking his last ties with the American Colonization Society and had begun publishing the *Emancipator*. In October Tappan and his colleagues founded the New York Antislavery Society.[19] They considered it practical to narrow their platform to "immediate emancipation which is gradually accomplished."[20] Garrison did not want to lose the momentum gained by the British West Indies emancipation act and pressed hard for a national organization dedicated to immediatism. Finally, at a hurried gathering in Philadelphia in December 1833, delegates from eleven states founded the American Antislavery Society. They elected Arthur Tappan as President and Garrison to

lead a committee to draft their "Declaration of Sentiments."
This "Magna Charta of the anti-slavery movement" was
entirely from Garrison's pen; it declared that, without
compensation to the slaveholder, the "slave ought to be
instantly set free."[21]

The impression made by the Declaration upon those
present was recorded by a Unitarian minister, Samuel J.
May: "there was a profound silence for several minutes.
There was but one thought with us all. . . . We felt that the
word had just been uttered which would be mighty,
through God, to pulling down the strongholds of slavery."[22] The convention stirred May, as if he had experienced Pentecost itself. In Garrisonian abolitionists like May
the religious overtones of part of the antislavery movement
are clearly seen. Contemporary descriptions reveal many
parallels to spiritual and ecclesiastical elements of Christianity; emotional fervor, communal support, biblical ter-
minology, the doctrine of nonresistance (nonviolence), a
catechetical approach to the young, preaching and prayers,
hymnology, remembrance of holy days and saints, gory
scenes of confessors and martyrs, and millennial hopes.
May's impressions of the convention as a "praying assembly"[23] lends credence to this observation. Of the three
regional strains of abolitionism, Western (led by Theodore
Weld, James G. Birney, Beriah Green, Elizur Wright, Jr.);
New York (the Tappans, Gerrit Smith, Joshua Leavitt); and
New England (Garrison, May, Oliver Johnson, Wendell
Phillips), the last named developed the most sectarian
religious abolitionism, with a compulsory fidelity to the
prophet, Garrison, and a confessional commitment to his
particular antislavery dogma. The Garrisonian brotherhood (and later sisterhood!), based as it was in Boston, the
Rome of the Unitarians, engendered a good deal of
support from individual Unitarians, but indifference, if not
opposition, from their official agencies and publications.

Religious antislavery as represented by the Garrisonian radicals was one pattern in the antislavery movement; it demonstrated a commitment to heart, religion, and agitation, rather than to intellect, philosophy, or pragmatism. The Garrisonians were radicals, agitators all, espousing a Christian anarchism, from whose ranks sprang up saints and martyrs.

One of the early martyrs in the Garrisonian hagiography was Prudence Crandall. This Quaker school teacher in Canterbury, Connecticut, had the opportunity to admit to her popular and successful girls' school, a "young [Negro] lady of pleasing appearance and manner." Impressed by the *Liberator's* encouragement of Negro advancement, she accepted the girl. Ignoring rising criticism from the town, she decided to open her school to "any qualified young lady of color." Canterbury was in an uproar. Andrew T. Judson, a local lawyer and an avowed colonizationist, led the opposition to her establishing a "nigger" school *anywhere* in Connecticut. It was a war between colonizationists and Garrisonian abolitionists. Town officials publicized their case in a letter to the American Colonization Society. They declared that the school threatened property values, that the Canterbury blacks (about ten to fifteen citizens) would claim equality with whites, and that such schools as Miss Crandall's would promote emigration of Negroes to New England and make the region the Liberia of America. On her side, Prudence Crandall had the continued counsel of Samuel J. May, publicity in the *Liberator,* and money from non-Garrisonian, Arthur Tappan. When Connecticut pushed through a "Black Law" in May 1833, Miss Crandall's school became illegal. She continued to teach and was arrested. She was imprisoned in a cell previously inhabited by a convicted murderer, and was brought to trial. The outcome of the trial was inconclusive and she returned to her school. The town treated her and her pupils with sadistic cruelty, poisoning their well with excrement, refusing them food and everyday services, and finally setting Miss Crandall's home on fire. She had recently married the Reverend Calvin Philleo, and on his insistence, she closed her school on September 10, 1834, and departed for Illinois.[24]

Harriet Martineau later called this period of antislavery activity the "Martyr Age." Garrison saw it as a "reign of terror."[25] Either title describes truly, if a bit hyperbolically, the era of violence and antislavery agitation in American history. The first phase of this terror included the swift spread of antislavery societies and ideas, and the unwavering opposition to them. The destruction of Prudence Crandall's school (1834); the mobbing of Garrison in Boston and the anti-abolitionist riots in Utica, New York, and Montpelier, Vermont (1835); the murder of Lovejoy (1837); and the burning of the Pennsylvania Hall (1838) were all a part of the first phase. The second phase included the rapid extension of the slave power into America's Western territories and, under the authority of the Fugitive Slave Law, into her Northern cities. The riots over the Jerry Rescue in Syracuse (1851); the rendition of Thomas Sims (1851) and Anthony Burns (1854); the bloody scenes on the Kansas prairie (1854–1856); the beating of Charles Sumner (1856); and the culminating martyrdom of John Brown (1859) were all a part of the second phase.

The mobbing of Garrison occurred on October 21, 1835. The anti-abolitionists had actually been after George Thompson, a well-known British abolitionist who had been encouraged by Garrison to lecture in America. Thompson was to appear before the Boston Female Antislavery Society, a group led by one of Garrison's most dedicated lieutenants, Maria Weston Chapman. Thompson never showed up, but a crowd of "men of property and standing" did appear. Garrison quietly informed them that the meeting was for ladies and said: "If *gentlemen*, any of you are *ladies*—in disguise—why apprise me of the fact, give me your names, and I will introduce you to the rest of your sex, and you can take seats among them accordingly." The mob, at first taken aback, became enraged and forced the ladies to adjourn their meeting to Mrs. Chapman's home; then they turned on Garrison. They dragged him onto State Street over the very ground, as Garrison proudly wrote, that had been "stained with the blood of the first martyr in the cause of LIBERTY and INDEPENDENCE, by the memorable massacre of 1770." Garrison, his clothes torn from his back and a rope about his neck, was spared from massacre by the arrival of the sheriff. For his own protection he was incarcerated.[26] Garrison was ecstatic: "It was indeed a blessed privilege to suffer in the cause of Christ."[27]

Some of the Boston "aristocrats and businessmen" had followed Mrs. Chapman and the twenty-five women of the Boston Female Antislavery Society to her house. While the men stood outside hooting and hollering, the ladies carried on their antislavery business inside. The following day, the Boston newspapers condemned the women for holding their meeting and thus provoking a riot![28]

The "blessed privilege" that Garrison enjoyed came also to Samuel J. May, not once or twice, but five times. May met determined opposition to his antislavery lecture tour through Vermont in October 1835. On October 21, the day the Boston mob attacked Garrison, some of the foremost citizens of Montpelier interrupted and finally halted May's address against slavery. And on the same day a mob in Utica, New York, shouted abuse and threatened lives at an antislavery meeting.[29]

Clashes like these were perhaps bound in the end to cost life, and two days later, Elijah P. Lovejoy's blood was spilled upon the altar of abolitionism. Educated at Colby College and Princeton Theological Seminary, Lovejoy then went out to Missouri to fight pro-slavery and the Roman Catholic Church. He worked as a school teacher and minister before becoming the editor of a Presbyterian newspaper, the *St. Louis Observer*. The cutting edge of Lovejoy's antislavery attack was tempered in a fire that burned alive a slave by the name of McIntosh. A Missouri lynch mob had barbariously executed the black right in the center of St. Louis for knifing a white police officer. After that, Lovejoy devoted ample space in his paper to the campaign against slavery. Pro-slavery vigilantes destroyed his press and threw him out of Missouri. Undaunted, he went to Alton, Illinois, and began publishing the *Alton Observer*. There he had another press destroyed by supporters of slavery and its replacement thrown into the Mississippi River. He tried to protect his fourth press with a rifle in his hands, and was cut down by an armed mob. Although Lovejoy disturbed exceedingly the sensibilities of many non-resistant antislavery workers, including Garrison, the 7th of November, 1837, became an abolitionist saint's day.[30]

Back East, the following spring, a mob smashed into Pennsylvania Hall, Philadelphia, and put it to the torch. It had cost $40,000 and been dedicated by antislavery workers to freedom of speech just two days before. The mayor, chief of police, and fire department of the City of Brotherly Love stood by and watched it burn to the ground.[31]

All these tragic events had a very positive impact upon the abolitionist movement. Many a timid reformer sitting on the fence of indecision fell off on the side of the abolitionists when he observed the trampling of basic liberties. Watching the mob attack Garrison made Dr. Nathaniel Ingersoll Bowditch an abolitionist; the Utica riot made Gerrit Smith, the New York philanthropist, join the cause of abolition; and the Alton tragedy drove Wendell Phillips and Edmund Quincy, two leading Bostonians, into the ranks of the abolitionist leadership.

C. PHILOSOPHICAL ANTISLAVERY

In addition to the wider attacks upon radical abolitionists, there were attempts in the Boston area to contest the hegemony of Garrison. One group of men who wanted to moderate Garrisonian radicalism formed the Cambridge Antislavery Society. Its membership was almost wholly Unitarian. It contained scholars and professors like Henry Ware, Charles Follen, Frederic Henry Hedge, and Henry Ware, Jr., men who, like the Garrisonians, wanted slavery to end, but who disagreed with the radicals' language, methods, and heated enthusiasm. The Society died in infancy with Follen going over to the Garrisonians.[32]

The distinct problem for some diffident reformers lay in their reluctance, and frequently in their categorical refusal, to enter into any kind of association. Several Unitarian educators and ministers, for example, William Ellery Channing, can be so described. They held a type of philosophical abolitionism that dealt with slavery in abstract terms, worshiped individualism, ignored emotional appeals, inculcated moderation, deplored unnecessarily disturbing the social order, favored a gradual emancipation scheme usually with compensation, were somewhat naive politically, and displayed a prejudiced paternalism toward black people. They simply did not see the problem of slavery as a paramount issue demanding their committed attention. The radical abolitionist found this ivory tower of individualism impregnable, and reacted against the intellectuals with frustration and acrimony. Garrison reserved for these advocates of philosophical antislavery verbal poison only slightly less potent than that he offered to slaveholders. "Especially towards Channing," remarked Albert Bushnell Hart, Garrison "felt all the bitterness of a radical against a liberal," and labeled Channing's essays on slavery "moral plagiarisms from the writings of the abolitionists."[33] The radical abolitionists never were able to welcome a philosopher to their company.

D. RELIGIOUS ANTISLAVERY BUFFETED: FAILURE AND SCHISM AMONG THE FAITHFUL

The radical abolitionists also failed with the churches. Here their failure angered and disheartened them. Preaching in favor of the holiest of causes, they envisaged a bountiful harvest of ecclesiastical recruits and assistance. Instead their admonitions seldom took root and were often thrown back into their faces. When Garrison gradually moved away from his rigidly orthodox Baptist position to a liberalism compatible with Samuel J. May's, the orthodox Protestants called him *infidel* and his movement *infidelism*— terms as incriminatory in that age of piety as *communist* and *communism* have been in ours.[34] The radical abolitionists rolled back such waves of abuse with their typical vitriol: Garrison called the Methodist Church a "cage of unclean birds and a synagogue of Satan,"   Congregational ministers, "implacable foes of God and man."[35] Stephen S. Foster fancied the inactivity of the church on antislavery as the "sorcery of a designing priesthood."[36]

In 1837 a few clerics, disgruntled over the conduct of the American Antislavery Society and especially the role played by Garrison and his coadjutors, issued *The Appeal of Clerical Abolitionists on Antislavery Measures*. The document disparaged Garrisonian methods and struck out against his employment of women as antislavery lecturers. This referred to Angelina and Sarah Grimké, two Quaker abolitionists from South Carolina, who were speaking extensively in behalf of the Society. Their clerical criticism fell on the involvement of women in all areas of the Society's work: antislavery fairs, petitions, tracts, and newspapers.

Garrison rebutted the *Appeal* with his characteristic gusto, chastising American clergymen as "blind leaders of the blind, dumb dogs that cannot bark, spiritual popes—that . . . love the fleece better than the flock."[37]

A schism in the American Antislavery Society was imminent. Away from Boston other antislavery reformers fretted over the woman question as one problem among many. The Tappans in New York wished to see a more evangelical orientation to antislavery programs, and felt convinced that Garrison's periodic skirmishes with various churches and clergymen precluded such hopes. Gerrit Smith, Henry Stanton, Elizur Wright, and Joshua Leavitt desired political action and deduced from Garrison's "No-Government" or nonvoting theory that little assistance would be forthcoming for this. The rupture took place at the annual convention of the American Antislavery Society in 1840.

Francis Jackson, a Garrisonian, presided over the assembly of a thousand delegates. He immediately appointed the fiery radical Abby Kelley to the business committee. Despite an uproar of protests, the assembly voted for her acceptance. The Tappans and other anti-feminists left the hall. The election of a woman to the committee, one of their number declared, "is throwing a firebrand into the anti-slavery ranks . . . [and] is contrary to the usages of civilized society."[38] "Firebrand" was an appropriate metaphor for Miss Kelley, but her excellent antislavery work earned her an office in the Society, "male chauvinist" objections notwithstanding. Following the departure of three other protesting men from the executive committee, Lucretia Mott, Lydia Maria Child, and Maria Weston Chapman took their places with the approval of the assembly. The delegates condemned political action and returned home.

Meanwhile the secessionists met to form the American and Foreign Anti-Slavery Society. They elected Arthur Tappan as president, made the *Emancipator* their official journal, denied any voting rights in their Society to women, and avoided the formation of a national antislavery third party.[39]

E. POLITICAL ANTISLAVERY

The flood of interest by many who were involved in the antislavery movement in political action could not be held back by Garrisonian theories nor by objections from the new American and Foreign Anti-Slavery Society. Myron Holley, Gerrit Smith, Joshua Leavitt, Elizur Wright, William Goodell, and the poet John Greenleaf Whittier began to weigh the possible political bargaining power the antislavery crusade could now provide. Since slavery had been recognized by law, they reasoned, it could be overcome by law. Moreover, blacks believed fruitful prospects might be obtained through political action. Only a few Negroes accepted Garrisonian ideas on nonvoting and political inaction. In April 1840 delegates met in Albany, New York, as the "National Convention of Friends of Immediate Emancipation" and held the first convention of the Human Rights Party or Liberty Party. They selected as their candidates James G. Birney for president and Thomas Earle for vice-president.[40]

Birney received only 7,100 votes, hardly enough to elect him president. But this fledgling Liberty Party gave the campaign for emancipation new life. Dwight Lowell Dumond in his typical exuberance for political antislavery called the party's birth the "most important event" since the formation of the American Antislavery Society.[41] In some ways it was. The Liberty Party and its successors, the Free Soil Party (1848) and the Republican Party (1854), provided a new forum for discussion, a new means of action. The antislavery drive had a new way to influence political directions, to change candidates, to amend the law and to make new laws. The old way of transforming the minds of

individuals, the spirits of institutions, through moral reformation would remain the same narrow, but less traveled
route of the Garrisonians. Reformers were being weaned
away from the American Antislavery Society and its ad-
vocacy of moral action.[42] "Steps [were being] taken by
the abolitionists," writes Louis Filler, "to secularize their
cause." Such steps not only made Garrison fume and rave,
but made philosophical antislavery advocate William Ellery
Channing complain as well: "I cannot but regret the
disposition of a part of the abolitionists to organize themselves into a political party."[43]

Yet political antislavery did not mean the *total* eclipse of
moral agitation. In order to secure the election of antislavery candidates and the passage of antislavery legislation,
the climate of opinion regarding antislavery in America still
needed to be improved. And for this the work of the
Garrisonian radicals was still needed.

In the election of 1844 Birney received 67,000 votes and
enough votes in New York to give the presidency to
Democrat James K. Polk. Antislavery voters had demonstrated some political muscle and their primary demands could no longer be easily ignored. Enough political
pressure existed in 1844 to end the Gag Rule (a rule that
had effectively tabled antislavery debate in the House for
eight years), to attempt to thwart the annexation of Texas in
1845 (though unhappily the election of the expansionist
Polk brought Texas into the Union), and to debate although not halt the Mexican War, 1846–1848.[44]

To increase their political clout the backers of political
antislavery were forced to widen their platform from the
single issue of abolition to a multiplicity of political goals.
The sharing of equal billing with nonextensionists, that is,
men espousing only a free soil position, caused a split in
Liberty Party ranks. Most members joined the Free Soil
Party formed in 1848 as a coalition of Liberty Party men,
New York Reform Democrats, and Antislavery Whigs. The

Free Soil platform was a slippery one for any steadfast advocate of antislavery, for it insisted on no interference with slavery already in existence. A disturbed backer, Frederick Douglass, felt obliged to warn the Free Soilers' convention in 1852 that the destruction of slavery, not just its containment, was *the* goal of the antislavery movement.[45] Not only had the antislavery movement been secularized by political action, but it had been corrupted as well.

Garrison had warned that political involvement with its attendant compromises would bring dilution, perhaps even dissolution, of the antislavery drive. In discussion of the patterns of antislavery the "political abolitionists" are usually thought of as the third-party men of the 1840s. However, the definition of a political abolitionist should include—and Garrison would undoubtedly agree here— those free souls who belonged to no antislavery society and yet were still fiercely abolitionist, men, for example, like Theodore Parker, who saw in power in politics the way to destroy slavery. Furthermore, the category should be stretched to include Antislavery Whigs like John Gorham Palfrey. The political abolitionist trusted in the pragmatic view of change through political development, believed in letting Yankee ingenuity find a political program that would work. He was open to compromise, open in some cases even to violence (here he could appeal to the American revolutionary political tradition). The political abolitionist was anathema to Garrison's idea of non-government and nonresistance.

F. NONVIOLENCE, NONGOVERNMENT, NONUNION

Garrison's testimony to nongovernment began in 1835 with his refusal to vote. Immediately preceding the foundation of the Liberty Party he undertook to sharpen his nongovernment theories, especially as they related to the United States Constitution. As the "chief apostle of radical non-resistance," Garrison's views forbade the use of violence even for righteous ends. Samuel J. May; Lydia Maria Child and her husband, David Lee Child; Abby Kelley; and Mrs. Chapman subscribed to Garrison's nonresistant position. From that position they logically advanced to the level of nongovernment and Christian anarchism. The debate along the way on whether the Constitution was a proslavery or antislavery document became intense; William I. Bowditch, Wendell Phillips, and Garrison argued its proslavery nature, while political abolitionists Frederick Douglass, William Goodell, and others maintained the opposite view.[46] The Garrisonian antislavery organizations would subject their anarchism to their own ballot box.

At the tenth anniversary of the American Antislavery Society, May 7, 1844, the meeting adopted a declaration of independence from Garrison's pen: Resolved,

> that the existing national compact should be instantly dissolved; that secession from the government is a religious and political duty; that the motto inscribed on the banner of Freedom should be, NO UNION WITH SLAVEHOLDERS; . . . and that revolutionary ground should be occupied by all those who abhor the thought of doing evil that good may come, and who do not mean to compromise the principles of Justice and Humanity.

The statement concluded with the honest and humble admission: "Ours is no anarchical movement but one of order and obedience."[47]

Three weeks later the motto "NO UNION WITH SLAVEHOLDERS" won by a vote of 250–24 at the annual meeting of the Massachusetts Antislavery Society. The majority present declared "it a first duty for [abolitionists] to agitate for the dissolution of the Union." A moral and nonviolent revolution had begun to secure the overthrow of the United States Constitution.[48]

G. *E PLURIBUS UNUM:* ANTISLAVERY UNITY AND TRIUMPH

When Southern slave-catchers entered Northern streets in pursuit of fugitive slaves, even citizens indifferent to antislavery reform became alarmed. Under the Fugitive Slave Act of 1850 the slave states became more aggressive in their attempts to reclaim "southern property." Each year during this period approximately one thousand fugitive slaves were reported missing by the South and legal procedures of the Act encouraged slavery to recapture its victims. Denied both a jury trial or court hearing in order to prove his freedom, any free Negro was open to possible seizure as a slave. A flush of fear crossed over the black community in the North. Within three days after the bill became law, forty ex-slaves left Boston for Canada. Several Negro churches dwindled in membership with the exodus of whole families. Some towns lost almost half their Negro population to Canada as a result of the law.[49] The second phase of the "Martyr Age" had begun.

The Fugitive Slave Bill was a part of the compromise package wrapped up by Henry Clay and carried through Congress under the leadership of both Clay and Daniel Webster. In a speech on the 7th of March, 1850, Webster vigorously urged compliance with the Fugitive Slave Bill—a piece of legislation, lamented Samuel J. May, the "baseness, meanness, cruelty of which, no epithet in my vocabulary can adequately express." George Ticknor, Jared Sparks, Samuel A. Eliot, and some eight hundred other Boston conservatives sent Webster a thank-you note for his speech and praised his effectiveness in calling again to their attention their duties under the Constitution. From the antislavery side, young Senator William Seward of New York, in a speech on March 11, denounced the compromise measures and extolled the concept of a "higher law" than the Constitution. In September 1850 President Fillmore signed the bill into law.[50]

The whole North seethed with excitement, especially Boston. In October 1850 slave-catchers arrived in the city in search of fugitive slave couple William and Ellen Craft. The Crafts, well-known to abolitionists for their spectacular flight to freedom, were quickly aided by Theodore Parker and the newly formed Vigilance Committee. The abolitionists secured their passage to England and to safety. Again in February 1851 slave-hunters circulated in Boston and seized Frederic Williams, or "Shadrach" as he was popularly known. They took him to the Boston courthouse to process his rendition, but traveled no further. Twenty Negroes rushed into the courthouse and spirited "Shadrach" away to freedom. President Fillmore called for an end to such forcible opposition to the Fugitive Slave Law and Webster condemned Shadrach's rescue as treason.[51]

The next attempt at slave-hunting in Boston succeeded. In April 1851 Thomas Sims, a fugitive from Georgia, was carried back to the state and publicly whipped as an example to other slaves contemplating flight.[52]

In Syracuse, New York, abolitionists prevented the return to slavery of Jerry McHenry. Samuel J. May and Gerrit Smith assisted in the rescue of Jerry and his flight to Canada. The antislavery workers in western New York thereafter celebrated October 1 as Jerry Rescue Day.[53]

Perhaps the most spectacular rendition of a fugitive slave occurred in Boston in 1854. In the spring of that year Stephen A. Douglas introduced the Kansas-Nebraska Bill, which explicitly repealed the Missouri Compromise and permitted the further extension of slavery into America's Middle West. Antislavery men were exceedingly upset over the bill and against such a background of hostile discussion Anthony Burns, a fugitive slave, was captured in Boston. Thomas Wentworth Higginson led a dramatic assault upon the courthouse wherein Burns was imprisoned. The sensational attempt left one guard dead, but failed to reach and release Burns. Before a crowd of 20,000 spectators, 2,000 men with a six-pound cannon marched Burns to the Boston wharves. There they placed him on board a steamer for Charleston. The cost of his rendition totaled $100,000.[54]

In order to prevent the fall of Kansas into slavery, Thomas Wentworth Higginson, Eli Thayer, Henry Ward Beecher, Lyman Beecher, and Edward Everett Hale spurred emigrants to swell the population of free-white labor in the territory. Particularly through the Emigrant Aid Company, they propagandized Kansas as a fertile prairie for the implantation of a new New England civilization.[55] Instead, the ground of bloody Kansas would yield up martyrs and spread its gore throughout the nation. It touched Washington, D.C., in 1856, when Charles Sumner vehemently challenged the South on the awful conflict in Kansas. Preston Brooks, a "model of plantation chivalry," struck Sumner from behind as the Senator struggled from his desk.[56] And it touched the western Virginia hills, when John Brown, whose hatred of slavery had festered in the violence in Kansas, descended upon the federal arsenal of Harpers Ferry. His ill-fated attempt to emancipate Negro slaves by force led him to the gallows and instant sainthood in the eyes of most antislavery reformers.

The blood of Kansas, the beating of Sumner, the execution of John Brown transformed the thinking of many peace-loving men and women. The attempts to extend slavery into the West, the Dred Scott Case of 1857, and the bungling compromise of the Buchanan administration exasperated antislavery reformers of all stripes and persuasions. With the election of Lincoln and the firing upon Fort Sumter there began a melting together of the various antislavery patterns of thinking and methodology. With the headlong clash of North and South, violence seemed God's solution to the problem of slavery. The darkening clouds of Civil War were viewed by abolitionists as God's will overcoming the sin of the nation and they saw their part in the conflict as members of the Lord's legions engaged in a holy war.[57] Kenneth Stampp writes that "by 1861 many antislavery leaders had concluded that force was the *only* means of reaching their goal. The strong religious element in this crusade mystically resigned itself to the will of an avenging God, for the shedding of blood would be His punishment for the terrible sin of slavery."[58] Alas, even the kind and gentle Samuel J. May cried out that he had preached a "war sermon."[59]

The war began not as a religiously inspired crusade; general support for emancipation even as a war measure was not readily available in 1861, but slowly public opinion moved toward accepting possible emancipation legislation. Once he perceived the direction of public opinion, no politician or statesman could ignore it. Hence in April 1862 Congress passed a bill of emancipation with compensation for the District of Columbia, and President Lincoln soon signed it. Then on September 22, 1862, Lincoln released his preliminary emancipation proclamation, and on January 1, 1863, he issued the Emancipation Proclamation itself, which ended slavery for those Negroes held in bondage in any Southern area then in rebellion against the United States. Celebrations occurred throughout the North and in the scattered parts under Union occupation in the South.[60]

As the war for the maintenance of the Union took on the added dimensions of a war to end slavery, antislavery reformers—even the Garrisonians—became more popular. Hereafter an honored place at ceremonies and councils was reserved for them. The Garrisonians experienced, of course, a good deal of soul-searching. After all, they had declared vocally their "withdrawal" from the Union. Still, just as they had bent their pacifist scruples under the weight of the "holy war," Garrison and most radical abolitionists, after an initial reluctance, made the necessary adjustment and supported Lincoln and the Union. They squeezed all the moral goodness they could out of Lincoln's antislavery measures.[61]

The abolition of slavery became a popular concept. Throughout the nation everyone could hear the death rattle. On April 8, 1864, the Senate adopted the Thirteenth Amendment and on January 31, 1865, the House concurred. By the end of the year three-fourths of the states had ratified the amendment. Only the death of the president could dim the brilliance of this mighty act. Garrison called it the "crowning victory" of the antislavery crusade. The Revolutionary Fathers had provided for slavery in the Constitution of the United States; now sons of a Second Revolution had wiped these provisions and all the horrors of slavery away in an act writ large:

NEITHER SLAVERY NOR INVOLUNTARY SER-VITUDE, . . . SHALL EXIST WITHIN THE UNITED STATES.[62]

2

Antislavery as Religion—1831–1840

IN my life "there was one great grief," wrote Samuel J. May, "that probably made the deepest religious impression my soul ever received." His favorite brother, Edward, accidentally bled to death while playing with him. Witnessing the horror of the ghastly scene and the hysteria of his mother, Samuel was distraught with grief. In order to console him, his parents permitted him to rest beside his dead brother. He "kissed his [brother's] cold cheek and lips, pulled open his eyelids, begged him to speak." Later, at Edward's funeral, their uncle, Samuel May, opened another coffin in the family vault and showed young Samuel how decayed the body had become. Uncle May explained that Edward's body also would decay, but assured the four-year-old Samuel that Edward "had gone to heaven with God and Christ and the angels. "Not surprisingly, May dreamt of Edward the evening after his funeral:

43

The ceiling of the [bedroom] opened, over where I was lying: a bright, glorious light burst in, and from the midst of it came down my lost brother, attended by a troop of little angels. They left him. He lay by me as he used to do, his head on my arm or my head on his. He told me how happy he was, what a beautiful place heaven was, how kind God and Christ were to him, and how the angels loved one another. There he lay until morning, when the ceiling above opened again, and the troop of angels came to bear him back to heaven. He kissed me, sent messages of love to father and mother, brother and sister, and gladly rejoined the celestial company.[1]

Many years later, May admitted that this extraordinary experience did much to substantiate his religious faith, and in the autobiographical material he left behind, he placed in immediate sequel to this mystical experience his recollection of his earliest encounters with Negro people. May's first contact was a classmate for three years "whose skin was as dark as a starless night, but whose spirit was as bright and joyous as a cloudless noonday." Moreover, the young Negro's participation in the class unexpectedly revealed to May and his friends an intellect equal to or exceeding their own. The second contact occurred when as a child May was knocked unconscious in an accident. When he awoke he found himself in the arms of a "large black woman" who promptly consoled him and carried him home. May never forgot his benefactress.[2]

These two themes—religion and race—placed in juxtaposition in the reminiscences of May's life, point in a graphic way to the understanding of the rise of the American Antislavery Society as a religious movement, within which the inner circle of Garrisonians emerged as a religious sect. This is not to say that every member of the Garrisonian group experienced a religious vision similar to May's—perhaps most did not—but Unitarians who were radical abolitionists experienced deficiencies in their denomination that abolitionist activity supplied.

May found in abolitionism a release of his pent-up feeling for a Christ-centered evangelical Unitarianism, whose energy needed to be expended against sin and on behalf of Christ and His people. Maria Weston Chapman and her sisters, Deborah, Anne Warren, and Caroline found in abolitionism community action and bliss that the Unitarian Church (and most churches) would not provide for their women. Lydia Maria Child, the daughter of a baker, enjoyed in abolitionism a social equality that gave her notoriety and usefulness, far exceeding any station she might reluctantly have been given in the Unitarian literary or social aristocracy. Abolitionism gave jobs, some full-time, to Unitarian clergymen like Thomas Treadwell Stone, Robert F. Wallcut, Samuel May, Jr., and even Samuel J. May. To Charles Follen, an intellectual immigrant, abolition gave expression to his acceptance and commitment to America's manifest destiny to be the society where human rights were most fully respected. Abolition was their life, abolition was their love, abolition was their religion.

John L. Thomas in his biography of Garrison has sketched this theme of abolitionism as religion. To Garrison, writes Thomas, "the energies of religious reform and the forces of abolition were one and the same. He only knew that he and his followers were Christian soldiers doing God's work in the world." Thomas supports the idea that the "American abolitionists constituted a religion and Garrison the leader of a schismatic sect within that religion. He took the formula for salvation of the religious revivalists of his day and applied it directly to slavery. 'Immediate emancipation' as he taught it was not a program but an attitude, an urgent warning that shut out thoughts of expediency or compromise."[3]

When contemporary observers of the Garrisonian agitation reminisced years later, they commonly mentioned the religious aspects of the abolitionist crusade. In 1879 Elizur Wright looked back upon the Garrisonian effort as a movement "purely religious."[4] The editor of the *Unitarian*

Review described in 1889, "the form of faith," the almost "new religion" of the abolitionists

> as a separate body, with its profession of faith and form of observance [which] had all that we could ask to make it a peculiar and in some ways a very beautiful and noble form of our common Christianity. It had its witnesses, its saints, its martyrs even, and its eloquent apostles. . . . Its deep sense of fellowship was such as to merge all the distinctions of race, wealth, social position, culture . . . or sectarian belief, in a common brotherhood. [It was] in the strictest sense a *religious* development, unique and peculiar, the outcome of the most vigorous piety and the intensest moral feeling, probably known to that day. [And it had] one article of faith . . . *The Negro* MUST *not be enslaved.*[5]

Thomas Wentworth Higginson, a political abolitionist, wrote in 1898 that the abolitionist fraternity was a "cult" possessing a "minimum of visible or potent machinery" but a "maximum of cohesion."[6]

Indeed, all the elements of a religion could be found in the Garrisonian fellowship. Garrison as their leader possessed the aura of a prophet, and even, to some people, of a savior. There were disciples, and on these a great commission rested. Most abolitionists underwent a conversion experience, a rite of initiation, a very definite point of reference in their lives at which uncertainty on antislavery gave way to the conviction of the truth of abolition. They had their evangelistic message, a concept of church, a sense of mission, and a form of worship. Their "theology" recognized fairly explicit "proofs" of faith, enumerated rather specifically the demonic forces at work against their cause, and taught a dogma both to bind them together and to secure the success of their goals. But like any sect, the original fervor eventually eroded and as others accepted their essential message of freedom for the slave, the confessional purity of their movement slowly dissolved or combined with other, secular, antislavery strains.

A. THE PROPHET

In October 1830 Samuel J. May had left the loneliness of his parish, the only Unitarian church in Connecticut, to visit Boston. There he heard Garrison lecture, and he was very impressed: "Never before was I so affected by the speech of man. When he ceased speaking I said to those around me: 'That is a providential man; he is a prophet; he will shake our nation to its centre. . . .' " Later at the home of a friend, May listened to Garrison illustrate plainly "that *immediate unconditional emancipation, without expatriation, was the right of every slave, and could not be withheld by his master an hour without sin.*"[7]

B. THE DISCIPLES AND SUNDRY CONVERSIONS

Among Garrison's disciples, Samuel J. May (1797–1871) most resembled the character of the beloved apostle of the New Testament. His gentleness earned him the adoration of his fellow abolitionists as their "Apostle John."[8] Gerrit Smith said he was the most "Christ-like man" he had ever known.[9] Bronson Alcott, May's brother-in-law, called him "God's Chore Boy," and Theodore Parker spoke of sweet, meek, and mild May as having a voice "made to pronounce the Beatitudes."[10] These pious encomiums may make May appear frightfully dull, but in fact he was not. He gained most people's appreciation, respect, and love, and for Garrison he was a particularly close and valuable friend.[11]

A graduate of Harvard College and the Divinity School, May served as his first church the impoverished Unitarian society of Brooklyn, Connecticut. Ministering to the solitary Unitarian church in the Orthodox Siberia was no easy task and May poured out his energy in tireless service. He began to publish a newspaper, *The Liberal Christian*, in 1823; helped found the Windham County Peace Society three years later; battled intemperance; and in 1834, fought beside Prudence Crandall to save her school. This last act caused dissension in the Brooklyn church. When it forbade May the use of the meeting house for antislavery meetings, he withdrew and became general agent for the Massachusetts Antislavery Society in 1835. The rigorous schedule of an agent shattered his home-life and his Unitarianism bore the brunt of an Orthodox attack upon the Society. These two considerations led him to resign, in 1836, whereupon he accepted a call to the Unitarian church in South Scituate, Massachusetts. May served there until 1842 when he was again forced to withdraw, this time in a dispute over abolishing the Negro pew. From 1842 to 1844, he headed the normal school in Lexington and then in 1845, undertook the Unitarian ministry in Syracuse, New York. He remained at this Unitarian outpost until his retirement in 1867.[12]

Before May had settled at Brooklyn he had visited Baltimore, Washington, and Richmond. What he saw of slavery sickened him and unsettled his views about it and even about himself. The thunderbolt of conversion struck him at the evening of Garrison's lecture against colonization: "That night my soul was baptized in his spirit, and ever since I have been a disciple and fellow-laborer of William Lloyd Garrison. [His lectures] gave a new direction to my thoughts, a new purpose to my ministry. I had become a convert to the doctrine of 'immediate unconditional emancipation. . . .' "[13]

If May epitomized the mystical and romantic Garrisonian evangelist, another disciple, Maria Weston Chapman (1806–1885), exemplified the rationalist administrator. An expert organizer and fund-raiser, her power among Garrisonians even rivaled that of Wendell Phillips and Garrison himself. At twenty-eight years old she entered abolitionist activity as the chief secretary of the Boston Female Antislavery Society, founded in 1834, then served as Counsellor for the Massachusetts Antislavery Society, 1841 to 1865, and on the Executive Committee of the American Antislavery Society, 1845 to 1863. She chronicled antislavery work in the series *Right and Wrong in Boston,* 1836–1840, and she edited the annual gift-book, *The Liberty Bell,* 1839–1855. When Garrison was absent she and Edmund Quincy edited the *Liberator.* Under her expert management the annual antislavery fairs added many dollars to the movement's treasury.[14]

If the radical abolitionists saw May as their St. John, then they lauded Maria Weston Chapman as abolition's "Maid of Orleans," the "Joan of our Ark."[15] Out of the pre-opening chaos of an antislavery fair she was known to bring order and efficiency with speed and dispatch.[16] In the heat of the conflicts among abolitionists, Chapman became more "religious than the Pope himself," and Garrison seldom lacked her protection.[17] Her services to Garrison "were inestimable," exclaimed his sons, "her cooperation with him perfect." They called her entrance into the abolitionist movement in 1834 her "baptism." To Chapman, Garrison was somewhat less than a deity, still she told her women friends that he had been "our Liberator," then she paused and said, "*The* Liberator."[18] As his adjutant, she carried the nickname given to her by abolitionist foes—"Captain Chapman"— and valiantly defended herself and abolitionism from many a goading obscenity.[19] "She was a doughty swordswoman in conversation, and wore armor," recalled her grandson, John Jay Chapman. "There was something about her that reminded me of a gladiator, and I sometimes wondered how she had ever borne children at all and whether she had nursed them. . . ."[20]

What did this amazing Amazon look like? Actually, she was no Amazon at all. She possessed an "exquisite beauty," observed Harriet Martineau. Like the princess Rapunzel, her golden blond hair seemed long enough to cover her to her feet. Her complexion was radiant; her profile, regal; and her eyes, steel blue. Truly, she was "beautiful as the day, tall in her person, and noble in her carriage, with a voice sweet as a silver bell, and speech as clear and sparkling as a running brook." She was a duchess, nay, a queen.[21] Moreover, to add to her beauty and "a phenomenal fund of physical health," she could boast a European education, a sharp intelligence and wit, and Pilgrim ancestry.[22] Men could melt as butter before Maria Weston Chapman, and they did; she managed Garrison, Phillips, and Quincy, Lewis Tappan confided, as "easily as she could 'untie a garter.' "[23]

One man who held his own with Maria was her husband, Henry Grafton Chapman, Jr. (1804–1842), a Boston merchant. He and Maria's sisters, Anne Warren (1812–1890), Caroline (1808–1882), and Deborah Weston (?) were all active Garrisonian sectarians. They were identified with, but sharply criticized the Unitarians.

Lydia Maria Child (1802–1880) was another Unitarian woman who was a leading disciple of Garrison. The daughter of a baker and the granddaughter of a weaver, Maria—she despised the name Lydia—grew up in rather simple surroundings. She and her brother, Convers Francis, enjoyed the riches of literature and she early demonstrated her own gifts as an author. She also early asserted an uncommon independence and protested male airs of superiority. In 1828 she married David Lee Child (1794–1874), a Boston lawyer and a member of the Massachusetts Legislature. She had already published her first three novels and edited *The Juvenile Miscellany*. Now, as a married woman in Boston, she continued her writing to great acclaim.[24]

David Lee Child had been associated with Garrison before the beginning of the *Liberator*, and when Mrs. Child met Garrison in 1832, she was immediately converted: "He got hold of the strings of my conscience," she testified, "and pulled me into reforms. . . . Old dreams vanished, old associates departed, and all things became new."[25] In 1833 Maria became more prominent in the abolitionist movement than her husband when she published her first contribution to the holy cause, one of the most effective tracts of the movement: *An Appeal in Behalf of that Class of Americans Called Africans.* Dedicated to Samuel J. May for his defense of Prudence Crandall, the small volume made a dramatic impact upon John Gorham Palfrey, Wendell Phillips, Thomas Wentworth Higginson, Charles Follen, and William Ellery Channing.[26]

Between 1841 and 1843 Maria edited the *National Anti-Slavery Standard*, the New York newspaper of the American Antislavery Society.[27] David also published antislavery literature, lobbied for abolition in Washington, and experimented with best sugar farming as a substitute for slave-labor sugar. Financial disaster followed his persistent but fumbling steps toward an ever-elusive goal.[28] The Childs worked equally hard for abolitionism, but their talents and maturity were not equal. Parker Pillsbury referred to David Lee as "the gifted husband of the more gifted Lydia Maria Child," and Deborah Weston wittily called the pair "Mrs. Child and Childe David."[29]

Another steadfast couple in the Garrisonian fellowship were Charles Theodore Christian Follen (1796–1840) and Eliza Lee Cabot Follen (1787–1860). Follen was an émigré from Germany, where he had been active in the Christian German *Burschenschaft* movement, fighting for republican ideals. A deep religious mysticism permeated this movement and Follen's Christian faith related directly to his political philosophy: "If men believed in the immortality of their souls," Follen taught, "there would be no slavery in this world, for all unjust pretensions and cruel distinctions among men, every proud elevation and servile humiliation, must fall before the acknowledged equality of immortal spirits." Follen lectured at the University of Giessen and the University of Jena before being forced to flee to America via Paris in 1824.[30]

Through influential friends Follen obtained a lectureship in German at Harvard. While in Cambridge he met Eliza Cabot, a pleasant, well-educated woman of a cultivated, but not a particularly wealthy family. Through Eliza, Follen became an intimate acquaintance of her pastor at the Federal Street Church in Boston, William Ellery Channing. The attractiveness of Dr. Channing's religion induced Follen, a Lutheran, to join the Unitarians in 1828, and the attractiveness of Eliza Cabot inspired him to join with her in holy wedlock that same year. Happily, Follen believed in the equality of the sexes. Eliza was nine years his senior and her two unmarried sisters immediately and permanently joined their household. The marriage flourished, however, despite continual financial hardship and each partner's commitment to a "mutual obedience to each other's superior judgement."[31]

In 1835, Follen lost his post at Harvard College and turned to the Unitarian ministry for employment. In 1836 he was ordained at Dr. Channing's church and served as an interim minister to the First Unitarian Society of New York City. Follen lasted there until May 1838, when he withdrew because of difficulties with the congregation, allegedly due to his antislavery preaching. Various "odd jobs" fed the Follens while Channing sought unsuccessfully to locate a church for his friend. Finally, a few souls in East Lexington, Massachusetts, in 1839 invited Follen to help build them a church and be their pastor at $600 a year. The good doctor was returning from a New York lecture series aboard the steamboat *Lexington* to dedicate his new church, when the ship sank in a blaze on Long Island Sound. Follen perished in the conflagration.[32]

When the *Liberator* began publication in 1831, Follen was drawn to the tiny office in Merchant's Hall to meet Garrison. He was inspired by the young abolitionist editor and after reading Mrs. Child's *Appeal* he joined the Massachusetts Antislavery Society. "I did not feel at liberty to stand aloof from a society," admitted Follen, "whose only object was the abolition of slavery." Eliza said he "loved and honored" Garrison and although he objected to some of the harsh language the radical abolitionists used, he served their cause faithfully. Follen was a vice-president and a member of the American Antislavery Society. After his death, Eliza Follen increased her literary efforts to keep the wolf from the door, but never ceased to aid abolitionism. She and her husband contributed significantly to the antislavery drive. It is rather sad that today Charles is remembered largely for introducing the German Christmas tree to New England, and Eliza for writing her immortal children's rhyme—"Three Little Kittens Lost Their Mittens."[33]

Six more disciples of the Garrisonian fellowship should be mentioned: Samuel E. Sewall (1799–1888); Ellis Gray Loring (1802–1852), and his wife, Louisa Gilman Loring (1791–1868); Francis Jackson (1789–1861); Henry Ingersoll Bowditch (1808–1892); and Edmund Quincy (1808–1877). All were Unitarian laymen and leading members of the Massachusetts Antislavery Society. Sewall and Loring (along with David Lee Child) had been at the foundation of the Society.

C. THE GREAT COMMISSION

On the cold slushy evening of January 6, 1832, a small group of men made their way along the dimly lit avenues of Boston's "Nigger Hill." Their destination was the African Baptist Church on Belknap Street. Meeting in the basement school room of the church, the men plotted a new organization to end Negro slavery in America. As a combination of rain, hail, and snow struck the basement window, the assembly's president, David Lee Child, called for the reading of the proposed society's preamble and constitution. The society's principles were clearly enunciated: 1.) Immediate emancipation. 2.) Slavery is sin. 3.) Color denotes political disability. 4.) Renunciation of violence and insurrection. Twelve men, the apostolic number, signed the document. Three refrained from doing so over qualms about the expediency of immediate emancipation—Child, Loring, and Sewall. Yet, soon they too would agree and become a part of this tiny apostolic band. They called their organization the New England Antislavery Society (later it would take the name Massachusetts Antislavery Society). The first American association with immediate abolition as its principal tenet was born.

As they left the building at the conclusion of their deliberations and entered the storm and darkness, Garrison remarked: "We have met tonight in this obscure school-house; our members are few and our influence limited; but, mark my prediction, Faneuil Hall shall ere long echo with the principles we have set forth here. We shall shake the nation by their mighty power."[34]

D. THE MESSAGE

Four years later, William Ellery Channing would question the policy of sending out antislavery apostles, who often possessed "indifferent intellectual and moral gifts." Lydia Maria Child replied that the early emissaries of Christ were not all equally gifted and like abolitionists their message was a very simple one. The abolitionists' principles, she declared, "are a resuscitation of doctrines preached by the apostolic seventy."[35]

There were aspects of the message of the abolitionists, of

course, that possessed no immediate parallels to the Evangel of the Bible. One idea that was similar, however, was that of being used as a tool of God; it was indeed His battle the abolitionists were fighting. They saw their cause as the "cause of Christ."[36] They acted in the mainstream of the "course of Providence," and God was using them as his instruments to accomplish his reformation.[37] It was a new reformation, said Maria Child, freeing men's minds from "every species of thralldom," and the greatest controversy since the Protestant Reformation. Maria Weston Chapman saw the "great work of Christianity" in their age in America to be abolition, and equated the work with former great conflicts with idolatry. "If there be any truth in the signs of the times," preached Charles Follen, "it is, that the Son of Man has risen upon this world, portending the destruction of slavery, and the vindication of the rights of man."[38]

The abolitionists, seeing themselves as a precious remnant of God and fighting with Him to destroy slavery, experienced both the divine assurance of being in the Lord's vanguard and also great loneliness. They were not fighting slavery with a comfortable host of allies in a redeemed North; rather, they fought slavery as a universal sin; the iniquity encumbered the entire American people, North and South. Even the abolitionists were not excluded and bore the shame of the birthmark of American slavery that spotted their souls. "Fellow-citizens!" shouted Follen at the New England Antislavery Convention in 1834, "we have all sinned together." When Mrs. Child pleaded for the abolition of slavery, she fully recognized that the withdrawal of God's blessing would accompany any persistence "in our iniquity." She placed the iniquity of slavery squarely upon her own broad shoulders and upon those of her fellow abolitionists. May aptly called America's predicament our "partnership in sin," and Mrs. Chapman compared an abolitionist's washing his hands guilty of slavery with Pilate—"*We ourselves* being in reality slaveholders," she confessed, "as Pilate was in reality implicated in the guilt of the death of Christ."[39] Yet, the abolitionists, tainted as they might be with slavery, alone possessed the true Gospel, and Mrs. Chapman advised all who wished to be delivered from the "curse of union in evil" to act with the American Antislavery Society. "Be baptized," she advised, "with the baptism that they are baptized with," for in all of America only the abolitionists, and *they alone, are right.*"[40]

The Garrisonian abolitionists not only admitted the universality of the sin of slavery in the sense of a catholicity of guilt, but also taught that the sin was all-inclusive. Slavery had so weakened the moral armor of America that every weapon in the arsenal of hell cut into the national fabric. In other words, as no citizen in America could escape the onus of the sin of slavery, no sin in America lacked its counterpart within the institution of slavery. Slavery contained all other sins; it was a satanic showcase of every kind of immorality. They were accused of preaching one idea, remarked Susan C. Cabot (1794–1861), Eliza Follen's sister and a Garrisonian devotee. But that idea "includes all others, for its aim is to overthrow a system which takes in and covers all the immoralities and sins that man can work upon the fair face of God's earth. Let one sin be mentioned which does not, almost of necessity, spring from the atheistic root of slavery!" Who can think of a greater sin than slavery? asked May. There is none, he quickly added. The answer for every American then was absurdly simple, the abolition of slavery must be immediate. They advocated immediate emancipation, May declared, "from the deep conviction, that few if any sins can be more heinous than holding fellow men in bondage and degradation, and in the assurance that men cannot leave off sinning too suddenly."[41]

The Garrisonian abolitionists gave warning: Either the North and the South terminated their respective forms of Negro slavery or they had to expect the divine retribution

of a massive Black insurrection. The "danger of servile and
civil war" increased, said Follen, as long as they continued to
ignore the slave's desire to be free. Slavery was a "true and
lasting source of insurrection," he cautioned and apathy
would escalate the violence that would finally descend upon
Americans or their descendants if they did not end the
ignominious institution. Safety and duty, May wrote, neces-
sitated abolition at once. Moreover, if free Negroes were
not permitted to rise in intellectual and moral worth, a
point would be reached where "in the providence of a just
God, they may throw off the yoke of their oppressors, with
vindictive violence." God would give them a Moses who
would teach them their rights, predicted May, and deliver
them out of white control.[42]

In putting into practice the ideal of the complete
brotherhood of man, peace could be maintained. This was a
major item in the gospel according to the abolitionists—all
men regardless of color were brothers. Such was the
message May unsuccessfully tried to convey to the opponents of Prudence Crandall's school. There was an "aristocracy of color," he told them, that had become their sad
heritage. May complained further that white people seldom referred to the blacks as Americans although many of
them had been there for more than a century and had
fought in the Revolutionary War. When Bowditch was
invited to participate in the Fourth of July procession of his
church's Sunday School, he urged the organizers to invite
the Negro Sunday School children to participate. They
should be given a cordial invitation so that "the unhappy
outcasts may feel that you really regard as a *practical* truth
that you really feel men are brothers, and born free and
equal. . . . Place yourselves under the banner for which the
blood of the colored man has flowed. . . ." His church
refused to invite any blacks and Bowditch withdrew. Susan
C. Cabot deplored this colorphobia. To discard a portion of
humanity, she complained, because white people did not

like their color or facial structure was "a form of atheism."
They were all children of God.[43]

But were the Garrisonians breaking down all distinctions
in American society? Mrs. Child said no; there was not the
slightest truth to the charge that abolitionists would force
uneducated blacks into the parlors of genteel whites.
Whites would mix with those Negroes, she explained, who
were equal to their own virtue and intelligence. Not *"every
privilege"* would be given to the freed blacks either, assured
Follen; they would have to be educated for society first. The
Garrisonian Salem Female Anti-Slavery Society stated
clearly in their constitution, "we are ready to acknowledge
[Negroes] as our friends and equals, whenever their
character and attainment shall justify it."[44]

The fear of possible amalgamation fed the colorphobia
and the abolitionists became very defensive on the issue of
mixed marriage. Follen disclaimed "as a sentiment utterly
foreign to abolitionists" any desire for miscegnation.
Neither the blacks nor white abolitionists desired any such
thing. Certainly the abhorrence of intermarriage, remarked Mrs. Child, was as strong to the black as to the
white. She assured any alarmed person, that there would be

> a sufficient number of well-informed and elegant colored
> women in the world, to meet the demands of colored
> patricians. . . . [Black men] will not be forced to make war
> upon their white neighbors for wives: nor will they, if
> they have intelligent women of their own, see anything so
> very desirable in the project. Shall we keep this class of
> people in everlasting degradation, for fear one of their
> descendants *may* marry our great-great-great-great
> grandchild?[45]

Notwithstanding the abolitionists' own difficulty in freeing themselves from the quagmire of racial prejudice,
their meetings and associations still reflected one of the
highest achievements in social, racial, and sexual equality

obtained in ante-bellum America. Germans mixed with Englishmen, women with men, blacks with whites, citizens with foreigners, poor farmers with scholars and Boston gentlemen. Something new, liberating, and exciting took place at their meetings, not the least being the sense of true community their membership displayed and enjoyed.[46]

E. THE CHURCH

"Ah, my friend," Maria Child wrote to Theodore Weld in 1880, "the *only* true church organization [is] when heads and hearts unite in the working for the welfare of the human race." She was commenting on the abolitionist brotherhood and she declared that selfishness and personal ambitions were suppressed in their fellowship. "The Holy Spirit did actually descend upon men and women in tongues of flame," she boasted. As her antislavery community took on the aspect of a church, a religious sect, the very individuality of its members became absorbed into a common abolitionist identity. Deborah Weston expressed her surprised when greeted on the street: "How do you do Abolition?" As readily as Evangelicals would sign themselves "Yours in Christ," abolitionist women ended their letters "Your *Sister in Freedom.*" Samuel J. May sensed the aspect of church in the abolitionist fellowship and drew parallels between it and the Pilgrims. His observation was sound. The abolitionists were not only a believing remnant in a wilderness of sin, they were a community of the covenant. They were the true Church within the fossil remains of the American institutional church. Maria and David Child attended the Unitarian Church in Northampton expressly because the minister was a member of the Antislavery Society. Had it not been so, Maria acknowledged, *"mein Mann"* would not *"kom da."* Maria also attended a monthly prayer meeting and found peace there, not because of any doctrinal or birthright affinity with fellow Unitarians in attendance, but because she recognized a "firm true antislavery spirit" was present.[47]

Outsiders could object to the abolitionists' methods and censuring language, but the "incorruptible fidelity and affection" abolitionists showed each other were enviable. A priesthood of all believers developed, whereby both lay and clerical leaders in the abolitionist party became "religious priests." They led Sunday worship and spoke the last words at the funerals of deceased members.[48]

The concept of the surrogate nature of abolitionism as church found one of its greatest champions in Maria Weston Chapman. If they desired to Christianize the nation, preached this high priestess of abolition, then they should strengthen the American Anti-Slavery Society, the only American institution founded on the Christian and republican idea of the equal brotherhood of man. "The American Anti-Slavery Society is church . . . to all who need . . . true religion. . . . It is 'the bright consummate flower' of the Christianity of the nineteenth century. [Join them] and find yourself the chosen of God . . . in a united, onward-flowing current of noble lives." With such enthusiasm, with such a perfect belief in God as being within their community, it is not hyperbolical to say with James Freeman Clarke: "I find here in the anti-slavery meeting a church of Christ, a church in deed and truth."[49]

F. WORSHIP

Worship is an integral part of any church and the "church of the abolitionists" was no exception. The annual meetings of abolitionist societies typically opened with prayer, followed by hymns, and finally an address— frequently an expository homily on abolitionist doctrine. For example, the second annual meeting of the New

England Antislavery Society opened with prayer, followed by "several appropriate hymns . . . sung with great taste and effect by a choir of colored children. . . ." At a local antislavery meeting arranged by Samuel J. May, the assembly opened with prayer, proceeded with the reading of a portion of Scripture, then hymn-singing, and finally, an address or, more appropriately, a sermon. Prayer as an essential component of worship manifested itself in various prayer circles that abolitionists held in their homes.[50]

A great part of the excitement of antislavery worship derived from the singing of hymns. The themes of the hymns sought to arouse a phlegmatic congregation and sentimentally to melt frigid audiences. Maria Weston Chapman and Eliza Follen exhibited a special genius for writing and compiling antislavery hymns. Mrs. Follen's *Anti-Slavery Hymns and Songs* and Mrs. Chapman's *Songs of the Free, and Hymns* were standard hymnals for antislavery worship.[51]

Mrs. Follen's hymn collection included such titles as the "Land of the Free and the Home of the Brave," "Remember the Slave!," "Auld Lang Syne" (for a change in missionary tempo!), "And the Days of Mourning Shall Be Ended," "Rescue the Slave," and "Lord Deliver!" There is no record as to which hymns were the most popular, but the hymn "On Hearing of the Sadness of the Slave-Children from the Fear of Being Sold," whenever sung, must assuredly have set records for precipitating tears.[52]

These hymns were composed for adult hearts, but children's minds were not to be neglected and Eliza Follen prepared hymns for them. Her *Hymns, Songs, and Fables for Young People* appeared in 1831, with an introduction by her husband. Some might object to the mixture of fare the book provides, explained Charles Follen, with its "gay and serious pieces . . . bound up together, but so it is in human life and human nature, and it is essential to the healthful action of a child's mind that it should be so." In other words the happiness of "Three Little Kittens" must be mixed with the somber, if not ugly reality of life. Fable and fact placed in juxtaposition reflect children's and mankind's true experience. The following song has not had the longevity of the adorable "Kittens," but there is the likelihood that while black men were slaves, this song of a solitary child who had lost his freedom made a greater impression on the young minds of white children and free black children than the three beloved kittens who lost their mittens:

THE LITTLE SLAVE'S WISH

I wish I was that little bird
    Up in the bright blue sky,
That sings and flies just where he will,
    And no one asks him why.

The slave boy wishes he were a little brook, a butterfly, a wild deer, a little cloud, any of these things to escape his bondage. And then he says:

I'd rather be a savage beast,
    And dwell in a gloomy cave,
And shake the forest when I roared,
    Then what I am,—a slave.

My mother calls me her good boy,
    My father calls me brave;
What wicked action have I done
    That I should be a slave?

They tell me God is very good,
    That his right arm can save;
O' is it, can it, be his will
    That I should be a slave?

O' how much better 't is to die,
    And lie down in the grave,
Than 't is to be what I am now,—
    A little negro slave![53]

Abolitionist holy days were occasions for families to gather for worship. Dr. Samuel Willard (1776–1859), a Unitarian minister and a Garrisonian who later went over to political abolitionism, told of his family's midnight vigil on the first of August 1838. This was the date the slaves in the British West Indies were to be set free and Willard and his family sang a hymn that he had especially prepared for the event. "If I ever felt devout," Willard recalled eighteen years later, "I believe it was then. . . ." Public services at his Deerfield parish had to contend with rowdies who removed the church's bell clapper and blew horns and beat pans while people within tried to pray for the new freedmen.[54]

Prayers to God alone would not bring emancipation unless His people were inspired as well to bring abolition about. The Garrisonians were quick to adopt the techniques of the camp meeting and revival. Skillful choirs, the finest orators, and fugitive slaves who testified were attractions to draw large crowds. Once people were gathered, speeches had to be extravagant in order to retain an audience's attention and attract them back again. Garrison and Mrs. Chapman were not satisfied until they could get a crowd angry. They knew that an angry audience meant an awakened audience. Moral forces could only work upon people who were tuned in on what was being preached. A sleepy or sleeping audience produced few converts to abolition. May used the common tactic of the frontier revivalist of mentioning sinners, in this case pro-slavery sinners, by name. In one address, May attacked Edward Everett and Daniel Webster, knowing fully well that such personal allusions were offensive to many of his listeners.[55] In the revivalist atmosphere of many of the abolitionist meetings, new individuals were added to the antislavery party, but the Garrisonians followed other avenues of missionary activity in their constant search for new members and more support.

G. MISSION

The active participants in abolition missions as in the
many missionary enterprises of Protestant churches were
women. Their leader was Maria Weston Chapman, who
personally believed she had "a mission to perform on
earth."[56] That mission lay in the expansion of the American
Antislavery Society and the destruction of slavery. As the
prime mover behind the antislavery annual, the *Liberty Bell*,
and the lucrative antislavery fairs, she provided a great part
of the budget of Massachusetts abolitionism. She was also a
champion of antislavery petitioning by women, believing
that the right of petition was a woman's "only means of
manifesting her civil existence." Mrs. Chapman brushed
aside taunts that petitioning was such "an odd *unladylike*
thing to do," by saying:

> We have never heard this objection but from that sort of
> woman who is dead while she lives, or to be pitied as the
> victim of domestic tyranny. The woman who makes it is
> generally one who has struggled from childhood up to
> womanhood through a process of spiritual suffocation.
> Her infancy was passed in serving as a convenience for
> the display of elegant baby-linen. Her youth, in training
> for a more public display of braiding the hair, and
> wearing of gold, and putting on of apparel. . . . Her
> summers fly away in changes of air and water; her winters
> in changes of flimsy garments, [and] in inhaling lamp-
> smoke. . . . This is the woman who tells us it is *unladylike* to
> ask that children may no longer be sold away from their
> parents, or wives from their husbands.[57]

As to the success of petitioning, Mrs. Chapman troubled
not. Whether men would be impressed by petitions and
moved to repentance she cared not. "We leave such cares
with God . . .; for [we know] what we have done is right and
womanly."[58]

The valiant ladies who made the rounds petitioning time

after time encountered disdain and opposition. When I bring around my petitions, exploded Mrs. Child, the "fairyland palaces" of high society become "cold and barren earth," but she wanted their names, not their fellowship. Boldly she continued. Marching straight to William Ellery Channing, she came away with his name on a petition to end slavery in the District of Columbia. Anne Warren Weston went petitioning along Boston's South Street and had a very rough time. One aggressive matron nearly killed her. In another area she added eight to ten names. She also was accosted by a Mrs. Bailey, who said she hoped all the abolitionist young ladies "who interested themselves in this matter would get what she supposed they were after namely nigger husbands."[59]

Obviously, not everyone the petitioners approached opposed their aims. The yards and yards of names sent to Congress attest to the support they gathered. Petitioning gave the women a fine opportunity to answer the assertions against immediate abolition and to sign up prospective members for the antislavery societies. Another way to reach both women and men was by the immensely successful antislavery fairs.

"Here at least," exclaimed Mrs. Chapman, "we are in our 'Sphere.' " The preparation of banners, the arrangement of the table displays, the pricing of the contributed goods, and the assigning of responsibilities were largely duties that Mrs. Chapman held firmly in control. Faithfully year after year she and her assistants contributed their donations and their time. All was not work without play, for the social meetings prior to the fair were great fun. "The glue and paste pots smoke there continually," Mrs. Chapman remarked, "—incense to the nose of an abolitionist."[60] The competition of civic pride was encouraged by preparing tables to represent particular communities, complete with a town's motto and plaque. Sales promotions like these at fairs close to Christmas increased sales nicely and, after 1835, each year brought a greater income than the year before. The first was held in the office of the Massachusetts Antislavery Society, December 16, 1834, and receipts stood at $360. The next bazaar, this time held at Mrs. Chapman's home, brought in $343. The Artists' Gallery was used in 1836 with gross receipts reaching $550. From 1837 to 1840, Mrs. Chapman held the fair in the hall of Marlborough Chapel, and abolition gained respectively $800, $1100, $1500, and $2001 for those four years.[61]

Especially memorable was the Antislavery Bazaar of 1840. Maria Weston Chapman had herself painted the banners that hung from the ceilings and walls, and had prepared the legends representing the towns and their offerings. Three hundred tickets were sold for the gala party held on the closing night of the fair. All the members of Boston abolitionism attended. The hall of the Marlborough Chapel, bedecked with flowers and fruit, glowed by the light of hundreds of candles. What made the evening a special affair was the presence for the first time of black participants. They had felt free at last to accept invitations to come on terms of equality and to take part in the festivities with their white friends. Their faces shone in the candlelight, recalled Caroline Weston, and there was a feeling among her friends that a "new era was inaugurated." She thrilled at the sight of Negroes and whites seated side by side at the same banquet table. A young Negro girl told Caroline the next morning of the happiness she derived from the party. *"It was like going to Heaven,"* she declared, and then expressed in a simple statement the pathos of her people: "I have had so much pleasure that now I am willing to die."[62]

H. PROOF OF FAITH

"How few now living on earth," reflected Maria Child in her old age, have any idea of the prayers, and tears, and inward struggles, through which [abolitionists] passed, in that arduous mission of rescuing millions of human brethren from the darkness and misery of slavery: to the young men and women of the present day, the fiery trials and hairbreadth escapes of that stormy period have the far-off sound of tradition, like the mob that stoned Stephen, and the wild beasts let loose upon Christians in the Coliseum. But the Cross stands in the Coliseum now, and colored men are in the Halls of Congress.[63]

In the reminiscences of the radical abolitionists the fiery trials of old age were always the sharpest memories. For proof that one had suffered for the cause was proof that one had actually had faith in the cause, that one had been a doer rather than a thinker, a confessor or martyr rather than an apostate from the only true faith. Legitimate abolitionists in the post-civil war years heard legions of counterfeit abolitionists pound their breasts and boast of their antislavery exploits. Higginson complained near the end of the century of being invited to antislavery reunions where he knew that the prominent speakers had had nothing to do with the antislavery movement or, what was worse still, had been bitterly opposed to it.[64] "Show us your scars!" became the challenge of authentic abolitionists. Having suffered for the slaves' sake was the proof of the one true faith.

All the radical abolitionists had experienced the painful effects of their revolutionary position. Mention has been made of Samuel J. May's being mobbed five times, of Garrison's ordeal of 1835, and Mrs. Chapman's sufferings with the Boston Female Antislavery Society. But the persecution of abolitionists did not always flare up in violence; most fequently it was a subtle strangulation of the normal relations between friends, scholars, businessmen, ministers, and congregations. Samuel J. May lost two churches over his antislavery activity, and Follen one. When the

Chapmans accepted the faith of the abolitionists, their friends condemned them and snapped all social ties. Bowditch was ostracized and warned that he "never would be successful in [his] profession" if he persisted in his abolitionism. The beloved and genial Ellis Gray Loring had to contend with slander and lies. Quincy's brilliant law career shone less brightly after joining the cause, and friends departed in droves. Maria Child used her honorary library privileges at Boston's Atheneum to research her *Appeal in Favor of That Class of Americans Called Africans.* She was the first woman ever to have use of the library, and as a result of the *Appeal,* she was the first woman to have her use of the library withdrawn. Sales of her novels and short stories declined precipitously and her income was drastically reduced.[65] To confess abolitionism in these initial years signified tremendous courage. "Those only who were ready," admonished Samuel J. May, "to take up the cross, to suffer loss, shame, and even death, seemed to us then fit to engage in the work we proposed."[66]

Ambiguity may creep into any martyrology and it should not be overlooked here. The Garrisonians were excellent propagandists and in their desire to demonstrate the general decline of freedom in America, they did not hesitate to point out the slightest injustice perpetrated against them. After all, the abolitionists knew the axiom: in the blood of the martyrs the church doth grow. For the Unitarian Garrisonians, perhaps the severest shock was the tragic death of Follen in 1840, for to a community that read with such clarity the march of God's justice in their country's history and in their own movement, the news that one of their number had been taken so cruelly, so unjustly, and so needlessly from them played havoc with their faith. Loring, recording this shock, said that for weeks it so affected him personally as to destroy all "his courage and faith." Eliza Follen fell into a pit of depression trying to reconcile with God the burden of the tragedy.[67]

The Massachusetts Antislavery Society gathering for its annual meeting a few days after Follen's death, unanimously voted to have Samuel J. May prepare a eulogy for him. The society approached each Unitarian church in Boston: one by one they refused the use of their halls for Follen's memorial service. Not even the eminent Channing could gain his own pulpit at Federal Street Church for the service to honor his dear friend. Saddest of all was the conduct of the East Lexington society, which refused Follen's friends the church that he himself had helped to build. Loring wrote in his diary that the churches answered almost uniformly—we *"have no apparatus to light the church."* For more than two months Follen's friends had to wait. Finally the society received permission to use the Marlborough Chapel. Nearly two thousand people packed the chapel to express in prayer, in eulogy, and in hymns their appreciation of Follen.[68]

That 17 April 1840 was Good Friday was not lost upon May. He drew parallels between Follen and Christ and the redemption of man. Channing in a eulogy given earlier than May's did not mention Follen's abolitionism.[69] May more than made up for Channing's omission. Follen's work for abolition, May preached, was the aspect of his character that was "the highest, holiest, [the] best of all." He had come to abolition as a gentle convert, "gentle as St. John," but one "who stood at the foot of the cross, in the face of the infuriated multitude." Because of his abolitionism he had been separated from Harvard and from his congregation in New York City. *"We can ask no higher evidence of his faithfulness,"* exclaimed May. Follen had made his witness. That he had been an abolitionist, "an avowed, active, official, immediate Abolitionist, is a testimony to the truth of our principles, and the general propriety of our measures. . . ." We have our martyr. The Unitarians, Garrisonian sectarians, May was saying, had their martyr. Follen had shown his proof of faith. "If there has been a man of this generation, who has borne the cross of Christ, that man was our brother. His testimony then is above all suspicion—dear, calm, unwavering. . . . He is gone. But, blessed be God! his testimony remains."

The service concluded with the singing of a hymn written by Mrs. Chapman. The two thousand present, bursting with pent-up emotion generated by May's impassioned eulogy, thundered

> Oh, Jesus! through our stricken souls,
>   Thy free, o'ermastering spirit pour,
> To bear us onward, through these rolls
>   The oppressor's wrath our steps before:
>
> That when our work on earth is done,
>   This true soul, taken from our need,
> May welcome us before thy throne,
>   With the glad myriads of the Freed![70]

I. DOGMA AND SCHISM

There is considerable irony in this apotheosis of Follen. He was certainly not on the far-left wing of the Garrisonians. He had fraternized with advocates of philosophical antislavery in the Cambridge Antislavery Society, and it is quite apparent that his opinions were slowly evolving toward political abolitionism.[71] This is not surprising; his background in European political anarchism was likely to influence him in this direction. But both these views— philosophical antislavery and political abolitionism—were anathema to Garrison, Mrs. Chapman, and other hardliners. His early death placed him in the pantheon of the religious abolitionists. Had he lived, his differences with Garrison probably would have dropped him into limbo—or hell—depending on how far he had chosen to differ.

By 1835 May could joyously repeat that nearly three

hundred antislavery societies had been established upon the fundamental principle *"that holding human beings as property is tremendous sin, and ought to be immediately repented of and forsaken."* In 1837 the figure of antislavery auxiliaries reached 1,006 and by 1839, 1,650.[72] Others besides Follen were quick to see the political weight such numbers could have. Dissension began to arise within the one true church of abolitionism, over the issue of the participation of women in the movement and the question of nonresistance and political participation.

Within the inner circle of Garrisonians there was little dissension regarding the woman question. May, at first, was slightly disturbed about the employment of women in the movement, but only for a short time. Opposition came more from the fringes of the American Antislavery Society and the Massachusetts Antislavery Society. Mrs. Child tried to defend antislavery participation by women in a meeting in Northampton, but with little success. The male leader ended the meeting by praying that those women, who "in the pride of their hearts desired to be leaders, might have humility given them."[73]

However, the question of nonresistance went right to the heart of the Garrisonian fellowship. Nonresistance was an enormously demanding position to maintain. "The Spirit of Non-Resistance," said May "is the highest attainment of the soul. . . . A true non-resistant must have the same mind that was in Christ." May felt he had not yet attained this position, and could not dare call himself a nonresistant.[74]

The bombshell, of course, that exploded the whole issue in the Garrison camp had been the Lovejoy affair. The abolitionists were committed to the use of peaceful means to free the slaves; now Lovejoy, whether they chose to claim him as one of their own or not, had brought violence to *their* side of the antislavery battle. Bowditch was exasperated by those abolitionists who extolled Lovejoy as a martyr. He could not see how one could support the eternal principles of justice by mutilating his brother men? Can it be that Lovejoy died a Christian? Was there anything Christlike in his death? Could he have borne his cross and have died meekly upon it? In the dark hour of trial should I think of *him* to be enabled to die as a martyr dies? Alas how blinded we are! No, Lovejoy is the *last* being on earth an abolitionist ought to think of, if he would be true to the cause he espouses. Abolition is pure and true. It needs no pistols or dirks. In its sublime strength it rises above such weapons.[75]

May was gloomier still: he thought the cause of antislavery was more "unpromising than it has ever been. I fear the *evangelical* character of our enterprise is or soon will be lost sight of and the catastrophe at Alton will do uncomparably more harm than good."[76]

Garrison called a peace convention in September 1838 and out of this was founded the New England Non-Resistance Society. Part of its Declaration of Sentiments repudiated all participation in politics. Mrs. Chapman, Anne Weston, Quincy, May, and other Garrisonians joined the Society, but the Declaration had gone further than many of them wanted to go. Mrs. Child for one was in a quandary. She did not know what to do with nonpolitical action and nongovernment theories and began to get depressed: "Much as I deprecate it, I am convinced that emancipation must come through violence."[77] The deterioration of dogma was beginning to show even among true believers.

The New England Antislavery Society had resolved at its annual meeting in 1835 "That it is essential to the progress of the Anti-Slavery cause, that its friends should understand and maintain its great distinctive principles, in all their purity and strength." Political action was discussed at this same meeting, but denounced as a corrupting influence. This was more than a sufficient reason for avoiding politics. Francis Jackson refused nomination for mayor of Boston by stating, "I do not want the antislavery course drawn into the 'whirlpool of politics,' " and besides, he added, he considered his position in the Massachusetts Antislavery Society "a more honorable position than to be Mayor of Boston." Others saw the abolitionists as just being used by each party, not strong enough to direct, and only an important bloc of votes to be directed.[78]

The dickering over political involvement, especially in the promotion of a third party; the woman question; and nonresistance brought schism at the meeting in 1840 of the American Antislavery Society. To be sure, the Unitarian Garrisonians stayed with the "Old Organization" over against Tappan's "New Organization," but the wrangling going on in the inner circle of Garrisonians—Sewall, Child, and Loring, who all favored political participation— brought much unhappiness to their abolitionist Eden.[79] Mrs. Chapman reveled in the strife: "The chaff has blown away in the recent storm—the cowardly have shrunk away from the brave, the traitor from the true." Others were not so enthusiastic. The divisions among the abolitionists upset May—they were not consistent with the "long-suffering spirit of the Gospel." Abolition seemed, he lamented, to be losing its "religious-tone." Mrs. Child came away from a tumultous meeting disheartened: "The moral elevation, the trust in God, which has usually inspired . . . abolitionist gatherings was wanting."[80]

3
Antislavery as Philosophy: The Prudent Party—1831–1842

Like the radical abolitionists, William Ellery Channing (1780–1842) also had tried to reconcile the death of Charles Follen with God's divine plan. But in his eulogy given before the panegyric of Samuel J. May, he accentuated the theological question of human pain and God's benevolence. The invalid Channing lived with pain and had incorporated the idea into his theology that suffering was "the intention" of the Creator. The "dark picture of the government of God" painted by Channing needed no human vindication of the goodness of God. His benevolence would explain itself.[1] Eliza Follen probably found little comfort in these words, and a good deal of discomfort in the fact that Channing, her pastor and friend, failed to mention the abolitionism of her husband.

Channing had remained silent on Follen's abolitionism, and, conscience permitting, he would have remained silent throughout the whole antislavery controversy. For he was a reluctant antislavery reformer. "All my feelings," he wrote to Lucy Aikin, in 1839, "and, I may add, my interest, dictated to me silence." But he was disturbed over the way the "professed abolitionists" pursued their reform. Although a "noble" band on the whole, they were "unwise and intemperate." They prejudiced the cause in the minds of "intelligent and influential people." No prominent leader would speak, and, therefore, Channing felt compelled to do so.[2]

As an individual, Channing felt obligated to speak out against slavery, but had no desire to join the abolitionists and try to mitigate the severity of their language and methods. He worked alone and deprecated associational action for himself and others. Two years before the New England Antislavery Society was founded, Channing had attacked societal action in his *Remarks on Associations*. He feared the tendency of some associations "to fetter men, to repress energy, to injure the free action of individuals and society." He lamented the power of societies to mold public opinion "tyranically." He placed his faith in "individual action as the highest good," and believed that individuals could accomplish the most good.[3]

The story of William Ellery Channing and the radical abolitionists, therefore, is one of tension. He could not join an abolitionist society in order to temper its methods and activities. He also could not successfully stand apart, criticize the abolitionists and, at the same time, secure the changes in their activity that he desired. He was not one of them. The Garrisonians did not understand him; he was too naive in his perception of slavery to understand the Garrisonians or to appreciate their tactics and style.

The emotions of the Garrisonians precluded calm reflection on the slaves' predicament. They believed an individual's right relationship with God required a belief in abolitionist principles. For Channing, however, an interest in antislavery reform was *but a single aspect of* an individual's right relationship with God. Abolitionism was the drums and brass section of a total symphonic approach to moral achievement. Channing refused to permit abolitionism a solo performance. The abolitionist ensemble was to be conducted in harmony with the other divisions in the orchestra of morality.

Channing remained aloof and tried to conduct. From his mind emanated the score, a perfect reading of the Divine melody. He related to Blanco White, an English friend, following the publication of his volume *Slavery:* "My aim was to oppose Slavery on principles, which, if admitted, would inspire resistance to all the wrongs, and reverence for all the rights of human nature." Channing had no doubt of the triumph of these principles, and his confidence was founded not on "events" or "outward progress," but on the power they exerted upon his own mind:

> In the response of my own soul to any great unchangeable truth, I hear the voice of universal humanity. I can conceive that my feelings are individual, but not any great conviction of the intellect, or lofty inspirations of the heart. These do not belong to *me*. They are universal.[4]

He tried to conduct and to achieve perfect harmony, for he was ill and meek and desired peace. "My tendency is to turn away from the contemplation of evils," he wrote to Mrs. Child. "My mind seeks the good, the perfect, the beautiful. . . . I am made of . . . poor material for a reformer."[5]

He tried to conduct America to a higher morality and freer religion than it had ever known, but his success was impeded by the noise of the radical abolitionists, and the dissonance that emerged and engulfed him weakened his spirit and hastened his death.

A. WILLIAM ELLERY CHANNING: SLAVES AND THEIR SAVIORS (1830–1835)

William Ellery Channing was the most distinguished clergyman in New England, a man with a worldwide reputation as a Christian moralist and philosopher.[6] As the minister to Boston's aristocracy, he moved in the circles of high society and bore the pressure of being a spiritual leader to wealth and influence. Maria Chapman acidly remarked that he "had been selected by a set of money-making men as their representative for piety."[7] Channing knew this, but sought not to be corrupted by the "aristocracy" whose "tendencies," he believed, "were hostile to those of Christianity and civilization." He hoped an "intellectual and moral" aristocracy would supersede America's conventional aristocracy. He would not achieve this by revolution—"I am anything but a revolutionist," he said— but by "the peaceful regeneration" of the world.[8] He tried to assist this transformation. His Federal Street Church became "the spiritual center of Unitarian Boston."[9] His preaching and the depth of his spirituality mesmerized his congregation.[10] In the loose fellowship of liberal ministers, he was early recognized as their head. When the American Unitarian Association was formed in 1825, Channing naturally was elected its president, but he declined to serve.[11] He became, and forever after remained, "the chief patriarch of Liberal Christianity."[12]

No cross emblazoned the shield of this patriarch; ironically, Channing's coat of arms carried the heads of three Negroes. His ancestors probably had fought to overcome the Moors; now their descendant carried on a peaceful crusade to overcome slavery.[13] He was exposed to slavery as a child in Newport, Rhode Island. Slaves waited on him at home and carried him to school. His father was a slaveowner and his grandfather had imported slaves. He was exposed to slavery while a tutor in Virginia. He came away with an abhorrence of the slaves' condition and a tender sympathy for the slaveholders' plight. He was exposed to slavery while convalescing in St. Croix, British West Indies.[14] He lived on a plantation with quarters that overlooked the slave village of the estate; his daily observations of the slaves worked upon his mind and the voice of conscience within begged to speak out.[15]

Channing first spoke out to his friends. To Joseph Tuckerman he wrote,"the West Indies have formed a dark page in human history. I know not a spot on earth, where man has done more to countenance the doctrine of total depravity."[16] To a Mrs. Codman he wrote that he sympathized with the slaves deeply and declared that the "infinite wrong [of slavery] cannot endure for ever in Christendom. It shocks me to think that Christians uphold it, for undoubtedly there are sincere disciples in the West Indies."[17] In a letter to Jane E. Roscoe of Liverpool, England, he provided page after page of his impressions of slavery in the British West Indies. He viewed slavery, he said, "with no small degree of . . . pain." The great evils of slavery, he felt, were of a moral nature. The slaves had sufficient food, adequate clothing for the Caribbean climate, and comfortable huts. To be sure, there were physical hardships. Slaves were forced by the "perpetual summers" of the West Indies to work all year. Their toil went entirely unrewarded. They suffered under overseers who were generally uneducated and undisciplined men. But the origin of their sufferings lay in moral evils. Their whole condition tended to degrade them to nearly the level of animals. This was the misery of slavery, said Channing, and it could not be expressed too strongly. "In these countries called Christian the largest part of human beings were iniquitously and forcibly reduced to a state which blights their whole nature, forbids all improvement and entails on them the misery of ignorance and vices."[18]

Channing also spoke out to his Federal Street congregation. Returning to the United States in May 1831, he preached on his observations of slavery the following month. He repeated to his people much of what he had told Miss Roscoe. In the British West Indies, he preached, there was the "mildest form" of slavery. "Still I think," he continued,

> no power of conception can do justice to the evils of slavery. They are chiefly moral, they act on the mind and through the mind bring intense suffering on the body. As far as the human soul can be destroyed, slavery is that destroyer.

The slave had no hope and lived for the moment. He sank into "a creature of sense," continued in "improvement as a child," abandoned himself to "great vices." Channing shared this information with his congregation because he believed that America had little sense of the reproach it brought upon itself. He wished Americans would duplicate the emancipation sentiment that had emerged in England. Slavery could not survive against "the excited moral conviction and reprobation of the civilized world." The lesson of the age was that "of sympathy with the suffering, and the devotion of the progress of the human race."[19]
It remained for Channing to speak out in print, to publish his opinions for the whole nation and world to read. But when he had returned to America, Boston was convulsed by Garrison's *Liberator*. *Slavery, emancipation,* and *abolitionist* were all explosive words. He timidly shelved the plans and first pages of an essay on slavery that he had begun to write while in the West Indies.[20] Time passed and the burden on his conscience grew heavy. His mind remained "painfully alive" to the subject of slavery. "I want to write, to act," he told Lucy Aikin in 1833, "but I must work alone, for I do not agree with the abolitionists, and I do not have the health, even if I had the ability, for a single warfare."[21]

Although frightened of the radical abolitionists, Channing began to be influenced by their propaganda and conversations. He was greatly impressed by Mrs. Child's *Appeal* and told her that the book had aroused his conscience to question whether he could remain silent on slavery any longer. Mrs. Child's opinions and publications were a constant inspiration to him. She more than anyone else, influenced him to participate in the antislavery movement.[22]

The abolitionists, aware of Channing's interest in antislavery reform, sought his help. Garrison wrote to him in January 1834, and admitted that not many influential people—Garrison used the words "not many mighty" people—had yet joined the "sacred strife." He warned that a "fearful responsibility" rested upon those who withheld their influence, and besought Channing to exert his prestige to save America from slavery. Apparently Channing ignored the letter.[23]

At the end of the summer of 1834, Edward Strutt Abdy, an English abolitionist, visited Channing at his Rhode Island retreat. Abdy immediately plunged into the topic of American racial prejudice and was surprised that Channing did not entertain advanced views on race. He was told that prejudice would end with time, "remonstrance on habits so long formed" did little good. If only "some great genius" among the blacks could excite sympathy and admiration for the race! Abdy found that Channing advocated segregated schools, and had himself originated the "African schools" of Boston. Channing only spoke of Negroes in the capacity of servants and laborers. He admitted that "prejudice was invincible, and that no effort, therefore, should be made to subdue it." His whole argument, said Abdy, was "the attempt of a philosopher, to find in the extent and intensity of a prejudice a reason for its continuance."[24]

Finally Samuel J. May, in the autumn of 1834, discussed

abolitionism with Channing at great length. Channing complained earnestly of the disruption and excitement aroused by the abolitionists. May listened patiently to Dr. Channing, a patriarch who indulged frequently in lengthy monologues, but then he burst out:

> Dr. Channing . . . I am tired of these complaints. The cause of suffering humanity, the cause of our oppressed, crushed colored countrymen, has called as loudly upon others as upon us Abolitionists. It was just as incumbent upon others as upon us to espouse it. *We* are not to blame that wiser and better men did not espouse it long ago. The cry of millions, suffering the most cruel bondage in our land, had been heard for half a century and disregarded. . . . You must not wonder if many of those who have been left to take up this great cause, do not plead it in all that seemliness of phrase which the scholars and practised rhetoricians of our country might use. We Abolitionists are what we are,—babes, sucklings, obscure men, silly women, publicans, sinners. . . . It is not *our fault* that those who might have conducted this great reform more prudently have left it to us to manage as we may. It is not *our fault* that those who might have pleaded for the enslaved so much more wisely and eloquently, both with pen and living voice than we can, have been silent. . . . We are not to blame, sir, that you have not so spoken. And now that inferior men have been impelled to speak and act against what you acknowledge to be an awful system of iniquity, it is not becoming in you to complain of us because we do it in an inferior style. Why sir, have you not taken this matter in hand yourself?

May shocked Channing with his unexpected rebuttal. After a period of silence, which seemed to May very long, Channing said: "Brother May, I acknowledge the justice of your reproof. I have been silent too long."[25]

On October 12, 1834, Channing preached as sermon on the anti-abolitionist mobs in New York City. He denied that

he stood "as the advocate of Antislavery associations." He
vigorously condemned their extremism but, perhaps heed-
ing May's reproof, declared that very often "it is the
indifference of the many to a good and great work, which
harries the few who cleave to it into excess." If men raised
up "just moral feelings aginst slavery," eventually this
"greatest calamity, scourge, curse, and reproach" of
America would yield. As an aristocrat appealing to aristocrats, Channing characteristically declared, "every superior
mind should be taxed to discern the safest and best means
of liberating the slave."[26]

The sermon created a stir. Follen called it an "abolition
sermon."[27] Abdy was told that it was the result of his
interview with Channing, but he doubted—and was probably right—that this was true.[28] The sermon was not an
"abolition sermon." When some members of his congregation wanted it published, Channing refused. "Were I to
publish, I should feel myself bound, not only to vindicate
more fully the invaded rights of Antislavery societies, but to
enlarge on what I deem their errors."[29]

Channing held elastic opinions of the abolitionists. His
seesaw statements were frustrating to anyone who wanted
to determine his true opinions. However, more often than
not his statements fell heavily against the abolitionists.
Privately in his letters, he attacked their lack of wisdom,
"injudicious operations," and "rashness"; called them a
"fallen party" who "hurt a good cause"; and said, "Happily,
the great prosperity of the country and the pressure of
business do not allow people to think much on the subject
[of abolition.]"[30]

Mrs. Child, Garrison, and Samuel J. May had all prodded
Channing to speak out in public. The publication of his
volume *Slavery* in 1835 must be considered, at least partially, the fruit of their pressure.[31] But it was a fruit somewhat bitter to their taste, for the essay condemned slavery
moderately and the abolitionists harshly. Still, it was from

the pen of an "idolized minister of a wealthy and conservative church," a man respected and admired for his moral authority more than any other man in Boston and New England, an aristocrat who cherished the esteem of aristocrats and men of influence. It was written by an invalid of fifty-five years of age. Channing's publication of *Slavery* was unexpected and courageous.[32]

Channing repudiated the slaveholder's claim of property in human beings. He demonstrated that man had sacred rights given to him by God, which slavery violated. He joined sympathy for the slave to a sympathy for the slaveholder. He outlined the evils of slavery and disproved those who perverted Scripture to support slavery. The means of emancipation, he said, belonged to the slaveholders themselves. "We have no right of interference, nor do we desire it." Gradual emancipation was a must. It would be "cruelty not kindness," to give to the slaves a freedom that they were unprepared "to understand or enjoy." He could not recommend colonization.[33]

He could not recommend abolitionism either. He devoted considerable space in his essay to deploring the physical attacks upon the abolitionists, and to attacking them verbally himself. They had done wrong; had produced newspapers with a tone often "fierce, bitter, exasperating"; had adopted erroneously "Immediate Emancipation" as their motto; were too democratic in their employment of women, children, and men—they accepted the "ignorant, the excitable, the impetuous"; they admitted "colored people" into their societies; alienated multitudes; and as an end result of their agitation seemed to have achieved nothing, and perhaps had retarded the cause of freedom and humanity.[34]

The first printing of 3,000 copies of *Slavery* was sold out in three weeks. Other editions quickly followed, and the essay was widely read and criticized.[35] The South thought Channing should have minded his business and kept silent.[36] From the border state of Kentucky, James Freeman Clarke gave a hearty "Amen" to Channing's moderate approach.[37] In the North, conservatives condemned Channing for "pouring oil on a conflagration."[38] Ellis Gray Loring found the essay "the most elaborate work on the *philosophy* of Anti-Slavery" he had ever seen.[39] Garrison called it "an inflated, inconsistent, and slanderous production."[40]

Garrison, the radical and prophet, led by his heart, directed by his emotions, impatient and daring, an agitator trying to change society, berated the work of Channing, the moderate and philosopher, who was led by his mind, directed by his reason, patient and prudent, a peacemaker trying to influence the individual. That they never mutually corresponded nor met to exchange ideas was abolitionism's great loss. The blame rests with Channing. Garrison desired an interview with him. Follen urged him to meet Garrison. The radical abolitionists saw his refusal to meet Garrison as "a stain" upon his antislavery record.[41]

B. A COMIC INTERLUDE—THE CAMBRIDGE ANTISLAVERY SOCIETY (1834).

Charles Follen had contacted Channing in July 1834, just after the Cambridge Antislavery Society was formed. It is likely that he asked him to join the new society. Channing declined: "I feel no freedom . . . to join any of your bodies, but the cause is dear to my heart."[42]

Although both Follen and Henry Ware, Jr., were said to have "concocted" the "little Abolition Society in Cambridge," the inspiration for the Society most assuredly was Ware's.[43] Henry Ware, Jr., (1794–1843), was the son of Dr. Henry Ware, Hollis Professor of Divinity in Harvard College. He had served the Second Church in Boston and was appointed Professor of Pulpit Eloquence and Pastoral Care at Harvard Divinity School in 1829. Extremely poor health delayed his acceptance of the post until October 1830, and greatly affected his activity thereafter. By 1841 he was forced to end preaching and teaching because of the further deterioration of his health. As a teacher in the Divinity School, Ware was respected and beloved by his students, and so continued to have great influence on the younger generation of ministers. The Society he helped organize and served as president reflected his desire to preserve individual opinion and promote the peaceful emancipation of slavery.[44]

The Cambridge Antislavery Society was the institutional representation of Channing's antislavery thought and of philosophical antislavery. It was a society of "gentlemen" who sought to moderate the "unreasonable violence" and "unchristian language" of the Garrisonians.[45] Almost all of its twenty-three members were Unitarians, and for the most part scholars and ministers: for example, Henry Ware, Sr., Sidney Willard, Charles Follen, Frederic Henry Hedge, William Henry Channing, and Charles T. Brooks.[46] Apparently, a few of these men at first gathered together quietly in a kind of caucus to propose ways to moderate the New England Antislavery Society. They desired to proceed slowly and without excitement, and in the light of this, decided against outside speakers, even Samuel J. May, until they themselves had established their own stance.[47]

At their first meeting, 4, June 1834 Ware presented what he felt the principles of the society should be: Slavery was wrong, must be removed, and all should work to end it. He added that measures for emancipation "must be conducted with great wisdom and gentleness, in a tone of Christian kindness and meekness"; that appeals for emancipation should be addressed "to the whites, especially to the slaveholders, satisfying them, by bold yet kind representations, of the sin and the dangers in which they and the whole country are involved"; and that it was "desirable to countenance and advance the efforts which are making to provide abroad a refuse for those persons of color who desire it, and to build up a colony for the establishment of Christianity and civilization in Africa."[48]

In the preamble and constitution of the Society that eventually emerged, the reference to colonization was dropped, the conciliatory attitude toward slaveholders was retained, and a call for the improvement in "the character and condition of the free people of colour"—including the establishment of better Negro schools—was added.[49] Channing said that he could subscribe to the provisions of the Cambridge Antislavery Society. Only his aversion to associations prevented him from joining.[50]

Ware then tried to no avail to introduce "temperate resolutions" at the New England Antislavery Society.[51] He proposed unsuccessfully a board of censorship for the *Liberator*, a proposal that Garrison's sons found "highly amusing." Six or seven "gentlemen" were to examine weekly all articles to be published in the paper.[52] He tried to get, with apparent failure, additional gentlemen interested in the Cambridge Antislavery Society. He told them that there were duties that obligated men to work for emancipation, duties to God, to the country, to the slaveholders, to the slaves. He did not oppose the Colonization Society. He listed the alleged evils that would arise with the success of emancipation measures: the loss of the white man's property, the worsening of the condition of the blacks, the dangers from insurrections, the difficulties over political rights for the blacks, and intermarriage. His approach involved an intellectual dissection of abolition, to expose all its responsibilities and problems to observation. His program was a steady, patient, and calm approach to emancipation.[53]

If Ware thought a society of men of influence could discuss emancipation amicably in the context of an academic salon and escape anti-abolitionist disapproval, he was wrong. Pressures were exerted on him by friends and associates to abandon his antislavery activity. Ware yielded. After 1834 he publicly made few antislavery statements.[54] His submission was primarily due to his feeble health. Even the most inquisitorial of Garrisonians, Samuel May, Jr., the cousin of Samuel J. May, acknowledged that it was for reasons of health that the invalid Ware could not cope with anti-abolitionist criticism. May appreciated the attempt of this "influential man" to do something for the cause, but still complained: "had he been more out-spoken and firm, it would have mightily encouraged the hearts of many of the younger [Unitarian] ministers who regarded him as a father, and would have been of the greatest value to the struggling friends of the enterprise."[55]

C. WILLIAM ELLERY CHANNING: ANTISLAVERY LETTERS OF A RELUCTANT REFORMER (1836–1839)

In May 1836 Channing attended a meeting of the New England Antislavery Society. He wanted to judge the Society for himself. He came away surprised and believed that the abolitionists were "improving by time" and "gaining wisdom by experience." He was very much impressed by an abolitionist speaker "of pure African blood." To hear this man was a revelation to Channing: "I felt that he was a partaker with me of that humanity for which I unceasingly thank my Creator. I felt on this occasion, as I perhaps never felt before, what an amount of intellectual and moral energy is crushed, is lost to the human race, by slavery." He noticed the absence of the "influential part of the community" at the meeting and found that the middle and laboring classes predominated. He recognized abolition's durability, for "with all its faults," he explained, it still was "founded essentially on religious conviction."[56]

Slowly, Channing moved toward the abolitionists. To

Harriet Martineau he wrote, "I am more and more willing to accept the enthusiasm of men in a glorious cause with all its errors." To Follen he wrote that the petitions to end slavery in the District of Columbia should be given special attention.[57] In the fall of 1836, in response to the destruction of James G. Birney's abolitionist press in Cincinnati, Channing published a twenty-six page letter to Birney that defended the freedom of antislavery discussion.[58] The *Letter* was "much less academic" than his essay *Slavery*. Amid his familiar doubts on abolitionist procedures, he now wrote that the abolitionists have "rendered to freedom a more essential service than any body of men among us."[59]

In August 1837 Channing composed an open letter to Henry Clay to oppose the annexation of Texas.[60] Channing gave several detailed arguments against annexation. His strongest argument held that the measure would extend and perpetuate slavery, and thus sink America below the civilization of the world. For this reason he could not accept fear of disunion as a sufficient cause for favoring annexation. Liberty was "a cause more sacred than union."[61] Channing's pamphlet was immediately circulated in Great Britain, France, and Mexico, and has been called the "most influential and widely circulated tract" in the decade of controversy over Texas annexation.[62]

In November 1837 Channing, greatly disturbed by Lovejoy's murder, headed a petition to secure the use of Faneuil Hall for a protest meeting. Mayor Samuel A. Eliot and the aldermen of Boston rejected the petition. They feared that partisan resolutions passed at the meeting would be taken as the opinion of the city, and that improper resolutions could injure the reputation of Faneuil Hall.[63] Channing addressed an open letter "To the Citizens of Boston," and told them that he neither represented nor encouraged the view of any particular antislavery party. He only wished for resolutions that would express opinion against mobs and violence and in favor of the freedom of the press.[64] A second petition for the use of Faneuil Hall was successful.

Channing did not want to speak because he was afraid that his voice could not be heard in Faneuil Hall.[65] But when 5,000 people gathered at the Hall on December 8, he reluctantly gave a short opening address. Another speaker presented Channing's resolutions in defense of the laws and the freedom of the press. After a tirade against the resolutions by James T. Austin, followed by an effective rebuttal by Wendell Phillips, the resolutions were passed by a large majority. Garrison pronounced them excellent, and Channing seemed to move yet closer to the radical abolitionists.[66]

He shattered such illusions a week later in a lengthy letter to the *Liberator*. Channing unfairly lumped Lovejoy together with other abolitionists. He suggested that they adopt peace principles and give assurance that another Lovejoy affair would not occur! He completed his letter by repeating his anti-abolitionist complaints.[67]

The antislavery strife wore heavily upon Channing; he much desired to mold the abolitionists into a pattern that suited his picture of ideal reform. In a letter to Mrs. Child in 1838 he urged the abolitionists to form themselves into a Society of Moral Preparation to cultivate moral influences within themselves. This activity would prepare them to reform the world in the wisest manner. Mrs. Child replied, *"Doing* is *preparing."*[68] And "doing" to Channing was painful. In a sermon on public unrest in 1838, entitled "Blessed Are the Peacemakers," Channing spoke from his heart when he cried, "Oh that we had the wings of a dove, that we might fly away and be at rest."[69]

In 1839 Henry Clay attempted to gain Southern support for his presidential ambitions by attacking the abolitionists and sanctifying American slavery. Channing felt compelled to answer Clay, and addressed an open letter to his close friend Jonathan Phillips.[70] Because Channing believed he would not write again on slavery, he wanted to "relieve [his] mind of all the burdens on the subject." He therefore touched a number of topics. He declared colonization a sham, a dream to remove slavery by draining it off to Africa—"a process about as reasonable as that of draining the Atlantic." He reaffirmed his trust in individual social reform: "I believe that, to produce moral changes of judgement and feeling, the individual, in the long run, is stronger than combinations." He defended the petition movement to emancipate slaves in the District of Columbia. He asserted the right of a slave to flee his bondage, and denied the right of anyone to return a fugitive to bondage. America's "sacred" Constitution, whatever it proclaimed, could not "sanctify injustice or repeal God's eternal law." Channing agreed slaveholders should be compensated for emancipating their slaves, but denied the slaveholders' right to indemnity. He included also his familiar criticism of the abolitionists. At the same time as he rose to praise them for their "generous sympathies," he stopped to chastise them for their zeal—especially in their attempts to over-come racial prejudice by failing "to respect . . . the usages of society." Finally, he once again offered his sympathy to the slaveholder:

> Could I liberate all the slaves, by misrepresenting the slave-holder, I would not do it. The primary work of a man is not to liberate slaves, but to be just, to render all their due, to do what is right, be the cost what it may.[71]

D. A TRAGIC INTERLUDE: THE SIMMONS AFFAIR (1840).

"I pray God," said George F. Simmons, "that I will always see my duty with clearness, and love it with heartiness; and when it is plainly before me"—here he could have repeated Channing's words—let me "do what is right, be the cost what it may."[72] George Frederick Simmons (1814–1855) graduated from Harvard College and the Harvard Divinity School. While not exactly a recluse in college, he did court "retirement" and was said to be "a lonely soul."[73] This solitary quality he retained the rest of his life. "His tastes and tendencies," said James Freeman Clarke, "were all in the direction of private study and labor."[74] Yet, whenever pressing issues of conscience arose, his was a reflex response. When members of the Harvard Divinity School faculty, for example, objected to a speaker (Ralph Waldo Emerson?) whom the students had invited to Divinity Hall in 1838, Simmons personally objected to Dean Palfrey, and defended freedom of speech.[75] Simmons was a brilliant and "true Christian scholar," a saintly spirit, "a man of genius," possessed with "a crowning gift of oratory" and an "acutely philosophical mind." When he graduated he was thought by his class to be the man most likely to succeed.[76]

Significantly, it had been Simmons, and not a Garrisonian abolitionist, who had responded to James T. Austin's attack upon Channing's *Slavery.* In an anonymous pamphlet written while he was still in Harvard Divinity School, he upheld Channing's views. He personally believed that Southern feeling not only could "be changed, but is daily changing." Slavery was wrong and the slave must be freed. Emancipation was possible, but must be gradual. "No prudent man," he said, "expects or wishes immediate abolition. The slave cannot yet be liberated with safety. He must still be restrained."[77]

On October 9, 1838, Simmons was ordained as an evangelist in Dr. Channing's church and immediately went to the Unitarian Society in Mobile, Alabama. He charmed the society with his quiet and gentlemanly manner and "splendid discourses." Few ministers fresh out of divinity school garnered as much praise as did Simmons. His congregation raved about him: "We are delighted," said one member. "He has won the whole society," said another. He is "universally admired," remarked a third. And by the standards of nineteenth-century salaries, they intended to reward him handsomely: "$3,000 this year, $4,000 the next, and $5,000 after that." The congregation grew rapidly as more and more people expressed interest in renting pews. He really has "immortalized himself," announced one wealthy laywoman. "If our church does not flourish it will be our own fault."[78]

On the night of May 19, 1840, four Negro slaves rowed Simmons out into Mobile Bay and placed him upon the brig *Emily* for passage to New England.[79] He had been forced to flee for his life. His crime had been to try to change Southern feeling on slavery by preaching two sermons.

On May 10th Simmons had preached a sermon on the kind treatment of slaves. The blacks, he admitted, were "brutish and unaspiring. They enjoy but an initiatory, and unsatisfied being, and must look forward to another world, even for that height of happiness, which *we* may possess in this." Their deficiencies in character were attributable to their ignorance and condition. Yet they were our brothers, although with "a coloured skin, and with faculties less apt," and like us shared "in the redemption of the cross." If laws prohibited the slave to be taught, then they were wicked and must be repealed. Simmons called upon his congregation to protect their slaves' homes and to make their family life more secure. The sermon was well received.[80]

On May 17th, Simmons had preached a sermon on the emancipation of slaves. He declared that if laws prevented emancipation, a slaveholder should hold his slaves as freemen, pay them, secure their domestic rights, protect them from wrong, and provide them with religious instruction. He advocated a kind of freedom within bondage. If a slaveholder respected the Christian concept of the brotherhood of man, he would not allow his slave to be degraded into a thing. *Thus will Christianity,*" Simmons taught, *eat out the heart of Slavery even while Slavery continues.* The servitude will not be a grinding bondage; but a mutual and fraternal dependence. While the outward condition continues the same; the virtual relation will be entirely changed.

In conclusion, Simmons confessed that he was not an abolitionist, but in fact had even opposed them. The sermon was listened to attentively, although one person walked out. But rumors spread the following day that as a result of the sermon some citizens were plotting to harm Simmons, and upon the urging of his friends, he fled.[81]

When Simmons returned to Boston he published the two sermons with a preface. He maintained that the opposition to him came from outside the church rather than within it. He exonerated the congregation of all blame, disclaimed any alliance with abolitionism ("Its spirit offends me"), and confessed his sympathy for the slaveholder. He had tried in the South to reach slaveholders as individuals. In New England, he said, he would have remained silent or urged the abolitionists "to moderation and charity."[82]

Simmon's experience in Mobile destroyed his career. He ceased to be an "accomplished orator," and became a "slow, hesitating, unimpassioned" speaker. After service as an assistant minister in Waltham, Massachusetts, and study in Germany, he accepted a call to Springfield, Massachusetts. When that city was troubled with a riot against George Thompson in 1851, Simmons preached two discourses in opposition to mobs. The sermon cost him his pulpit. How ironical, said James Freeman Clarke, that such a quiet and introspective man as Simmons, "whose tastes led him away from antislavery agitation," should twice lose his pulpit for expressing antislavery views.[83] He spent his last years serving a tiny, isolated congregation in Albany, New York. Contracting typhus, he died at the age of 41, and exchanged, his necrologist said, an "earthly hope for heavenly fruition."[84]

E. WILLIAM ELLERY CHANNING:
EMANCIPATION AND DEATH
(1840–1842)

In 1840 Channing was greatly impressed by a pamphlet by Joseph John Gurney on the results of emancipation in the British West Indies. Gurney visited Channing, told him of his favorable observations, and inspired him to write his own pamphlet. Entitled *Emancipation*, it appeared in November.[85]

The tract consisted of lengthy quotations from Gurney's work, and Channing's own observations. He was pleased to see that the West Indian Emancipation was the work of Christianity. Devout Christians had accomplished it and their work was an inspiration to him, for he believed it added much to the evidence of Christian truth. In light of the English example he castigated the American churches. Southern churches taught the rightfulness of slavery and Northern churches on the whole ignored it. He spoke of the debasing aspects of slavery and remarked, "were it not debasing, I should have little quarrel with it." He tried to calm those who feared the introduction into American life of a massive, free Negro population:

> I should expect from the African race, if civilized, less energy, less courage, less intellectual originality, than in our race, but more amiableness, tranquillity, gentleness, and content. They might not rise to an equality in outward condition, but would probably be a much happier race. There is no reason for holding such a race in chains; they need no chain to make them harmless.[86]

Faithful to his belief in individual action, he urged individuals to continue to oppose slavery "freely and fully." It was not enough "to think and feel justly"; one had to speak out. Reversing his earlier stand, he now especially encouraged women to work to end slavery, since its "chief victims" were of their sex. Speak to your husbands, to your sons, to your daughters, to your female friends about slavery, he said. To those who objected that this was not "proper work" for women, Channing exclaimed: "What! Do I hear such language in a civilized age, and in a land of Christians?" The work of women "is to be a minister of Christian love, . . . to sympathize with human misery."[87]

Individuals were to abstain from political action against slavery in the South as if it were slavery in a foreign country. They could and should free themselves from all obligations to use national law and their own state law to support slavery. Northern abolitionists were to treat the South as an impregnable bastion of slavery, impossible to be breached by national law. But if fugitive slaves escaped from the bastion and came North, they "should meet aid rather than obstruction." Then Channing made a boast that coming events proved false. In Boston, Massachusetts, "it is next to impossible that the slave who has reached us should be restored to bondage."[88]

He devoted some space in *Emancipation* to revealing his displeasure over the move of some of the abolitionists to organize an antislavery political party. Their party was bound to be corrupted and swallowed up by one of the major parties. The abolitionists' strength, he felt, had always been "in the simplicity of their religious trust, in their confidence of religious truth." He had even hoped that they would "gradually become a religious community, founded on the recognition of God as the common, equal Father of all mankind," of the union of every human soul with Jesus Christ, and of the brotherhood of man. He thought he saw in the principles of the early abolitionists a "struggling of the human mind toward . . . Christian union." Channing was adamantly firm in his opposition to political action. If nothing but political action could remove slavery, he said, then slavery must continue: and if we faithfully do our part as Christians, we are not responsible for its continuance. We are not to feel as if we were bound to put it down by any and every means. We do not speak as Christians when we say that slavery *must* and *shall* fall. Who are we, to dictate thus to Omnipotence?[89]

But Channing himself became somewhat politically involved as a result of the "Creole Case" of November 1841. The *Creole*, an American ship carrying a cargo of slaves from Virginia to New Orleans, Louisiana, had been seized by the slaves aboard and forced to sail to Nassau in the Bahama Islands. The British authorities in Nassau freed all the slaves except the actual mutineers, who were jailed. Daniel Webster, as Secretary of State, demanded the return of the slaves as mutineers and murderers, and as the "property" of citizens of the United States. The British refused and declared that the slaves were freed when they touched British soil. Channing marshaled evidence from political leaders and friends to write a two-part tract entitled "The Duty of the Free States."[90]

In the first part of the pamphlet he upheld the freedom of the escaped slaves, hoped they remained free, and chastised Webster for his remarks. In the second part, he devoted attention to the duties of the free states in regard to slavery. He heartily affirmed that they were to insist upon emancipation in the District of Columbia; to work "earnestly and resolutely" to amend the Constitution, in order to release the North from obligations to return fugitive slaves; and to dissolve the Union rather than to annex Texas.[91]

Throughout Channing's antislavery activity he was unable to satisfy either the radical abolitionists or conservative Unitarians. On several occasions both groups severely embarrassed him. In January 1842 he called upon Maria Weston Chapman "in a pastoral capacity" to urge her to participate in worship at the Federal Street Church or at least somewhere. She boldly testified to her dedication to the abolitionist faith and "excommunicated" the Federal Street Church. To mortify Channing as completely as possible, she praised Theodore Parker.[92] The conservatives of the Federal Street congregation humiliated him by refusing to permit him to let the Antislavery Society use the church for a meeting, and by canceling his offer of the church for the abolitionists' eulogy of Follen. Slowly he became estranged from his congregation. He preached only four times in 1840, and not once in 1841. On April 7, 1842, he preached for the last time in Federal Street Church.[93]

Channing spent part of the summer of 1842 vacationing in the Berkshire Mountains. When he discovered that no provision had been made by the local people to celebrate the anniversary of the West Indian Emancipation on August 1, he prepared an address and spoke to the villagers in Lenox.[94] Channing used the occasion to marvel once again at the West Indian Emancipation as a "Christian enterprise." Jesus Christ was the liberator of the slaves. The act of emancipation was "a sign of the triumph of Christianity . . . a new proof of the coming of Christ in his kingdom." Thus the movement for emancipation in America must be kept free of political involvement. The North had but one weapon to use—"moral force, the utterance of moral judgement, moral feeling, and religious conviction." Channing concluded by fervently praying:

O come, thou kingdom of heaven, for which we daily pray! Come friend and Saviour of the race, who didst shed thy blood on the cross to reconcile man to man, and earth to heaven! . . . Come, Father Almighty, and crown with thine omnipotence the humble strivings of thy children to subvert oppression and wrong, to spread light and freedom, peace and joy, the truth and spirit of thy Son, through the whole earth![95]

It was his last public prayer; he died two months later.

Lucretia Mott praised the Lenox Address. Channing, she believed, had redeemed himself at last. She told Mrs. Chapman to publish the address far and wide.[96] Another Garrisonian said Channing had climbed "the path of Christian humanity" and had nearly embraced the radical abolitionists.[97] Oliver Johnson pointed out that the Lenox Address was completely devoid of Channing's familiar attack on the Garrisonians. He felt it was a "hearty endorsement of their cherished principles and measures."[98]

After Channing's death, the radical abolitionists' praise contrasted with the Unitarian conservatives' disapproval of Channing's antislavery involvement. Dr. Francis Parkman lamented to a fellow Unitarian minister that Channing had "meddled" with abolitionism at all. In so doing he had lost "that eminent position" and had parted with "that *beautiful* influence" which he had among them. Parkman and his fellow conservative clergymen—Samuel Kirkland Lothrop, Alexander Young, and Ezra Stiles Gannett—were the ministers who officiated at Channing's funeral. "What a set they had," said Maria Child," To bury the old clothes of a living man. . . . The dead burying the dead with a witness." And Theodore Parker stood among the bereaved and thought what a "fearful mockery" was the spectacle before him: Parkman, Lothrop, Young—"the gnat, ass, [and] glutton, at the lion's funeral."[99]

With the death of Channing and Ware, and as a result of the experience of Simmons, the ideal of calm, reflective, patient discussion and influence in the abolitionist crusade faded. Antislavery as philosophy had lost its greatest exponents. When they died, the prudent approach to antislavery activity largely died with them.[100] It was an approach that in so many ways failed. The Cambridge Antislavery Society—that "robust organization," Garrison's sons called it—did not live beyond a few months.[101]

Simmons's gentle word to Southern slaveholders had nearly cost him his life. Channing's criticisms of the abolitionists brought few changes among them. His proposals to end slavery stopped short—once Northerners had done all they could to clear their individual consciences—at the Mason and Dixon Line. The slave in the Southern bastion remained a slave. In other respects it had been a success. It made a contribution to public opinion. Channing's reputation enabled his writings to reach gentlemen who would never have picked up the *Liberator* nor read a radical abolitionist pamphlet. Public opinion was altered a little more because of Channing's work, Simmons's testimony, and Ware's "academic antislavery salon."

4

Antislavery as Politics: Voting No to Slavery—1840–1850

A. JAMES FREEMAN CLARKE: THE PRACTICAL ABOLITIONIST

IN a lonely frontier outpost of Unitarianism, a young minister concluded a synopsis of Channing's *Slavery* for the *Western Messenger* by writing: "To all which we say, Amen." Among Unitarians, James Freeman Clarke (1810-1888) made one of the most remarkable pilgrimages in antislavery thinking. Upon graduation from Harvard Divinity School, in 1833, he took charge of the year-old Unitarian congregation in Louisville, Kentucky. There in the midst of slavery he served seven years.[1] He developed conservative views on slavery not because of the mildness of the institution in Kentucky, but because of the sincerity and humanity of so many of his slaveholding friends and parishioners—to say nothing of his slaveholding relatives. Clarke even declared that Kentucky slaveholders were overly indulgent with their slaves. "It is not doing what is just and equal," he told his congregation, "to give liberty and indulgence to a servant which he has not self command enough not to abuse."[2]

Clarke was of course no friend to slavery, only to slaveholders. "The system of slavery," he wrote to Margaret Fuller, "colours everything" in Kentucky. He attributed the violence and corruption of his environment to slavery.[3] Yet he placed no blame on the slaveholders. When Clarke reviewed Channing's *Slavery* in the *Western Messenger* in 1836, a reader objected because, although Clarke had condemned slaveholding, he had written that a slaveholder was not necessarily a sinner nor was immediate emancipation right. Clarke answered his critic by writing that at first even the Apostles did not rebuke slavery, and that second, the slaveholders merely practiced the Golden Rule in not immediately emancipating their slaves. For the slaves once freed would be unwilling and unable to work and without training and intelligence they would steal and starve. Throughout his life Clarke continued to maintain that the slaveholder was not a sinner nor slaveholding a sin.[4]

While holding these views, Clarke deplored the activities of the radical abolitionists. Their principles were false and their program brought evil to the slaves and their masters. The "Providence of God" was "secretly working" slavery's downfall; abolitionists (and pro-slavery advocates) worked *against* God in vain.[5] Writing in the *Western Messenger* on Lovejoy's murder and the burning of Pennsylvania Hall, he upheld freedom of speech, but insisted that he was not defending the abolitionists. Their course, he declared, was "foolish and wicked."[6] Some publishers lost subscribers for advocating abolitionism; Clarke lost subscribers to the *Western Messenger* for not advocating it.[7] Rather, he supported colonization as a "means of great good" and an indirect way to end slavery. When his close friend William Henry Channing became an anti-colonizationist, Clarke was ready to defend his own pro-colonization stand.[8]

Clarke's view of the "Simmons affair," therefore, was predictable. Reluctant to discuss Simmons as an "enthusiast or fanatic" in the pages of the *Messenger,* he sought the reasons why a "sensible and prudent man" should have taken such an "extraordinary" step. Simmons undoubtedly had been motivated by his conscience, but had *not* acted rightly. "A Christian minister in a slave holding state," admonished Clarke, *"ought not,* under present circumstances to preach on the subject of slave-holding." With proof-texts from the Bible to support his view, he said that since Christ avoided speaking on the subject, ministers certainly could and should do the same! He believed that the Mobile congregation would recover "from this injury, and flourish as before."[9]

When he arrived in Louisville, Clarke had made the choice between preaching Unitarian doctrine or a practical Christianity. He decided on the latter.[10] His views on antislavery before and after 1840 reflected this choice. The most practical way of handling slavery in a Southern milieu, he believed, was to proceed quietly and ever so moderately—avoiding both ivory tower isolationism and religiously enthusiastic abolitionism. The practical bent of his personality was reinforced by "the natural, hardhearted practicability" of his Western environment.[11] But a practical approach to emancipation of slaves in Kentucky meant proceeding very slowly, and this agonized Clarke. When he felt that no longer could he effectively serve his congregation, he looked longingly toward New England. "Everyday I become more of an abolitionist," he wrote to his future wife, Anna Huidekoper, in 1839. A year later he wrote to his sister that he would like to labor in Boston, being "ready to strike a good blow for freedom."[12]

Clarke left Louisville in June 1840 and visited his brothers in Chicago. In the First Presbyterian Church he lectured on "The Evils of Slavery." After considerable travel throughout the Northern states he returned to Boston in 1841 and founded his free church, "The Church of the Disciples." He wanted the church to be a "church of Christ" rather than a Unitarian congregation, built not on "coincidences of opinion," but on "coincidence of practical purposes." The purpose of his congregation was to assist its members "in working out [their] slavation." Various committees were set up, including one on slavery. Clarke led the Church of the Disciples until his death in 1888.[13]

At home in New England, Clarke throve and felt free to plunge wholeheartedly into the antislavery campaign. He became the friend of many of the radical abolitionists, so his attitude toward them changed, although he still could not accept their methods and never did join an antislavery society.[14] Since they permitted their speakers full freedom, he accepted invitations to speak at their meetings. He disagreed with the Garrisonians that the true way to abolish slavery was to attack the Church or the Union.[15] He did not advocate blind reverence for the Union and Constitution, but to dissolve the Union was revolution and revolution was wrong when reform was possible.[16]

Clarke dated his conflict with slavery from the year 1840. His path to emancipation as a "practical abolitionist" was through the use of the ballot-box. He supported the Liberty Party, the Free Soil Party, and the Republican Party.[17] The North, he maintained, was greatly implicated in slavery. The North was fettered to the institution by the Constitution, it shared responsibility for slavery in the District of Columbia, it returned fugitive slaves to the South, and it continued to protect slavery in Congress.[18] The North sent men to Congress who were more interested in Southern trade than Northern principles. This situation could be changed by letting moral questions enter politics and overcoming the "national sin [of] slaveholding" through political action.[19] Clarke was always accused of preaching politics instead of the Gospel. "*My* Master has taught me," said Clarke, "that the real Gospel is that which breaks every yoke and lets the oppressed go free."[20]

B. JOHN PIERPONT: THE MORALIST OF POLITICAL ACTION

Within the sanctuary of his free church, although Clarke could preach "politics," others in New England suffered. An ecclesiastical trial at the Hollis Street Church in the south end of Boston was concluding its work in 1841. John Pierpont (1785–1866) faced an ecclesiastical council of Unitarian leaders for preaching temperance and anti-slavery. Pierpont had continually defended political preaching. In a sermon preached in January 1839, entitled the "Moral Rule of Political Action," he objected to the "gross" misconception that political action was completely different from moral action. He explained that if one as a moral agent

> would effect a moral object, and that object may, . . . best be effected *by means* of political instrumentalities—the aim, i.e. of the body politic—the act, in itself considered, without reference to the motive to the act, or to the end to be attained by it, or the law that is to pass judgement upon it, is a political act; but considered *with* reference to all these things, it is a moral, at the same time that it is also a political act. It is a moral act performed *by the means* of political instrumentality.[21]

Pierpont voted only for legislators who upheld public morals and who obeyed "God rather than men." He refused to vote for those who did not exhibit morality in politics. Would he abandon party loyalty over moral issues? Yes, indeed. "When 'True to party,' " he answered, "means

'False to God,' it is time for me to quit it. . . . When my party [runs] away from morality, [it runs] away from me." One must exercise his right to vote and to use political influence, he remarked, for it was a Christian's duty to place in office those who would be faithful to reform.[22] The primary reform to Pierpont was antislavery.

Pierpont supported the Liberty party, and thus had traveled a long way from his days as poet for the Essex County Federalists thirty years before. His poetry was now at the service of the antislavery movement. He had graduated from Yale College in 1804; tutored children on a South Carolinian plantation, studied at the Litchfield Law School, and was admitted to the bar in Newburyport; failed at law and business; graduated from the Harvard Divinity School in 1818; and was ordained at the Hollis Street Church in 1819. For twenty-five years he served this prestigious and influential church to the mutual satisfaction of himself and his people.[23]

Pierpont had been a colonizationist, but moved over to abolitionism when he read Garrison's attacks upon colonization. He parted with Garrison over political action. He saw in 1838 that antislavery reformers could exercise an effective veto over the two main political parties if they would remain united. Sooner or later, politicians would have to listen to them.[24] At the Hollis Street Church where he was already noted for his practical sermons that avoided abstract and dogmatic theology, he began to preach on the "political issue" of antislavery.[25] When he alternated this theme with sermons on temperance the conservative politicians and liquor merchants in his congregation began to complain. The "Seven Years War" of John Pierpont began. By 1840 relations between him and his parishioners were so poor that an influential party in his congregation demanded his resignation. Pierpont held fast and an ecclesiastical council met in July 1841 to review the charges against him.[26]

Pierpont had ably defended himself in letters published

in the *Christian Register,* which prompted one sympathetic Unitarian clergyman to write that he had "gained a great victory" but to warn that " 'another such would ruin him.' As soon as the water gets smooth, after this tempest, I should think he had better make sail for another harbour."[27] Pierpont expected a favorable outcome to his trial even though conservatives predominated on the Council. He was deeply disappointed. In their verdict they did not recommend his dismissal, but still expressed "their disapprobation" of his conduct![28] Theodore Parker called the Council a modern "Sanhedrin."[29] Pierpont stubbornly continued his ministry, but finally conceded defeat. He resigned May 10, 1845, and "made all sail" to the small, insular, and newly organized First Unitarian Society in Troy, New York.[30]

C. THEODORE PARKER: THE AMERICAN REVOLUTIONARY REBORN

Theodore Parker (1810–1860) wrote to Pierpont and praised his lonely stand: "Nothing has happened for years so reflecting disgrace on the Boston clergy as your departure for the city [;] . . . their disgrace is your glory."[31] Parker had had his own battle with the Boston Unitarian conservatives. He had preached "a manifesto of transcendentalist Unitarianism" entitled "The Transient and Permanent in Christianity," on May 19, 1841. In 1842 he had published his controversial "Discourse of Matters Pertaining to Religion." In 1843 conservative Unitarians had invited Parker to discuss his views with them. They complained that his theology was not Christian. Some criticized him for his attack upon the Hollis Street Council. When they asked him to withdraw from the Boston Association of Ministers, Parker refused.[32] He would not abandon his church just as he would not abandon his country. He believed that liberal Christianity and American liberty must be preserved and reformed from within. Parker, the moderate revolutionary, spent his life preserving and reforming "the dream of history" and "the hope of humanity"—democratic institutions.[33]

Parker's grandfather, Captain John Parker, was commander of the Lexington minutemen in the American Revolutionary War. His grandfather's musket always hung above his desk. Intensely proud of his heritage, Parker was dedicated to political action and to a thorough commitment to democracy.[34] When Parker came to his first parish in West Roxbury in 1837, he planned to be a scholar rather than a reformer. He had chosen the West Roxbury congregation primarily because of its proximity to the great libraries in Boston and Cambridge. At first scholarship did absorb him; he devoted ten to fifteen hours daily to literary labors. He did not deliver his first antislavery sermon until January 1841. When he spoke again from the pulpit on slavery in 1843, it was to repeat this sermon.[35]

In it he declared that the North attempted to gloss over slavery in silence. For New Englanders to do this was to repudiate their revolutionary tradition and their allegiance to liberty. He praised the Garrisonians, but differed from them in his understanding of antislavery. If the Constitution of the United states sanctioned slavery, then as human law it was open to amendment: "What voters have made can voters unmake."[36]

A Garrisonian present quickly reported the sermon to his fellow believers. They were pleased that Parker had "come out" against slavery. Edmund Quincy mistakenly concluded that Parker had proclaimed the Antislavery Society as one of the "chief . . . manifestations of Christianity in the present age, without any Emersonian or Channingian qualifications." But he accurately reported that after this Parker would be aiding the abolitionist cause.[37]

Yet not until 1845, when Texas was annexed, did Parker

emerge as a major antislavery reformer. This grandson of Captain Parker saw American liberty menaced by the slavocracy's dominance in Washington and extension into the West. He began to advise and to coax the few antislavery congressmen and senators to increase their opposition to slavery. He saw slavery as the "one great practical question in America" to which all the other problems of the country were fastened. *The* problem demanded "practical measures"—that is, to Parker, "political measures"—for solution. As one of his biographers wrote

> [Parker] believed in politics . . . as the instituted agency for carrying ideas into effect. He did not stand outside of politics, as the [Garrisonian] abolitionists did: Rather he stood above them, as one who would make them serve his turn. He voted; encouraged voting; counted the actual and reckoned the possible votes; interested himself in the candidates to be voted for; stirred up the enthusiasm of constituencies; marshalled his armies of ballots as a general his myrmidons; all the time ringing out his prophetic call to conscience, and impressing on men the majesty of the eternal law.[38]

The reason Parker waited until 1845 to come out firmly against slavery was not only his preoccupation with scholarship, but also the unpopularity of the subject. He later declared that his sermon in 1841 and other antislavery activities offended his West Roxbury congregation and forced him to preach against slavery with the "greatest circumspection." However, when he became the minister of the Twenty-Eighth Congregational Society in Boston, the free church formed for him in 1845, he ceased to be circumspect. In his free church, Parker was a free man, and he quickly made up for his previous timidity.[39]

D. THOMAS WENTWORTH HIGGINSON: THE POLITICAL ABOLITIONIST OF NEWBURYPORT

The ministries of Theodore Parker and James Freeman Clarke made a great impression upon young Thomas Wentworth Higginson (1823–1911). Under Clarke's influence at the Church of the Disciples, Higginson entered the Harvard Divinity School. Upon graduation in 1847 he accepted an invitation to become minister of the First Religious Society of Newburyport. At his ordination Clarke gave the charge. He urged Higginson to rebuke the sin of slavery from his pulpit.[40]

Higginson had seen slavery on his uncle's plantation in Virginia and at slave auctions in Baltimore.He read Mrs. Child's *Appeal* and Harriet Martineau's "The Martyr Age in America," and then entered the antislavery movement. During his ministry at Newburyport, he was drawn to the Free Soil party in 1848 and became actively involved in politics. The pro-slavery feelings of Newburyport were very deep and the young minister faced a revolt in his congregation. Unafraid, he invited a fugitive slave to speak in his church, shared his pulpit with fellow political abolitionists, including Theodore Parker, and attacked Zachary Taylor's nomination for president as the work of the disciples of "ultra-slavery." His people became increasingly uneasy. "What his old Whig parishioners will do," declared his close friend Samuel Johnson, "no mortal knows." The answer came soon—hard pressed by a small, wealthy, contingent of his congregation, Higginson resigned in September 1849. After a period of relative inactivity, he took charge in 1852 of the Free Church in Worcester, a "Jerusalem wildcat" organization founded upon the model of Parker's Boston congregation, and devoted to antislavery and free religion. Higginson had found a perfect home.[41]

E. THE MINISTER AS A POLITICAL CANDIDATE

The antislavery Unitarian minister who was politically active during the 1840s had several Unitarian political leaders to inspire him. One example of an antislavery Unitarian politician was John Albion Andrew (1818–1867). He was drawn to the Church of the Disciples by the "practical Christianity" of James Freeman Clarke,[42] and won to antislavery by Mrs. Child's *Appeal*. But he never joined an antislavery society and he declared: "I am not a come-outer. I am a stay-inner."[43] He always remained faithful to the processes of democratic government and the duties of citizenship. Devoutly religious, he filled his speeches with a profusion of biblical passages and Christian phrases. Because of his pious politics, he was subjected to "great abuse and vilification." He taught Bible classes at his church, preached intermittently for Clarke and the minister of the "Baptist Church for colored people." He was a vigorous opponent of slavery and a lawyer for fugitive slaves. He moved from the Whigs to the Free Soilers to the Republicans. He was the ideal candidate for governor of Massachusetts at the opening of the Civil War. He won by the largest popular vote ever cast for a governor of Massachusetts up to that time.[44]

Another Unitarian political leader was John Gorham Palfrey (1796–1881). Palfrey was at first minister of the influential Brattle Street Church and then Dexter Professor of Sacred Literature at the Harvard Divinity School. Entering politics in the 1840s, he served as a state legislator, as secretary of state of Massachusetts, and as a representative to Congress. He believed that the Garrisonians were irresponsible reformers and joined the Cambridge Antislavery Society. But in 1844 he inherited a number of slaves from his father's plantation in Louisiana, and immediately set about with great effort and considerable expense to free them. This experience and the annexation of Texas caused him to see clearly the political implications of slavery. Palfrey became a true believer in Free Soil.[45]

Still another Unitarian politician was John P. Hale (1806–1873). He was a "compulsive churchgoer," a leader at the Unitarian Church in Dover, New Hampshire, and a faithful parishioner, correspondent, and friend of his minister, the Garrisonian John Parkman. Hale began his political career as a state legislator in 1832 and became Congressman of New Hampshire in 1843. The issue of the annexation of Texas weakened his allegiance to the Democratic party and with the help of Antislavery Whigs, Independents, and Liberty party men, he was elected to the Senate in 1846. In 1848 he was nominated by the Liberty party, and in 1852, by the Free Democrats (Free Soilers) as their presidential candidate. Hale remained in the Senate until 1864.[46]

To these examples of successful Unitarian antislavery politicians must be added the unsuccessful candidates. In 1842 John Greenleaf Whittier wanted the Liberty party to capitalize on the publicity created for John Pierpont by the Ecclesiastical Council. After consulting several political abolitionists and finding "perfect enthusiasm" on their part for Pierpont, Whittier induced the Liberty party convention to nominate the Hollis Street pastor. Pierpont declined, however, preferring to devote his time to free his pulpit from control by the pews.[47] But to the disgust of his Garrisonian friends, he still campaigned for the Liberty party.[48]

In 1842 Pierpont also preached one of his most "treasonous" sermons. He called the surrender to the South of a fugitive slave an act of the "morality of a Judas." If in his "heaven-bound journey" he saw that the Constitution of the United States stood in his path, he declared; "It shall not hinder—it shall help me on my way; for I will mount upward by treading it under my feet." Conservatives asked reformers to cherish the memory of the forefathers of the Constitution, but when the work of our forefathers became incompatible with God's commands, then Christians could not obey both "our dead fathers" and the "Living God." They must choose. To Pierpont the choice was clear. [49]

Pierpont felt exiled in Troy, New York, and when the opportunity arrived in 1849 to be minister of the First Congregational (Unitarian) Church in Medford, Massachusetts, he eagerly accepted. Parker immediately sent him a note of welcome: "I understand that [you are leaving] the Trojans [to] come nearer to us. 'Of course' you won't think of preaching about *Politics,* or any of the matters which demand *Reform.* No you will *preach the gospel.*" While in Medford, Pierpont ran for Congress on the Free Soil ticket in 1850. A poor third-place finish ended his career as a political candidate, but not as a political preacher. Then that career ended as well. In 1858 his congregation declared that he had been "unwisely persistent in preaching politics." Pierpont resigned.[50]

Whittier also promoted Higginson as a candidate of the Free Soil party for Congress in 1848. The Newburyport minister accepted and began to "stump" for the party. He did not believe that he could possibly win, but sought to play the role of "spoiler" and defeat the most pro-slavery candidate. His campaign, of course, aggravated his already disgruntled congregation. His mother wrote:

> And so you are fairly entered again on a political career—safe—because on the unpopular side. Therefore I don't complain.[51]

Indeed it was unpopular; the Free Soil party polled a dismal 73 votes in Newburyport.[52]

The Compromise of 1850 brought Higginson again into the political arena. The political abolitionists who opposed the Compromise thought that if all antislavery voters, whatever their differences, would unite, they could halt the spreading power of the slave states. Once again on Whittier's recommendation, the Free Soil party nominated Higginson for the third district of Massachusetts in Congress. Higginson distributed 4,000 copies of his campaign manifesto, "Address to the Voters of the Third District."[53]

He explained that he sought to tell the truth, regardless of whether it secured him votes. "It is of great importance that [votes] should be neither gained nor lost by a misunderstanding of the truth," he said. The Free Soil party followed a course of *political* and *moral* agitation. The party attacked the compromises that surrendered the Wilmot Proviso, conceded too much to Texas, and produced the infamy of the Fugitive Slave Law. Citizens could combat the Fugitive Slave Law, explained Higginson, through state legislation to protect citizens from the Law's grasp, through agitation for its repeal, and by constitutional amendment. As *voters* had a duty to try these proposals, but as *men*, Higginson declared—and in this he went beyond the position of the Free Soil party—they had a duty "TO DISOBEY IT," and to accept the legal penalties. "The most valuable citizen is he who obeys the laws when his conscience is not outraged,—and when it is outraged; disobeys and takes the penalty." In conclusion Higginson said, "we must legislate openly and actively on the side of freedom." The Free Soil party was pledged to this course; if another party, "truer and wiser in freedom's cause" arose, he would support it.[54]

Higginson obtained 21 percent of the vote and finished third. He found as had Pierpont that a "politician" in the pulpit or a "pulpiter" in politics was an undesirable.[55]

In 1848, friends urged Parker to enter politics. Their suggestion was not new; he had been asked before. But to be a congressman or senator had no appeal for him. There were two objections, he declared. First of all, no one would vote for him. He doubted that any town in the state would give him any post above hog-catcher, and even for that he possessed a distinct disability: "A man in spectacles could not well run after swine." Second, he felt that his place was the pulpit and not the politician's stump. His role would be solely as correspondent, critic, and "chaplain" to the antislavery politicians in Washington.[56]

F. THE POLITICAL EVENTS AND TACTICS

In 1845, the year of the Texas annexation, Parker opened his lifelong friendship with Charles Sumner and began his work as a pastor and critic to political leaders. Higginson attended meetings and prepared petitions to protest the annexation. Pierpont and Palfrey, as well as several Garrisonians, addressed a letter to the clergy of Massachusetts and asked them to defeat annexation by putting pressure on the state's representatives. The year before, Clarke had proposed the formation of a "great League" of antislavery men to oppose all candidates who supported the annexation of Texas. He himself had supported Henry Clay in 1844 as the only presidential candidate who was opposed to annexation *and* could possibly win.[57] After Polk had been elected and the momentum toward annexation increased, he told his people not to despair of parties or of the nation.[58] Later on in 1845, he again called for a great Northern league of all parties pledged to vote for the best men.[59]

The eventual annexation of Texas and the beginning of the Mexican War in 1846 reinforced Clarke's belief in the need for a "Great Northern League for Freedom." In sermons to his congregation he explained exactly what he meant. The members of the League would be pledged not to support anyone who was not opposed to slavery. This *"abstinence pledge"* would be binding upon all members. A candidate would be considered opposed to slavery if he could support the League's four great measures, namely, to abolish slavery in the District of Columbia, to halt the interstate slave trade, to abolish by amendment the pro-slavery clauses in the Constitution, and to halt the extension of slavery. The League would not nominate any candidates itself. It would hold social meetings like those of the Odd Fellows, but all secrecy would be avoided. It would finance lecturers, "local lodges," newspapers, and tracts. The practical effect of the League, said Clarke, would be to control the outcome of close elections. Until a consensus of antislavery opinion was achieved in the North, the League could well be potentially the best tactical weapon of the antislavery party.[60] Clarke's League never became a reality. His belief that the various factions of the antislavery movement could be united was idealistic and premature.

The political abolitionists along with the other antislavery men were horrified by the Mexican War. Clarke wanted our armies withdrawn and the invasion, plunder, and conquest ended. "Our mission on earth is not that of Genghis Khan, of Attila, of Caesar, of Napoleon," he declared, we should not desire Mexican soil; we have enough for our own use for a century. Pierpont also attacked the slavocracy's insatiable appetite for land—"to conquer, occupy, hold, and ultimately to absorb, after the pattern of Texas—the whole of Mexico, to the isthmus of Darien [as] Slave Territory. . . ."[61]

Parker measured the war's cost against the funds provided for libraries, art, and education. The drain of the Mexican War upon men and resources was appalling.[62] It was an "aristocratic war, a war against the best interests of mankind," a war to extend slavery. Those who did not oppose the war, said Parker, were guilty of "moral treason." The war corrupted its own armies; ten percent of the American soldiers in Mexico deserted. When the soldiers or "trained murderers" came home morally ruined, they were unfit to work. The war had cost much, and hopefully it had taught us much. Its lessons had taught us, Parker declared, to teach our children in turn "that such a war is sin, and [that] slavery [is] sin."[63]

The times were grim, but Clarke found hope in having Palfrey in the House and Hale in the Senate. Theodore Parker praised Palfrey's political testimony, and Higginson saw in Joshua R. Giddings's work in Congress an attempt "to arouse [the] nation from sin."[64] Much hope was placed in a political awakening of the people, in the work of the North's antislavery representation in Congress, and upon the progress of the Free Soil party.

In the expression of his faith in political change, Parker started with the primary level of politics—the people. All great questions, he taught, were to be decided by the people of America. In our country all men were voters and our democracy developed and instructed "the mind of the nation."[65] The trouble in the 1840s was that America's politics were chiefly directed by the merchant class—a "politics in which money is preferred, and man post-poned."[66] The "Plutocracy of the North" with its feudal monetary powers shared the same concerns with the "Slavocracy of the South." They were children "born of the same mother"—irresponsible power.[67] When a democratic government "follows the eternal laws of God," declared Parker, "it is founding what Christ called the kingdom of heaven." But here in America our leaders in power made laws for their own benefit. Slavery and business protected themselves and the nation was made subservient to the "politics of pedlers."[68]

Parker accused the nation's political leaders of not opposing slavery. Out of the thirty-one New England members of Congress, no more than five could be considered antislavery men. In forty-eight years out of sixty, a slaveholder had been president of the United States. Sadly the men who controlled New England politics "love to have it so." If either party thought it could gain by supporting antislavery it would become antislavery immediately. But each party knew that it gained nothing by supporting antislavery. The people would act politically to overthrow the apparently immovable status quo, whether by constitutional or unconstitutional action. "The action of the people of a nation," Parker remarked, "must be political action."[69]

Parker evaluated the role of the Free Soil party in December 1848. Men of uneven talents and discordant allegiances, he admitted, represented this party, yet he hoped that their motto "No more slave territory" would soon be replaced by "No slavery in America." "The revolution in ideas," declared Parker, "is not over till that is done, nor the corresponding revolution in deeds while a single slave remains in America." The Free Soil party must go forward. Although it faced the powerful interests of the South, "the ultimate power of the genius of freedom is certain."[70]

The concept of Free Soil was that the freedom of the North, not the slavery of the South, would be extended to the West and Southwest. But with the Fugitive Slave Law of 1850 the North found its free soil threatened. When Daniel Webster spoke in behalf of the Law and the protection of the Union, the political abolitionists protested. Parker was particularly severe with Webster and said his conduct was comparable with that of an Austrian or Russian politician, or a Benedict Arnold. Clarke thought the stir created by Webster's speech propitious for the election of Free Soil candidates. Their good showing, he believed, would record the judgment of Massachusetts on Webster's stand. He urged Sumner, Higginson, and others to campaign, especially for Palfrey.[71]

Opposition to the Fugitive Slave Law was an important part of Higginson's campaign message. Parker also rallied opposition to the Law in sermons to his congregation; they responded with applause and stamped their feet. He said that clergymen regarded the Fugitive Slave Law as not their

"official business." But the "official business" of a clergyman, statesman, or mechanic was second to his personal
duty as a man. Parker did not like violence, but he felt that
he must do all in his power to prevent the return of a
fugitive slave. He felt that the fugitive had "the same
natural right to defend himself against the slave-catcher, or
his constitutional tool, that he has against a murderer or a
wolf." A man who seized a fugitive, "in that moment of
attack alienates his right to life," and if no other escape was
available, Parker would "kill him with as little compunction
as [he] would drive a mosquito from [his] face."[72]

On October 15, 1850, warrants were issued for the arrest
of two members of Parker's congregation, the fugitive
slaves William and Ellen Craft. Quickly the Vigilance
Committee formed to protect fugitives gathered with Dr.
Bowditch, Loring, Jackson, May, Jr., Phillips, Douglass,
Lewis Hayden, and others. They proposed to scare the
Southern kidnappers out of Boston. Parker was chosen to
inform the two slave-catchers that their lives were in danger.
William Craft was armed and hidden in the home of Lewis
Hayden. Ellen stayed with the Lorings. Would the Vigilance Committee actually use force? Parker said he would.
Higginson declared that although he abhorred bloodshed,
a man might need to defend his inalienable rights by
physical force. Fortunately, no one had to use a fist or fire a
shot. The intimidation of the kidnappers worked and they
fled Boston. Parker gave the Crafts a legal marriage and
sent them on their way to England.[73]

Clarke felt that a constitutional view of the subject of
fugitives required proper safeguards for the rights of free
Negroes. Northern legislators had been driven to pass the
Fugitive Slave Law out of their regard for property and
southern threats. Were we to pass any law the South
demanded? he asked. Surely the "freedom of freemen is at
least as deserving of security, under the constitution, as the
slavery of slaves."[74]

Politicians proceeded, said Parker, on the idea that the State was for a portion of the people and not for all the people. Three million slaves were not recognized as citizens. If we protested this situation, the politicians laid "their fingers on our lips." They believed government was chiefly for the protection of property, and that all men were to obey laws even if their consciences opposed those laws. They called for conduct that emulated Judas Iscariot. They offered ten dollars to betray a fugitive; Judas took thirty pieces of silver to betray Jesus. "It was," Parker bitterly declared,

> as honest a fee as any American commissioner or deputy will ever get for a similar service. How mistaken we are! Judas Iscariot is not a traitor; he was a great patriot; he conquered his "prejudices," performed "a disagreeable duty" as an office of "high moral and high principle;" he kept the "law" and the "Constitution," and did all he could to "save the Union;" nay, he was a saint, "not a whit behind the very chiefest apostles." "The law of God never commands us to disobey the law of man." *Sancte Iscariote ora pro nobis.*[75]

Parker did not fear the talk of disunion. If the Constitution failed, Americans should dispense with it and put a new one in its place. No danger to the Union yet existed. If the people of Massachusetts had really thought there were any danger, they would have gathered a force of a hundred thousand armed men. Still, if the Fugitive Slave Law were enforced in Massachusetts then, Parker believed, the Union ought to be dissolved. The South had gone too far. She had spat upon the North. She had gotten largely what she had wanted. But "let her come to take back the fugitives," warned Parker, "and trust me, she 'will wake up the lion.' "[76]

The long pilgrimage in antislavery thinking of the men described here had come to an end with the Fugitive Slave law. They all had advocated change through the use of the ballot, but the inherent violence of the Law had produced violent actions even from Christian ministers like Parker and Higginson. But although the pilgrimage led only *some* political abolitionists to violence, *all* had taken a pilgrimage. Clarke had moved from colonization in the slave environment of Kentucky to political antislavery in Boston; Pierpont from the Federalists to Liberty partymen; Parker from scholarship to reform; Hale from the Democratic Party to the Liberty Party and the Free Soil coalition; and Palfrey from slave owner to, very quickly, emancipator. Youth and discipleship shortened the pilgrimage of Higginson and Andrew. Both were only children when Garrison's *Liberator* appeared. Both had Clarke as a mentor and Parker as an inspiration. The route of their pilgrimage was already clearly marked.

All were somewhat late to the cause. They wanted to reform society, a slow process, rather than remake society—what the Garrisonians either naively thought and pathetically hoped could be, or arrogantly demanded should be—an instant achievement. All these men were either political candidates or campaigners. They worked to preserve, to refine, and to reform democratic institutions. They worked hard to influence public opinion. Their campaigning was intrinsically a blend of morals and politics. Unconsciously, or perhaps consciously, their political action began to blend with the "moral action" of the Garrisonians.

PART II

The Patterns Merge

5

From Sect to Church: The Flagging of Religious Enthusiasm—1840–1860

As the invasion of the North by Southern fugitive slave-hunters increased, so Northern antislavery sentiment increased. In reaction the South became more and more defensive and unyielding in its demands for the protection and extension of slavery. Men from Georgia, South Carolina, Virginia, and other Southern states, stalking through the streets of Northern communities in search of fugitive blacks, pushed the nation into the second half of the "reign of terror" between pro-slavery and antislavery partisans.

Unity among the advocates of antislavery could have helped to enlarge antislavery influence, but, of course, incidents like the schism of 1840 prevented a united front against the Southern invaders. The true believers, the

Garrisonian sectarians, were severely tried on the one hand by the infighting and intra-party restructuring that had to take place in the 1840s, and on the other hand by the violent events of the 1850s. As the faith of some of them was severely shaken, the faith of others became more dogmatic and uncompromising. Potential recruits to Garrisonianism during this period seldom measured up to the standard of radical abolitionist dogma. The phenomenon arose of people who believed in the methods and ideals of the Garrisonians but refused to join them. Fewer were converted, and there was less religious enthusiasm. A stabilization and secularization of their program slowly but steadily progressed as the Civil War approached. Political methods seemed more reasonable and in many ways providentially required. Were the radical abolitionists secularizing their religious movement or was Providence equipping American politics for a religious crusade? No matter, the trend was clear—religious antislavery and political antislavery were becoming one. The patterns of antislavery merged as the 1850s were preparing America for a great holy war in which radical abolitionists, political abolitionists, and the few remaining advocates of philosophical antislavery would take part.

A. THE FAITH DEFENDED—THE AFTERMATH OF THE SCHISM OF 1840

Maria Child smiled when the political abolitionist John Pierpont told her he was going to try to stand between the two parties, the old organization and the new organization. She realized that few antislavery reformers were that sure-footed. To Maria Child the rupture of the American Antislavery Society in 1840 was about freedom and conformity. The Garrisonians cherished their freedom too much to expel any individual who wanted women to vote at abolitionist meetings, or who desired non-resistance, or who wished to promote disunion. She observed that the lines between the two groups fell, quite unintentionally, along a denominational pattern. Most of the old organization were Unitarians and Hicksite Quakers, and most of the New Org (as Mrs. Child was wont to call it) were Calvinists of one profession or another. Pierpont desired to work between the two. Well go ahead, said Mrs. Child, but do not forget:

> The bigoted always get somewhat of assistance from the liberal, by virtue of their liberality of opinion; but it works all *one way*. The Unitarian is often brought to give his money and his word to advance some Calvinistic purpose; but the Calvinist is too narrow to aid Unitarians, even in a good work. . . . Old organization is, in the same way, often brought to help some scheme of New Org; but the reverse, never.[1]

The sorting of the lambs took place quickly, and it was not possible for an abolitionist to stand discreetly between flocks or pass from one to the other. Ellis Gray Loring felt that if the antislavery organizations could not rise above their intra-party quarrels they would assuredly die, but although he favored political action, he cast his lot with the old organization.[2] Samuel J. May hurriedly sent a note to Mrs. Chapman and pledged his allegiance to the old organization, "where I hope to be found," he declared, "so long as I live."[3] For Mrs. Chapman the quarrel between the old organization and the new one was "the noblest struggle for freedom, that ever delighted the centuries."[4] To a true Garrisonian "the *wrong kind* of antislavery" could only be considered as "the anti-Christ."[5] With heresy running rampant, the Garrisonian flock were warned to be on their guard. "The very *elect*," cautioned Henrietta Sargent (1785–1871), "are in danger from false brethren."[6] But the "elect" survived and in 1845 Eliza Lee Follen judged the old organization to be ascendant.[7] How could it have been otherwise? God was with them.[8] Moreover, He evidently had infused their society with a divine wisdom. How else could one explain the assurance with which Mrs. Chapman boldly declared: "There never was a Society that equalled the American Anti-Slavery Society for sagacity. In all emergencies that have happened since its foundation, it has never made a mistake, that was of the slightest importance."[9]

The three problems related to the schism of 1840, nonresistance, the woman question, and political action, had great influence on the forms that Garrisonian activity took during the period 1840 through 1860. The first of these concerns, nonresistance, was held by all the Garrisonian Unitarians, including a new fellow traveler, William Henry Furness (1802–1896), who began to assist radical abolitionism in the 1840s[10] The nonresistant position, Mrs. Child believed, was natural to abolitionists since nonresistant principles and abolitionist principles were identical. "I never saw a truth so clearly," she told Ellis Gray Loring: Nonresistance was a panacea for all ills of life, social and civil. It was "the *only* one for a disordered world," declared Mrs. Child, "a sovereign cure for all ills that flesh and spirit are heir to."[11]

When the Mexican War of 1846–1848 began, radical abolitionists saw both their abolitionist and nonresistant "principles" trampled upon. The war brought the possible extension of slavery and the loss of life. Thus, doubly offensive to nonresistants, the war was naturally condemned by all the radical abolitionists. Every step America took in that awful war, lamented Samuel J. May, plunged the nation deeper in guilt. Let our soldiers "be commanded to repent," advised May, "which means turn back, . . . and let our nation confess before God and the whole world, that we have done a grievous wrong."[12]

During the 1840s the nonresistant philosophy of the radical abolitionists reached its greatest height, but with the tragic events of the 1850s a gradual erosion of their nonresistant "principles" occurred.

However, the Garrisonian attitude on the woman question remained constant. If anything, the support for the employment of women in all phases of the abolitionist drive steadily increased. There were obvious reasons for this appreciation. First of all, their leader, Garrison, had committed himself to battle for women's social and political rights. Thus, when his wife gave birth to a girl in 1844, the proud Garrison announced: "We shall demand for her the rights of a human being, though she be female."[13] He permitted no second-class discipleship for women in the abolitionist ranks.

Second, the small size of the Garrisonian sect did not permit the rejection of assistance by women. *"Our Zion,* alas!" cried Maria Chapman, "has but 'a single man to each ten yards of wall!' "[14] Everyone who would work was accepted, and "trusty females" were eagerly sought.[15] Whenever the women were absent, for example when Maria Chapman, Eliza Follen, and Susan Cabot visited Europe for extended periods of time or when Maria Child suffered bouts of depression and inactivity, their loss was sorely felt.[16]

Third, some of the Garrisonian women saw the parallel significance of Negroes' rights and women's rights. Intrinsically the battle for the one was bound up with the other.[17] The exuberance of a Mrs. Chapman or an Abby Kelley Foster, who appreciated their own sex and exerted their talents of leadership, were great examples for more timorous women like Henrietta Sargent and Eliza Follen.[18] As the abolitionist movement grew, the women's rights principles of Maria Chapman, Abby Kelley Foster, and Maria Child grew with it.

Finally, the Garrisonian movement could ill afford to lose

the extremely valuable assistance provided by the women. It was obliged to acknowledge the excellence of the work performed by women. Their valuable financial contribution to the movement through their annual fair continued. Mrs. Follen held small weekly gatherings of friends to work on the fairs. Meeting in different homes she endeavored "to fan the embers to a flame" wherever abolitionist activity showed an initial spark or wherever established abolitionist fires were beginning to cool.[19] She penned many a letter in soliciting goods for their bazaars. "Come and help us do something towards building up a temple of a truer freedom" than we now own, she wrote. "Help the regeneration of our much abused liberty," she pleaded. "Can you send some fruit for our refreshment table?" she asked. "We fear the multitude may not be fed and only the miracle of anti-slavery love will meet the demands for food." All these requests were made in the name of the "holy cause."[20]

Anne Weston described her work behind the long tables at the bazaars as much more difficult than manning a revolution barricade in Paris. Ellis Gray Loring commented drolly that the ladies at the fair made most of their money by selling to one another.[21] But the hard work and sororal selling added much money to the movement's treasury.

The 1840 fair, as noted previously, netted $2,001. By combining shrewd planning, the ever-increasing interest in antislavery activity, and high quality merchandise from sympathizers in Europe (the result of contacts of Mmes. Follen and Chapman), the ladies by 1855 more than doubled the net proceeds of the 1840 fair and in 1859 tripled the 1840 figure. The most religious of sects, if not corrupted and secularized by financial success, can sometimes assume a certain arrogance and fastidiousness. Mrs. Chapman admitted that the $6,000 raised in 1859 was good money, but complained about competing fairs that were springing up and hindering the "grand primal work." For the radical abolitionists were working toward "the Liberation of a continent, and to the salvation of a world" she said. Naturally, the Garrisonian sectarians had to be more discriminating now. Antislavery fairs had nearly ceased their usefulness, she declared. Having gained respectability, the radical abolitionists deserved and desired "big cash donations."[22]

The third wedge in the cleavage of 1840, the question of political activity and its offspring the campaign for disunion, was heatedly debated by the Garrisonians.[23] They believed that since the South contributed toward the election of each administration, abolitionist support of the administration would be in part support of pro-slavery organization. Hence, in Mrs. Chapman's opinion, the abolitionists had always to be in opposition to every administration, whether Whig or Democrat. When some abolitionists proposed their own political party as a new alternative, the Garrisonians believed that the party would fall speedily under the control of the major parties. Their religious dedication to moral action precluded political action. Political results could only *follow* moral methods, said Mrs. Child. The Liberty Party and political abolitionists were putting the cart before the horse. Ellis Gray Loring and Henry Ingersoll Bowditch, however, both favored political participation and rejected disunion. They appreciated a politician like John Gorham Palfrey, and rejoiced in the success of political antislavery. Yet, they considered moral methods as essential in obtaining abolition and would not resign from membership in the American Antislavery Society nor desist from supporting it financially.[24]

Given the general political climate in America, radical abolitionists did not believe that political action could accomplish anything positive in the 1840s. They all agreed that the "moral climate of the country had to be prepared before they could participate in political action.[25] The annexation of Texas, extending slavery as it did, helped advance disunion sentiment.[26] It also demonstrated the strength of the Southern juggernaut in Congress. The radicals believed that slavery had destroyed the Union; as propagandists for disunion they simply recognized this fact.[27] Most radicals supported Higginson's Disunion Convention of 1857. Two weeks before the convention, Garrison made the telling remark at the twenty-fifth anniversary celebration of the Massachusetts Antislavery Society, that if the schism of 1840 had not occurred he thought emancipation might have been already achieved.[28]

B. THE FAITH SHARED—FELLOW PILGRIMS ALONG THE WAY

New members joined the Garrisonian sect in the 1840s, but their allegiance differed from that of members converted in the 1830s. Instantaneous conversion gave way to a slowly evolved conversion to the urgency of antislavery participation. In this category, the archetype among Unitarian ministers was Samuel May, Jr. (1810–1899). Others recognized the correctness of the Garrisonian methods and approach, but did not join the American Antislavery Society. One outstanding Unitarian fellow traveler in this category was William Henry Furness (1802–1896). He was with the Garrisonian sectarians, but not of them.

Samuel May, Jr., was a cousin of Samuel J. May, under whom the younger May served his ministerial apprenticeship in Brooklyn, Connecticut. He absorbed antislavery ideals both from his cousin, and from his mother, Mary Goddard May (1787–1882). Upon his graduation from the Harvard Divinity School in 1833, he was soon settled over the new Unitarian society in Leicester, Massachusetts. Lydia Maria Child's *Appeal* influenced him greatly and he identified himself with the Massachusetts Antislavery Society. Yet, his convictions developed gradually and not until

1840 did he truly become an outspoken abolitionist. In that year he helped organize the Leicester Antislavery Society and went to New York as its delegate to the annual meeting of the American Antislavery Society. Three years later, he traveled to England and lobbied among English Unitarians in behalf of Garrisonian abolitionism. Returning home he became a nineteenth-century Tomas Torquemada, roasting all prominent Unitarian ministers for their lack of antislavery fervor with the same diligence that the Spanish Inquisitor had pursued Roman Catholic heretics. Ezra Stiles Gannett, completely exasperated by May's activity, called him "the most dangerous man in Massachusetts." When May held an anniversary celebration of the West Indian Emancipation at his church in 1845, his congregation began to get restless. May resigned the following year and, after several months of supply preaching, he entered his eighteen years of service as the General Agent of the Massachusetts Antislavery Society.[29]

In Philadelphia, William Henry Furness of the First Unitarian Society slowly moved toward the position of the Garrisonians. When Pennsylvania Hall was destroyed by an anti-abolitionist mob in 1838, he preached a sermon to his conservative mercantile congregation on freedom of speech. He carefully avoided any implication that he was speaking in behalf of abolitionism.[30] However, at a Sunday observance of the Fourth of July in 1839, he attacked slavery. The Philadelphia pastor broached the subject again on January 3, 1841, and then again on the occasion of the National Fast, on May 14th.[31] In that sermon, Furness told his congregation, "we cannot remain silent and indifferent [any longer] and be guiltless."[32]

The tempo of Furness's antislavery preaching increased until hardly a Sunday passed in which he did not mention slavery either in his sermons or prayers.[33] Between the period 1841 to 1846, he painfully saw some of his parishioners walk out during his sermons, cancel their membership, lodge protests against him, and nearly succeed in removing him from his pastorate. But Furness survived this disaffection and continued in his antislavery.[34]

But what kind of an antislavery reformer was he? By every measurement except actual membership in the American Antislavery Society, Furness was a Garrisonian. The antislavery crusade was "the major interest" in Furness's life and ministry.[35] He believed slavery to be sin; it could only be abolished through moral persuasion.[36] Abolition was "the holiest of causes," thought Furness. "It is the Christianity, the Religion of our Times."[37] He disavowed political action and believed as a "pastor of a Christian Church," he was "*ex officio* the presiding officer of an antislavery society."[38] Finally, he had the admiration of the Garrisonians and they welcomed him to their work. "Furness is among the prophets!" exclaimed Maria Child, when he ran into trouble for preaching antislavery. "May the priests diminish and the prophets increase." And what greater endorsement could any man or woman have than Mrs. Chapman's, who said Furness had come finally "into practical fellowship with American fellowship with American abolitionists."[39] Yet, Furness's reluctant course to abolitionism haunted him. Many years after emancipation had been achieved, he remarked, "I have always considered myself an 11th hour man in the sacred Cause without the excuse of the men in the Parable whom no one had called to work. I was called by the Divine Voice and I ran and hid myself, for I was a long time afraid."[40]

C. THE FAITH CONTINUED—PROSPERITY OF THE HOLY CAUSE

"To me," Furness told his congregation, in 1851, the abolition movement "is profoundly and especially religious."[41] Throughout the 1840s the Garrisonians' commitment was religious. The cause, with its attendant persecutions, was the "main purpose" of our lives, said Maria Chapman, and she thought the Garrisonians best comprehended the words of Christ "Inasmuch as ye have done it unto one of the least of these my brethren ye have done it unto me!"[42] Their understanding of the slaves as Christ's brethren enabled many of the radicals to persist in their work. As timid Henrietta Sargent remarked, "It is that mankind is dear to him that I would relieve and serve the [slave], feeling in so doing I do it unto him—without my knowledge of Christ, as the head of every man, the bound, as well as the free, I could not be an abolitionist."[43] Henry Ingersoll Bowditch confided to Mrs. Chapman that, although he was a Christian originally, he could not join the abolitionist radicals, but the abolitionist martyrdom "proved the height of the *christian love*" they had reached. Once he accepted that he was called to "the holy cause" by "a message on high," he realized that he had been a slave to public opinion. He now recognized a "feebleness" of language in discussions of slavery or reprimands of slaveholders. Was one to pat a slaveholder on the shoulder, Bowditch asked, and say, "Look here my dear fellow, you are a naughty person. If you don't behave better I shall have to do something severe."[44]

No, answered Samuel May, Jr. The abolitionists met on Sundays "to 'preach the Gospel' " and they spoke "more truly and impartially" than most American ministers. They approached the slaveholders out of their love for them and brought a message of repentance. They did not want the dreadful sin of slavery to engulf them.[45] "We must so act and speak to those who are blind through sin," wrote Susan Cabot, "that their hearts may burn within them, and their eyes will be unfastened and they will kneel and worship the law of right as the law of their being."[46]

Thomas J. Mumford (1826–1877), converted to Garrisonianism through his mentor, Samuel J. May, proposed during this period "a romantic idea of a new 'company of Jesus' devoted to the overthrow of slavery."[47] There are no details of his proposal, but in the missionary endeavor to lead the slaveholder to repentance, such "a company" was not needed. For the widening impact of the Garrisonian sectarians could be seen in the antislavery legions attending their functions in the 1840s and the 1850s. The annual "Pic Nic" celebrations of the British West Indian Emancipation were a good example of the growth of opinion against slavery in the North.

A theological student had proposed in the *Liberator* of June 24, 1842, the idea of holding an annual picnic to celebrate the first of August 1834. Samuel J. May endorsed the idea. The August Firsts were seen as an abolitionist holiday to match—probably to the consternation of patriotic conservatives—the fuss and feathers of the Fourth of July. The "Fourth" celebrated an incomplete revolution; the "First" celebrated a new revolution. Attendance at the various antislavery picnics around New England varied from 800 at Dedham's Temperance Grove in 1842 to 6,000 to 8,000 at Tranquillity Grove in Hingham in 1844.[48]

One should not underestimate the meaning of the British West Indian Emancipation for radical abolitionists. Indeed, it constituted a holy day, an anniversary that celebrated, said Samuel J. May, an occasion "more auspicious to the cause of the poor and oppressed," then any other event since the birth of Christ.[49] The massive August First camp meetings included Bible readings, antislavery songs and hymns (every person held an antislavery song sheet or an *Anti-Slavery Hymn Book*), orations, prayers, offerings, and the reading of letters from the abolitionist leaders unable to be present. Every reference to emancipation in their letters received the hearty response of "Amen!" from the crowd. The abolitionist singing group, the Hutchinsons, or the local antislavery choir led the singing of soul-stirring favorites, bound to bring tears and applause. Each picnic was preceded by a procession through the local community with bands and banners and the ringing of church bells; the procession for the Hingham meeting in 1844 reached a mile and a half in length![50]

The radicals made a conscious attempt to involve children in the antislavery movement in general, and in the antislavery picnics in particular. Remembering the words of Jesus, "Let the little children come unto me," the abolitionists issued the call, "Let the children come, that they may imbibe the spirit of devotion to the cause of impartial and universal freedom, and be prepared to take the place of their fathers in the warfare with oppression.[51]

In her juvenile magazine, *The Child's Friend*, Eliza Follen recorded the impressions the antislavery picnic at Dedham in 1843 made upon a young lad, Hal. The letter probably was written by Mrs. Follen herself. The procession and the beautiful banners excited Hal—especially one that showed "a fine figure of a black man" breaking his chains, with a face so full of joy that Hal "thought it almost handsome." Then in a remark designed to disquiet many a conservative parent with pangs of guilt, Hal said, "And mother I do wonder that I never heard you or father speak of the 1st of August." Hal then reported the various slogans on the banners, mentioning particularly those by Unitarians. His emotions were touched by a boy who recited a poem called "The Christian Slave," and Hal was moved to say that "if the men don't all do something about slavery soon, we boys had better see what we can do, for it is too wicked."

After a tasty lunch, more speaking and some "real good singing" followed, but what pleased Hal most was an address by an almost "white" fugitive slave who spoke very well. The orations ended with the singing of "Old Hundred." Hal described the scene to his mother:

Now dear mother just imagine a grand grove of tall pine trees, with their branches crossing each other, so as to look like the arches of a grand cathedral, with the blue sky for a ceiling, and at least fifteen hundred people joining most of them with their voices, and all looking as if they did with their hearts in singing "From all who dwell below the sky," and to that glorious old tune: it seemed to me as if the spirit of old Martin Luther was there. I never had such a feeling of awe in my life. I wanted you and father to be there; I never felt so religious; England may be forgiven a thousand sins for this one act. Why do not all christians rejoice in this day?[52]

Hal's letter in the *Child's Friend* brought the wrath of the Boston *Courier* down upon Mrs. Follen. The daily newspaper criticized her magazine as "dangerous." Not only did it give children early biases against slavery, it could also possibly corrupt their morals and religion! A Unitarian clergyman inanely rebutted the *Courier's* criticism. Children should be taught that slavery is an evil, his argument went, if only for the reason that so many New England sons went South. They accepted slavery and treated their Negroes more harshly than Southerners were prone to do. This was because they were used to the hard work of the free laborer. Therefore Mrs. Follen's magazine taught children the wrongs of slavery. When their children became slaveholders, parents could safely say that they were "not responsible for the sin."[53]

Because such a great number of people were involved in the antislavery picnics, it quickly became apparent to the Garrisonians that they could not insure that platform speakers would maintain the purity of abolitionist doctrine. The introduction of "alien" antislavery dogmas by political abolitionists and pseudo-abolitionists weakened the religious enthusiasm of the picnics as they became an accepted annual event. By the 1850s the "religious" procession had disappeared and the "Sunday School-like features" of the picnic's program had been dropped. Henry Ingersoll Bowditch nervously noted at one of the very first anniversary picnics the intrusion of non-Garrisonians upon the

radicals' territory. He was especially perturbed by a few
Unitarian ministers who implied that they were "rather
superior in certain Christian virtues" to the Garrisonians.
He complained to Mrs. Chapman that these men seemed to
be pushing the radicals aside in order to carry on the cause
of the slave by themselves. "Now, I rejoice to see such
evidence of regeneration in the Unitarian body," Bowditch
told her cynically, and would be willing to stand aside and
let them take "the Standard and bear it to victory. *I* believe
the Unitarians, [however,] *as a body,* are as rotten as ever
upon this subject and woe would the slave's cause be were it
to rest chiefly upon them."[54]

D. THE FAITH SHAKEN—THE REIGN OF TERROR OF THE 1850s

By 1850 charter members of the American Antislavery
Society had been working to overthrow slavery "immediately" for nearly two decades. For some, patience and
endurance had worn thin; for others, faith and hope were
disappearing. The awesome events of the 1850s: the Jerry
Rescue, the Sims and Burns renditions, the Kansas out-
rages, the terrible attack upon Sumner, and, finally, John
Brown's raid into Virginia were incidents to perplex
anyone devoted to moral action and peaceful means. The
Garrisonian devotion to these methods weakened and, for
many, evaporated, when the South after years of threaten-
ing left the Union.

In 1851 Daniel Webster went on a grand tour of the
country to rally support behind the Fugitive Slave Law.
When Webster emphasized in Syracuse, New York, that
opposition to the Law was treason, Samuel J. May and other
members of the local vigilance committee were present in
the audience. A few months later May faced the threat of
legal action for assisting one William McHenry, popularly
known as Jerry, to escape the clutches of slavehunters.[55]

The rescue of Jerry played havoc with May's peace principles. He confessed to Garrison that "he could not preach
non-resistance very earnestly to the crowd," which clam-
ored for Jerry's release.[56] Moreover, as a result of the
Jerry rescue litigation, May took a greater interest in politics
and sought the help of political abolitionists John Gorham
Palfrey and William Henry Seward.[57]

In Boston in 1851 political abolitionists Wentworth
Higginson, Theodore Parker, and others, had been unable
to thwart the rendition of Thomas Sims. Henry Ingersoll
Bowditch, a Garrisonian who had repudiated nonresistance in arming himself to protect the Crafts, observed
Sims's sad return to slavery. When Sims was placed aboard
the brig *Acorn* at sunrise to be returned to Georgia,
Bowditch was there. In "the depths of sorrow" Bowditch
viewed with dismay the body of police with drawn swords
protecting Sims's captors. He heard Sims's last words
before the vessel departed: "And is this Massachusetts
liberty?"

A stranger climbed on top of a crate on the wharf and
urged all to join with him "in religious services for the
departing missionary of liberty." Bowditch responded:

> With my whole heart I sprang towards the spot, and
> there, with heads uncovered, under the broad expanse of
> heaven, and with the light of morning just breaking over
> the water, that stranger offered a prayer that touched all
> our souls. We felt the need of prayer; nay, we felt that on
> that only could we rest. For a week, night and day, we had
> labored in vain, and now that all was finished, we fled to
> the God of justice and humanity. Under the arms of the
> [stranger] were clustered the rough Presbyterian, the
> rigid Catholic, the liberal Unitarian, the youthful skeptic,
> and all influenced by one and the same spirit of prayer.[58]

Bowditch wished for revenge; he hoped that the ship
might flounder in the storm that arose the following day.

Then he remembered the words of the dying Christ: "Father, forgive them; they know not what they do!" Bowditch prayed aloud and "a sweet peace ... stole imperceptibly over [his] soul." He perceived clearly that a struggle was likely to ensue that would end "with the sacrifice of life."[59]

No event so rankled the radical abolitionists as the Fugitive Slave Law. While traveling by stagecoach, Maria Child clashed with a defender of the Law. She "burnt" the stranger "up like a stroke of the sun, and swept his ashes up after him."[60]

Then in June 1854 the radical abolitionists saw five companies of United States troops drag Anthony Burns back to slavery. Human government had once again, remarked Furness, "interfered with the discharge of Christian duty."[61] Our government had by this law set a "fountain of deadly poison in our midst." The hour was dark, for Massachusetts had done obeisance to the Slavocracy: "Let her hang her monuments of the Revolution in black. . . ."[62]

Mrs. Child fretted over the rendition of Burns as one more encroachment of slavery upon the North. "My very soul is sick," she cried, "in view of these things." The depressing events only increased the melancholy Mrs. Chapman was experiencing. She poured out her heart to James Russell Lowell: "I used to consider it mere cant," she wrote, "when I heard the old country folk say in their stolid way,—'nothing but *religion* can satisfy the immortal soul.' I have known long since what it means." It meant, she continued, "the thing, whatever it is, that makes us forget ourselves in our fellow creatures—*that* remains, when the personal presence of our other grief is removed. THE CAUSE has been the Paraclet [*sic*] to me. [THE CAUSE] has been all-comprehending . . . to me."[63]

Abolitionist spirits fell further when the news of the bloody conflicts between pro-slavery and free state forces in

Kansas filtered back to New England. The South had penetrated the North to seize slaves and now she moved West to extend the boundaries of her slave-pen. She ruled Washington and had struck down the Massachusetts senator who dared protest her intrusion into Kansas. Maria Child hurried herself preparing garments and relief boxes for Kansas sufferers. Their plight tormented her and she was convinced that God had decreed that American had "to sink, sink—till it touches bottom." She also worried about Sumner's health and would awaken from nightmares of murdered settlers in Kansas or of the bleeding Sumner. It has been "the night" within my soul, she grieved. "To labor so *long* against slavery, and yet to see it always triumphant!"[64]

The penultimate event before the holy war, of course, was John Brown's raid at Harpers Ferry. "I apprehend," said Samuel J. May, "it is but the beginning of sorrows; the pattering of the rain before the hurricane."[65] The languishing faith of the Garrisonians quickened. Maria Child in particular found new "youth and strength" in the "sublime martyrdom" of John Brown. His example gave her "renewed zeal for the righteous cause" and she saw a similar effect on multitudes throughout the North.[66] She offered to tend Brown's wounds and when insulted by Governor Wise of Virginia, she initiated a correspondence with Wise. Later the correspondence was printed and some 300,000 copies were distributed. She scurried from door to door in Wayland, Massachusetts, and secured 300 signatures on a petition in behalf of two of Brown's men.[67] Furness collected money in Philadelphia for Brown's family and the treasury of the American Antislavery Society contributed money to Brown's defense and his family's needs.[68]

But neither Mrs. Child, Furness, Samuel J. May, nor other radical abolitionists condoned Brown's methods. They agreed with Mrs. Chapman that Brown's way was not their way, although the man himself was "heroic and saintly." Brown's act, said Mrs. Chapman, was "*not* murder, treason, conspiracy, as the world understands those words." Mrs. Child could not subscribe to Brown's methods, but now after this scare in the South, what other methods could be used? An insurrection would be terrible to white women and children, but black women and children had for generations suffered without protection. "My *duty* is clear to me," she at last acknowledged, "I must stand by the poor slave. . . . Shirking and quivering at every nerve, I would *still* do it, if I *knew* their pathway to freedom must be 'over their masters' bodies.' . . . It is a trying position, but I must be true to principles of *freedom*, as well as to peace."[69]

E. THE FAITH SECULARIZED—THE FUSION OF CHURCH AND STATE

In 1858 Maria Chapman covered Weymouth County in pursuit of names for a petition to remove Judge Edward G. Loring from office for his part in the rendition of Burns. From house to house she went, urging people to sign the petition as an act of "common humanity, Love of Liberty, Patriotic State Sovereignty, disunion from Sin, [and] Loyalty to righteousness." With her long skirts and bonnet she marched straight into the local sawmill and went among the millhands. She shouted "a few Anti-Slavery truths in a voice shriller than all the music of the sawing." The workers, plainly overwhelmed by this blond apparition among the lumber and sawdust, took her pen and inkpot in hand and signed the petition. I got all their names in "a twinkling," Mrs. Chapman boasted. Her hunt for signatures was most successful. Collecting 800 names, she was astonished how wide-awake people were on antislavery.[70]

Indeed, antislavery propaganda and the reign of terror of the 1850s had extended antislavery sentiment. Most

Northerners were at least against the extension of slavery and the emotional issue came more and more into public and political discussions. With Frémont's candidacy in 1856, the Garrisonians broke ranks on the issue of political participation.

Eliza Follen, in a tract addressed *To Mothers in the Free States*, said mothers could help end slavery through influence on their sons. A mother's teaching could lessen the votes for a fugitive slave law or a Nebraska bill.[71] Naturally, logic led some mothers to say, why wait for my son's vote, when my husband could vote right away against slavery? Maria Child, therefore, urged her father and husband to back Frémont in 1856. She herself "would almost lay down [her] life to have him elected." Frémont was riding the wave created by the abolitionists. The "old abolitionists," said Mrs. Child, were beginning to see the results of their twenty-five years of work, for the masses were beginning to be swayed. It was too bad that women could not vote, for they would certainly have helped Frémont win. When he lost, Maria Child felt as if she had just buried her mother.[72]

Samuel J. May came out openly for Frémont in a Fourth of July oration at Jamestown, New York. May admitted that Frémont's party did not offer everything an abolitionist would wish, but it had the best possibility of saving America within it and he would support it. Garrison charged his old friend with infidelity to his peace principles. But May saw it otherwise. Frémont's election could avert civil war or at least throw responsibility for a war upon the slaveholders. For twenty-five years May had not troubled himself about politics, but now he was impressed by the public tragedies. The Republican Party was headed in the right direction. "They will be obliged to go much further for God and humanity than they foresee. So I am going to urge them forward into an advanced position from which they cannot recede." So important was the election to May and his

Syracuse congregation that he told James Freeman Clarke that they were too occupied with politics to entertain the American Unitarian Association Convention![73]

Garrison's criticism of May was unjustified in the eyes of Maria Child. She also disliked Garrison's attacks on Sumner and Henry Wilson. The Garrisonians were a noble and true band, but their impact was not so great as that of an "extensive political organization." The Republican Party was in the ascendant and, although Mrs. Child had no great confidence in the party, it was still "better dan nothin," as her housekeeper said of husbands. Maria Child remembered that the abolitionists had said in their early years that eventually abolition would be completed by politicians. Twenty-five years ago they would have rejoiced to have a man like Giddings, Sumner, or Wilson. Now we have them, said Mrs. Child, and may God bless them![74]

Mrs. Chapman speculated that the political and religious traditions were basically antislavery all the time. Their consciences were on the side of the abolitionists, but their temporal concerns drove them against the abolitionist party. "That's why," explained Maria Chapman, "they showed so much bitterness towards us." A Unitarian minister wrote to Samuel May, Jr., in 1858 and declared that all the antislavery activity in his area was political. The antislavery feeling that Mrs. Chapman speculated upon, was surfacing, because Northern temporal and political concerns were coalescing with antislavery interests. Samuel May, Jr., who had not voted in twenty years, told an English friend that the Constitution still disenfranchised the Garrisonian abolitionists, "nevertheless, as between existing parties, we cannot but desire the success of that one which the Slaveholder most fears" and will help check slavery's growth and promote the spread of freedom. In the present context this party is "undoubtedly" the Republican Party.[75]

Antislavery religion and antislavery politics were coming together to destroy slavery. Both church and state needed a cleansing and the antislavery movement was helping to bring this about. "Nothing is so indispensible to the purification of the American Church as well as the honor of this Republic," said Samuel J. May, "as the entire extirpation of Slavery. It defiles everything it touches." Maria Chapman put her trust in associations to bring this about— "Not [voluntary] associations as machinery only or as churches only, but as *both*." She did mean tying together of church and state, but "a *fusion*" of church, self, and government working as one to cast out the "Demon, PENALTY," that is, man's interference with God— prominently seen in slavery. Her concept saw fruition in the civil war that lay just around the corner. She desired and hoped for some "great earthquake"—that was what some people would call it, she said—until they found that is was a "resurrection."[76]

6

The Ascendancy of Political
Antislavery—1850–1860

A. GOVERNMENT BY GOSPEL

THE Fugitive Slave Law, declared James Freeman
Clarke, had demoralized the Church: the "atheism" of
ministers who backed the rendition of fugitive slaves
supported his view. It had demoralized great men:[1] Webster had with alacrity, John Pierpont wrote, unleashed
"human-blood-hounds" to track down hapless Negro
people.[2] It had demoralized political parties: the platform
statements of the two major parties, remarked John
Gorham Palfrey, revealed that the "bill of untenable
abominations" was to be sustained as the law of the land and
its opponents would be "choked off" from uttering their
"honest protest."[3] The Whig party of law and order, said

145

Clarke, supported the South, which had broken the law and fomented disorder. The Democratic party supported the only "aristocracy in the land"—350,000 slaveholders.[4] These two major parties had capitulated to power and money, "trading politicians and political traders."[5] The Fugitive Slave Law had caused "tumult and outrage" in the North and had demoralized the region: a half-million free Negroes had no more security than a horse.[6]

Theodore Parker, as Boston's chaplain to fugitive slaves, wrote to President Fillmore and demanded that their "inalienable rights" be respected. Fillmore apparently ignored the letter, and directed that the Fugitive Slave Law be faithfully executed.[7] As chairman of the executive committee of the Vigilance Committee of Boston, Parker distributed petitions to ask Congress to repeal the Fugitive Slave Law, and to urge the Massachusetts legislature to pass strong "personal liberty laws."[8] He tried these peaceable means to help the fugitives, if these failed there were always other ways. He wanted to work under the Constitution, but there were limits to compromise:

> In matters of Interest compromise is never out of place; in matters of conscience never in place. . . . I am responsible to nobody; I look at Principles and ask, *are they right, just, agreeable to the Constitution of the Universe?* If so they must be kept.[9]

Parker's statement could be taken as the general view of the political abolitionists during the 1850s. In the decade, various Unitarian political abolitionists were tempted to compromise on "matters of conscience." Pierpont had been warned by his Medford parish to desist from preaching politics and had lost his post. Sadly this great reformer in his seventy-fifth year begged to continue to preach and to serve, but he was denied a permanent post. He was "rather out of line." No Unitarian church, he said, wanted to hear anyone who had anything to say "about *rum* and niggers."[10]

Orville Dewey, acting as an emissary for the Unitarian Church in Washington, offered the church's pulpit to James Freeman Clarke on one condition. "If you say," he wrote, "that you *will not* take a pulpit, when you cannot preach upon slavery, that ends the question." Clarke remained at the Church of the Disciples. Palfrey was asked whether he would be interested in a professorship of history at Harvard College. At the same time he was admonished that an active part in the "politics of the day" would be "incompatible with an office in the College." Palfrey replied that he had other plans, and he stated quite plainly that should he ever again become a member of the academic community, he would regard the "proprieties of my position, and the welfare of the College." Anything more than that, he politely stated, the College "would not probably expect."[11]

Political abolitionists found themselves repeatedly responding to the question of political preaching, or in Palfrey's case, "political teaching." Webster told us, said Parker, that religion was excellent except when it interfered with politics.[12] Good conservative doctrine demanded that the pulpit be free of political preaching; that the "politics of the day," the public issues of the day, were to be treated during the week. The Sabbath was reserved for piety, worship, and prayer. But in their free church congregations Clarke and Parker were not bound in their political activity. The Church of the Disciples functioned as a hall for political lyceums as well as services of worship, and Clarke himself publicized and presented political lectures. In the campaign of 1856 he gave a lecture called *The Ethics of the Ballot Box; or Christian Principles of Voting, with Their Application to the Next Election.* Two years later he gave a series of lectures on the theme "Good Men for Public Office." In one lecture he delineated his vision of a Christian state: All the public offices of the country were filled by good men inspired by their Christian faith. The Union was viewed by the world as the "majestic leader of the human race." America had emancipated and educated its slaves. As a redeemed nation it achieved its "manifest destiny" to be a "Christian democracy" governed upon the "principles of the Gospel." An impossible vision to realize? Clarke did not think so. Already, he said, we were the "only nation which [had] order without soldiers, law without a police, and religion without an established church."[13]

In another lecture in the series he suggested ways to achieve his idea of government by gospel. First, everyone should vote. "Joyful and terrible," he said, "should be the voice of the people uttering itself through the ballot-box— terrible to the wicked servant, joyful to him who had done well." Second, everyone should vote for good men. It was better to vote for leaders with principles year after year without triumphs than to carry elections by voting for "Mr. Facing-both-ways." Eventually the good men would win. Third, everyone should insist upon the nomination of men of virtuous private character.[14]

Parker cared less about the private virtue of a candidate than about his public virtue. Charles Sumner had once told him that he, Sumner, was in "*Morals* and not in *Politics*." Upon Sumner's election to the Senate, Parker wrote, "I hope you will show that you are still in Morals *although* in Politics. I hope you will be the *Senator with a Conscience*." If an antislavery politician lacked public virtue, Parker was quick to censure him. He called Henry Wilson to task for regarding ambition and popularity too much, and told him to follow Sumner's example as one who had "grown morally" at his post in Congress! Wilson kindly acknowledged Parker's mild censure, and Parker soon praised the Senator's heroic service in the cause of freedom.[15]

Both Parker and Clarke held strong views on civil disobedience. Parker maintained that obedience to law depended upon the justice of law, upon whether it was a part of God's natural law—not upon whether a law was constitutional. Unjust law should be disobeyed. But he saw two degrees in disobedience, passive and active. The latter was "resistance," doing something against the law: Parker had counseled fugitives to slay those who obstructed their flight to freedom. The Fugitive Slave Law, he taught, violated conscience and was forced upon Bostonians by bayonets, guns, and cannon. "If the people consent to suffer it, it is because they are weak; and if they consent to obey it, it is because they are also wicked."[16]

To obey the Fugitive Slave Law, said Clarke, was to disobey God, to corrupt society, and to threaten the credibility of the Constitution and the dissolution of the Union. In counseling disobedience, he did not foresee a rampage of lawlessness sweeping the North. Few men who counseled disobedience to a particular law would set out to overthrow every law. The risk of fine and imprisonment remained a deterrent. "Good men obey the laws mainly from conscience," preached Clarke,

> bad men mainly from fear, and the majority of men from self-interest. The great majority of laws are such a kind that they can be conscientiously obeyed. It is only *now*, when the rights of our neighbor—of a poor colored brother—are trampled upon, that we appeal to conscience and refuse obedience.

Only the best man disobeyed wicked laws and in so doing they made other men better. "If you wish law to be obeyed universally and thoroughly," he warned, "do not teach men to trifle with their conscience." To those who objected that the concept of a higher law brought disorder and anarchy, Clarke admonished,

> Let a race of men be formed, who will never do what they think God has forbidden, no matter who commands it,

and you have a race of men who will maintain order, who will assure the peace of the state, and on all of whose steps prosperity and power will attend.[17]

A growing feeling against the intractable political power of the South moved the political abolitionists to advocate greater radicalism and even violence. Moral persuasion, said Pierpont, did not seem to be able to disenthrall the North from "our Southern masters." Parker traveled widely throughout the West on the lyceum circuit and through a careful statistical presentation demonstrated that the "South [was] the master of the North." Northern society, morality, and industry, he said, were being adversely affected by the cancer of slavery.[18] He thought effective machinery existed under the Constitution to arrest slavery's advance, and he became angry with politicians in Washington who stubbornly maintained that they were powerless. Did not the Constitution guarantee to each state a "Republican Form of Government"? Then slavery should be subject to the powers of Congress as were *"Popism, Czarism, Hereditary Nobility,* or *Hereditary Monarchy."* If South Carolina established a papal government, Congress would force it to reinstate a republican government. Slavery was an anti-republican as popism and, therefore, should be swept away.[19] Congress, of course, was not likely to confront South Carolina as Parker hoped; that confrontation would come in 1861, when the state established an "independent" government. Then force would be used to reinstate a republican government without slavery. Parker would not have been averse to the use of that force.

B. "THE FIRST ACT OF VIOLENCE": THE RENDITION OF ANTHONY BURNS—1854

When the Vigilance Committee in Boston met to deal with the seizure of Anthony Burns in May 1854, Parker was one of those who expressed willingness to use force to save Burns. He and Higginson became members of an executive committee of six who advocated violence. "Remember that to us," wrote Higginson to a friend, "Anti-Slavery is a matter of deadly earnest, which costs us our reputations today, and may cost us our lives to-morrow."[20] And it nearly did. Leading a rescue party up the courthouse steps to free Burns imprisoned inside, Higginson received a sabre slash in the face. A courthouse guard was stabbed to death. Lewis Hayden, Boston's leading Negro citizen, fired a shot in Higginson's defence and grazed a United States marshall. Parker later exclaimed, "Why did he not hit him?" The disastrous, uncoordinated attack upon the courthouse failed to save Burns, and Boston antislavery reformers were plunged into outrage, despair, and mourning. Boston had become, said Palfrey, a den of "Knaves, pirates, cannibals."[21]

This "first act of violence" in the 1850s began the steady procession of events of brute force leading to Harpers Ferry. Parker, Higginson, and several others were indicted for their part in the raid. Higginson bragged that he might plead not guilty because he and his fellow attackers had a right of access to the courthouse. James Hackett Fowler (d. 1889), a student at the Harvard Divinity School, was overjoyed by Higginson's indictment. Fowler himself had *only* been thrown into a "loathsome cell by the ruffian police of Boston," and then released. But his brief imprisonment had been a glorious experience: he had suffered the "most shameful physical abuse, [his] head being smashed against a stone wall by their brutal hand clenched into [his] black hair. But all this did not silence [his] tongue." Their martyrdom, he told Higginson, would result in much good. "Let us be ready for any sacrifice for our own integrity and the truth."[22]

Undoubtedly Fowler was disappointed when the indictment against Higginson and Parker was quashed. Certainly Parker was disappointed. He had wanted to test his part in the Burns case in court, but had to be satisfied simply with the publication of the massive "Defence" he had prepared for the trail.[23]

In their sermons preached on the Sunday following the rendition of Burns, Parker and Clarke revealed no loss of faith in political action. However, Higginson, still in a state of excitement, preached change by revolution rather than change by ballots. His sermon, entitled "Massachusetts in Mourning," was published in the *Worcester Daily Spy* and reprinted as a pamphlet. Reformers could use ideas and moral suasion as weapons, he declared, but when they were confronted by pistols, clubs, and soldiers, then physical resistance was necessary. Had enough men supported him, Higginson believed that he could have rescued Burns. "Calm, irresistible force, in a good cause, becomes sublime," he preached. If the attack on the courthouse did nothing more than force the South to guard her slave with hundreds of soldiers, "it was worth a dozen lives." For despite the increase in antislavery sentiment, the South beat the North *more and more easily every time.* The only path to reform the nation was revolution, and Higginson believed revolution had begun: "If you take part in politics henceforward, let it be only to bring nearer the crisis which will either save or sunder this nation—or perhaps save in sundering." These were strong words, but no other words were adequate. Slavery had reduced America to a "state of barbarism." Life was difficult in these times and Higginson proclaimed:

I can only make life worth living for, by becoming a revolutionist. The saying seems dangerous; but why not say it if one means it, as I certainly do. I respect law and order, . . . [but] while Slavery is national, law and order must constantly be on the wrong side.

Freedom needed defenders. Higginson hoped that Massachusetts would not again be found wanting.[24]

Clarke had just returned from Meadville, Pennsylvania, and therefore had missed Higginson's attempt to free Burns. In his sermon on the rendition, Clarke admitted his great remorse for Massachusetts: "Now would be the time for this community to put on mourning— . . . because Honor is dead, because Humanity is dead, because Massachusetts has been placed, and by her own acts, beneath the feet of Virginia." At first the relationship of freedom in the North to slavery in the South had been one of superiority, but because of the North's continual display of weakness the relationship had changed to one of equality, then inferiority, and at last subjection.[25]

The cowardice of public officials in Boston did not bother Clarke so much as the timorous behavior of the Unitarian churches and clergy. The officials of Boston were but "creatures of public sentiment," whereas the Unitarian churches of the city had the teachings of Channing, Follen, and Ware to instruct them. Yet, in these churches were those who had done the most in the community "to lower its moral sense" on the subject of the Fugitive Slave Law. They voted for it. They defended it. They enforced it. If revolution, civil war, or dissolution of the Union occurred, the fault would rest with those who had sought to appease the South by concession. In his testimony against the North's cowardice in face of the South's dominance, Clarke therefore agreed with Higginson. But he had different proposals for overcoming Northern weakness.[26]

Clarke's suggestions were actually a reiteration of his old idea of a "Great Northern League for Freedom." First, he

said, all the friends of freedom should unite in one great
Northern party. Second, the "calmest, coolest men" should
be nominated and elected. Third, no man should be
supported for any state or federal office who did not openly
pledge to repeal the "popular sovereignty" clause of the
Kansas-Nebraska Act, to support jury trials for fugitives, to
forbid the extension of slavery, to prevent the admission of
any more slave states, and to dissolve the Union if any of
these measures could not be secured. Fourth, he called for
individuals to dedicate themselves "to labor and pray and
speak and suffer for the cause of Universal Freedom," to do
more for the slave, to speak louder in his behalf, to "enlist in
this warfare for life."[27]

Parker's sermon on the rendition of Burns, called the
"New Crime Against Humanity," proposed suggestions
quite similar to those of Clarke. He wanted calm, systematic,
and deliberate action. He desired a convention of citizens
of Massachusetts and a general convention of all the
states—presumably Northern states—to organize for
"mutual protection" against the Fugitive Slave Law. New
and forceful personal liberty laws should be passed. Men
should be elected who would execute these laws without
timidness.[28] Cohesion between antislavery forces of all
persuasions seemed to Parker and Clarke especially necessary just then; the rendition of Burns had helped to provide
the climate wherein a great Northern antislavery league or
party was likely to become a reality.

C. CANNONS FOR KANSAS AND FREEDOM WITH FRÉMONT—1856

Slavery had risen like a "great black flood," preached
Clarke in the spring of 1856, and "we shall raise a dam
against it in the Western Missouri and turn it back from
Kanzaz."[29] He shared some of the exuberance of those who

heartily supported emigration to Kansas. The battle to save Kansas from slavery was a "noble and heroic enterprise," a war between "Michael and his angels on the one side, Satan and his angels on the other."[30] Higginson felt compelled to fight in this war, and following an enthusiastic meeting at his Worcester Free Church in behalf of the free state settlers, he departed for Kansas. Traversing the contested areas of the war-weary state, he could not have been happier. "I saw there the American Revolution," he told a meeting of Garrisonians upon his return, "and every great Revolution of bygone days . . . still [alive]." Higginson had been the representative in Kansas of a militant group that assisted emigration to the territory. His men were well armed and prepared to fight.[31]

Although Parker lamented that the conflict in Kansas had to be won by bullets and not ballots, he joined in the militance of the occasion. "Thank God," he wrote to Sumner, "I can buy a sword without selling my shirt." To John P. Hale he wrote that he had shrunk his book budget: "I may want the money for cannons." Parker raised hundreds of dollars to aid Kansas.[32]

Clarke's congregation also opened their hearts and pocketbooks to the cause. They packed clothing for New Englanders who had underestimated the cold of a prairie winter. And they sent funds to fugitive slaves who had been stranded in Kansas. Less inclined to violent action than either Higginson or Parker, Clarke purchased several shares in a conservative emigrant aid society rather than back Higginson's militant agency. He asked assistance from men of all political parties for the sufferers in Kansas. "These men stand in the breach fighting our battle," he declared. "They stand to resist the extension of Slavery and the aggression of the Slave power."[33]

In the context of the bloody conflict of Kansas, the beating of Sumner seemed to Parker to be almost a natural happening. The event has "not heated me in the smallest,"

Parker preached to his congregation; "my pulse has not beat quicker than before; . . . for this assault on Mr. Sumner is no new thing." He had talked with Sumner many times before about the violence of the South. He knew that the Senator was ready for it. The attack did not surprise either Sumner of Parker. If South Carolina was permitted to beat a black man in Charleston, it was not illogical that she would beat a white man in Washington. But the attack upon Sumner actually had greatly disturbed Parker. Writing to John P. Hale, he confessed, "I wish I could have taken the blows on my head—and not he, at least *half of them.*"[34] To meet this challenge of Southern violence he recommended to his people to elect in the year's presidential campaign a man who was neither a "knave" nor a "dunce."[35]

Parker had mused in his journal in 1851 that if he had devoted as much time to theological reflection as he did to political participation on the slavery question he could have contributed a great deal to theological literature. I was born to be a philosopher, he thought, and events call for a *"stump orator."*[36] In 1856 his alternate vocation dominated his attention. He knew all the leaders of the Republican party, many of them intimately. He hoped that emancipation would come through having one of their number in the White House. With skill and organization, he believed, the Republicans could capture the presidency. If Conscience Whigs, revolting Democrats, Northern Know-Nothings, Republicans, old Liberty party men, and Garrisonians banded together, it could be done. He listed as his preference for the Republican nomination, Seward, Chase, and Hale, in that order.[37] He greatly admired William Henry Seward, but supported the Republicans' nominee, Frémont. The presidential election of 1856, Parker believed, was the most important presidential election since the nation's first.[38]

James Freeman Clarke was a very eager campaigner for Frémont and well informed in political organization. To his friends in Pennsylvania he sent several recommendations on campaign strategy. First of all, they should learn the political composition of every section of the state in order to discover how "every voter" intended to vote. Next they should organize Frémont Clubs in every community and use them to canvass voters and to distribute campaign literature. Then they should sponsor a series of "camp meetings" in remote sections of the state so that no group of voters remained unreached. Finally, to support these efforts, money should be collected from within and from without Pennsylvania.[39]

In his own state of Massachusetts, Clarke portrayed the presidential campaign as a battle between "Civilization and Barbarism." The issues in the election, he lectured, were not questions of tariffs, trade, or taxes. Mankind was the issue, not money. It was a question of "human rights and human freedom," not only for the black man, but for every man. The election would pit the interests of Democracy against those of a "tyrannical Oligarchy, between Freedom North and South and Slavery everywhere, between Peace and Union on the one hand, Civil War and Division on the other." Christians who desired their country to be a Christian country in deed as well as word should vote for the Republican party. Protestant clergymen of every denomination were "openly and earnestly" supporting Frémont because they saw this election was one between "Christ and the Anti-Christ." This did not imply that Buchanan was the Anti-Christ and his opponent, Frémont, had messianic attributes. No; slavery was the Anti-Christ for it denied the Bible to God's children. Northern Christianity was simply uniting with that political movement which would stop slavery's expansion.[40]

Preoccupied with his revolutionary enthusiasm, Higginson did not vigorously campaign for Frémont. He was on the committee of Worcester citizens who ratified Frémont's nomination. He was also asked by Worcester Republicans to run for the Massachusetts state legislature, but he declined, saying that the Free Church demanded this attention. A reason closer to the truth was probably his temporary lack of interest in moderate political antislavery. Having witnessed the "revolution" in progress in Kansas, he had in mind far more radical proposals to end slavery than to campaign for John C. Frémont. "Kansas fever" drove him to see that victory over slavery lay in the disruption of the Union: "I am sure that the disease is too deep for cure without amputation." For his part, Parker would not propose disunion as long as hope for Frémont's election existed. Yet, he admitted, "If Buchanan is elected, I don't believe the Union holds out three years. I shall go for dissolution."[41]

D. A UNION OF "SPUN-GLASS": THE DISUNION CONVENTION OF 1857

Higginson was the prime mover behind the "State Disunion Convention" of January 1857. He was convinced that disunion sentiment was widespread as a result of the repeated triumphs of the South. At the twenty-fifth anniversary celebration of the Massachusetts Antislavery Society, he declared, "You first told us the "secret of anti-slavery, and told it in one word—Disunion! . . . As God is in heaven, our destiny and duty are to be found there. It is our only hope."[42] The call for the Convention was headed by Higginson and Thomas Earle, the old vice-presidential candidate of the Liberty party in 1840. "The greater part of the signers," wrote Higginson to John Gorham Palfrey, "were active supporters of Col. Frémont's Election, and the object of the Convention is to consider the question of Disunion, not as a Constitutional scruple, but as a practical measure." Both Garrisonians and political abolitionists predominated at the meeting; Garrison himself served as one of the vice-presidents. Parker was invited, but had a prior engagement. He was pleased about the meeting; it showed that the North had some manhood still. Yet, reneging on his intention to "go for dissolution," he objected to disunion. Would it not leave "four millions of 'poor whites,' and four millions slaves, to their present condition"? The citizens of the North had to bring these people out of their bondage, "peaceably if [they could], forcibly if [they] must." He had believed that emancipation could be achieved without bloodshed. Now he said, "I believe it . . . no longer."[43]

The newspapers severely criticized the Disunion Convention. Higginson thought it had been a success. He was proud that a dozen of America's "most eminent men" had written more than seventy manuscript pages to the Convention. Disunion now could be openly discussed and advocated as a viable political program. In July, Higginson, Garrison, Phillips, and 6,400 other antislavery citizens issued a call for a National Disunion Convention to meet in October. Signatures to the call were obtained by sending petitions to antislavery leaders in communities throughout the nation. Nearly 300 were signed and returned, the bulk coming from Massachusetts, Ohio, Pennsylvania, New York, and Michigan.[44]

Like Parker, Clarke could not advocate disunion. When he spoke at the August First anniversary celebration at Abington, Massachusetts, in 1857, the *Boston Courier* criticized his association with the disunionists of the Massachusetts Antislavery Society. The Garrisonians, he told the *Courier* in rebuttal, allowed him perfect freedom to speak his mind, and he never pleaded for disunion. Disunion required a conviction by the Northern states that liberty was greater than Union. If this conviction were realized, slavery would end and make the dissolution of the Union unnecessary. The radical abolitionists were not likely to harm the Union. "Its chief danger is from those who seem to think it made of spun-glass." These "Union-savers" remained in a "perpetual panic," and their fright encouraged slaveholders to threaten continually the dissolution of the Union. Slavery not disunion, declared Clarke, was the "one dark, deep, poisonous plague-spot of the land"; to remove it was the "greatest cause of the age."[45]

Apparently Clarke and Parker were among a host of dissenters from Higginson's disunion platform. Not enough enthusiasm existed for it, and not enough support could be obtained. "The march of events proved too strong for us," Higginson later wrote. The proposed "National Disunion Convention" never took place.[46]

E. "NEITHER TREASON NOR MURDER": HARPERS FERRY—1859

Parker did not feel that the Garrisonian abolitionists gave the "political workmen" of the antislavery movement enough credit. The radical abolitionists could easily be outspoken, but Sumner, Seward, and Chase had to weigh their thoughts carefully before speaking on antislavery. They were owned by the people and had to widen their personal views to be reelected.[47] Parker waited upon them to develop nonviolent or violent political solutions to end slavery, all the while impatiently advising fugitive slaves and their rescuers to use violence.

In a speech in the hall of the State House before the Massachusetts Antislavery Society in January 1858, Parker noted the great political change in Northern antislavery thinking. The first remarkable indication of the ascendancy of political antislavery was the fact that the Massachusetts Antislavery Society could now meet in the hall of the State House. Only a few years ago this would have been impossible. The antislavery reformers had gained political power and the Legislature of Massachusetts had begun to do what they asked. He also alluded to the fate of the Northern senators who had voted for the Kansas-Nebraska Bill. Of the ten who had sought reelection, only one was successful. Thirty-nine of forty-two Northern representatives who had voted for the Bill had lost reelection.[48]

Slavery had to be overcome, Parker declared, either "politically, or else militarily." If emancipation was not achieved peacefully soon, then it would be gained through bloodshed. "The negro will not bear slavery for ever," he preached; "if he would, the white man will not." A victory by the Republican party in the presidential election would prevent the further extension of slavery. If the North would choose an antislavery president in 1860 and implement the principles of the Declaration of Independence and the preamble of the Constitution, America would be totally and truly free. But the Republicans had to change their approach to slavery. Parker called for aggression:

> We must attack Slavery—Slavery in the territories, Slavery in the district, and, above all, Slavery *in the Slave States.* Would you remove the *shadow of a tree?* Then down with the tree itself. There is no other way.[49]

A few days after Parker's speech, Higginson received a letter from John Brown, who wrote: "I have been told you are both a true *man*: and a true *abolitionist*; 'and I partly believe,' the whole story." Brown sought funds to accomplish "BY FAR the most *important* undertaking of [my] whole life."[50] His plans intrigued Higginson: "I am always ready to invest money in treason," he wrote to Brown, "but at present have none to invest."[51] In the ensuing months he became more and more committed to Brown's "secret service." Parker and Samuel G. Howe were involved in the plans. John A. Andrew sent funds. It became gradually clear to most of Brown's supporters that he intended an invasion of the South.[52]

An armed crusade to emanicpate slaves had been a fear
shared by William Ellery Channing and the advocates of
philosophical antislavery. The Garrisonians also rejected
such proposals. Higginson undoubtedly desired to change
their minds. In 1858 he spoke to the May meeting of the
American Antislavery Society. Referring directly to servile
insurrection, but refraining from mentioning Brown's
plans, he declared:

> Behind the long years of cheerful submission [of Negro
> slaves] there may lie a dagger and a power to use it when
> the time comes. . . . We speak of the American Slave as if
> he was never to do anything for his own emancipation.
> We forget the heroes of Santo Domingo, in fact great
> negro heroism has already been shown and thus charges
> of timidity are wrong.[53]

Higginson had touched an important point. Not only did
some people fret over the possibility of a servile insurrection; incongruously many Whites doubted that manliness
or heroism was an attribute of the Negro race. Among
political abolitionists, with the exception of Higginson, it
was uniformly believed that blacks lacked aggressiveness.

Higginson's conviction of the heroism of Negroes originated in his experience of *following* the black confederate
who led the attack upon the courthouse in 1854. This
"experience was of inestimable value to [me]," he wrote,
"for it removed once and for all every doubt of the intrinsic
courage of the blacks." In Parker's mind, however, there
was "no doubt [that] the African race is greatly inferior to
the Caucasian in general intellectual power, and also in that
instinct for Liberty which is so strong in the Teutonic
family. . . ." But although the blacks lacked the "general
power of mind, or instinctive love of liberty equal to the
whites, they are much our superiors in *power of cunning,* and
in *contempt for death*—rather formidable qualities in a servile
war." The Africans, he believed, were "not very good at the

sword," and while not exactly cowards were a very docile people.[54]

To support his opinion of Negro meekness and to illustrate the "sad history of the African race," Parker told the story of a fugitive slave. The slave was an "entire negro," whose grandfather had been taken from the Congo coast. He was married and had children. One day his master beat him so severely that both of his arms were broken. They were badly set and healed deformed. His master offered to sell him his freedom, but after he had raised half the sum, his master tore him from his family and sold him "down South." While on board the river steamer taking him southward, the slave had the opportunity to slay his sleeping guards with an axe. But he recalled the Lord's command, "No murderer hath eternal life," laid down his weapon, and was sold into slavery. Later he escaped to Boston and told his story to Parker. "What would you have done?" he asked Parker. "I would have slain my kidnappers," Parker replied, "and then trusted that the act would be imputed to me for righteousness by an all-righteous God!"[55]

Parker's low opinion of Negro masculinity was also reflected in his concern over the "Africanization of America." "Any Anglo-Saxon with common sense," he wrote, "wishes the superior race to multiply rather than the inferior."[56] And it was best that they procreate separately. The "regressive" nature of the South was a partial testimony to amalgamation. The "ethnological sluggishness of the African element" had been mixed into the Southern population.[57] Parker, as an activist and one who was deeply imbued in the revolutionary spirit of 1776, had no patience with "sluggishness," whether suggested or real. In the black race it was very real: "The negro is slow," observed Parker in the West Indies, "a loose-jointed sort of animal, a great child."[58] Sadly, Parker was not above using racial slurs. Writing from the West Indies in 1859, for example, Parker longed to participate in the Republican party battles and to speak on the Fourth of July in Boston, but could not, he said, because he was "sick as a miserable nigger."[59]

The robust and sometimes vulgar language of Parker was not the style of James Freeman Clarke. Still, Clarke's general view of the Negro corresponded with Parker's. The black did not have the "sturdy self-reliance of the Anglo-Saxon," he wrote, and was "easily depressed by unkindness."[60] The alleged inferiority of the Negro could not be affirmed without further proof. Still, he admitted there were racial differences. The Negro race, for example, manifested some "very striking traits." It was an "affectionate race," he declared,

> kindly, full of sympathy, naturally polite, tasteful, religious, with keen perceptions, with profound magnetic natures, living very near to nature, catching instinctively some of her mysteries, and knowing her secrets as our cold Saxon observers never are able to know them.

The warm, religious nature of the Negro impressed him very much. Although the Negro race may "always be inferior in some respects," its great sensitivity could give it leadership in the arts and religion. America would have "no real living art" until the blacks were educated to be the nation's artists. And although some said that God permitted Negro slavery in America in order to produce black missionaries for Africa, Clarke saw God's hand directing the blacks to "stay and Christianize us."[61]

Clarke believed that one of Christianity's good works, the destruction of racial prejudice, had top priority.[62] At the same time he lauded the establishment of a retirement home for "aged colored women" "equal" to the one already existing for white women. His mother and all of the best families, the Cabots, Jacksons, Goddards, and Higginsons, supported this "separate but equal" charity. The home gave rebuttal, thought Clarke, to those in the South who taunted the North over its bad treatment of Negroes.[63]

Parker believed that the Negroes would eventually take "their defence into their own hands, especially if they [could] find white men to lead them." Perhaps this belief motivated him somewhat to assist John Brown. He was naturally disappointed when Brown was captured at Harpers Ferry and sentenced to death.[64] Brown's failure also disturbed Higginson, who had hoped that the incursion into Virginia would end accusations of the "apparent feebleness and timidity of the slaves."[65] He visited Brown's family in North Elba, New York, and hoped, through Brown's wife, to persuade Brown to consent to a rescue attempt. Brown wisely declined. Any escape plan was almost certain to fail. Brown's family greatly impressed Higginson and he wrote to his mother:

> [Harpers Ferry] is the most formidable slave insurrection that has ever occurred, and it is evident, through the confused and exaggerated accounts, that there are leaders of great capacity and skill behind it. If they have such leaders, they can hold their own for a long time against all force likely to be brought against them, and can at last retreat to the mountains and establish a Maroon colony there, like those in Jamaica and Guiana. Meantime the effect will be to frighten and weaken the slave power everywhere and discourage the slave trade. Nothing has so strengthened slavery as the timid submission of the slaves thus far; but their constant communication with Canada has been teaching them self-confidence and resistance. In Missouri especially this single alarm will shorten slavery by ten years.[66]

Generally, the political abolitionists tried to separate the man from the event. They praised Brown but usually disapproved of his methods. The wisdom of the raid was questionable, but as John A. Andrew remarked, "John

Brown himself was right. I sympathize with the man"; and, he continued, "I sympathize with the idea, because I sympathize and believe in the Eternal Right."[67] Andrew's pastor, Clarke, preached on the Harpers Ferry Affair after word was received of Brown's death sentence. He blamed the whole tragedy upon the pro-slavery mentality of the North and the South, and especially upon the "false conservatism of the North" and the "low condition of the religion of the country."[68]

F. THE TRIUMPH OF POLITICAL ABOLITIONISM: THE ELECTION OF ABRAHAM LINCOLN—1860

James Freeman Clarke wrote to a dying Theodore Parker in Europe, in the fall of 1859, that the political prospects of the Republican party were far from encouraging. If the Republicans could take Pennsylvania, he felt that they could gain the White House, but unfortunately, as in 1856, political organization in the state was poor. A new kind of politics was needed. The people had to be enlightened on the issues. Voters had to be canvassed. Tracts and lecturers had to be sent wherever most needed. The election could be won by an effective distribution of information and "thorough agitation."[69]

Once the presidential race in 1860 was fully underway, Clarke was in the middle of the excitement. Parker, who had created so much public support for the Republicans, died in May before the Republican convention met in Chicago. He had favored the nomination of Seward, with Chase as his second choice. Lincoln's nomination would probably have disappointed him, but would have still received his support. Higginson backed Lincoln and urged the Worcester Convention of radical political abolitionists to do the same. Although the Republican party platform repudiated John Brown's raid and advocated a mild antislavery stance, there was hope that better things would follow a Republican victory.[70]

On the Sunday evening before the election, Clarke made a final attempt to rally support for Lincoln. Speaking to a large congregation of voters at the Church of the Disciples, he praised the pioneer work of the antislavery reformers: Phillips, Garrison, Parker, William Ellery Channing, Samuel J. May, Mrs. Child, the Follens, Pierpont, Giddings, Sumner, and John P. Hale. They had created the Northern antislavery sentiment that would now encourage and enable Abraham Lincoln to complete their task. If the Republicans won, the antislavery hosts of past and present could take credit for the victory. No doubt it pleased Clarke that at least a kind of spiritual "great northern league for freedom" had at last materialized. In delivering this political lecture in his church, Clarke disavowed partisan politics; his lecture was solely in the interests of Christianity. To be fair, he outlined the platforms of the four political parties, but no one could mistake his preference. The main question of the election was human slavery. Only one party platform was in accord with Christian principles. "This election," declared Clarke, "will determine the moral progress, the virtue, education, and Christianity of coming millions."[71] A few days later he shared in the exuberance of a Republican victory. After two decades of patiently voting on the losing side, Clarke had this time voted for a winner—Abraham Lincoln. It was a victory "born of endurance," full of hope and great expectations.[72]

Part III

The Patterns Framed

7

To Move a Mountain: Unitarian Individuals and Institutional Unitarianism—1831–1860

AS individual Unitarians discovered the immediacy of antislavery reform, they expected their denomination to participate and even lead the movement. They were bitterly disappointed. As far as the Unitarian Garrisonians were concerned, the interracial fellowship they enjoyed and encouraged spotlighted their denomination in a glaring and embarrassing way. The segregation of Negroes into separate pews went against the laws of humanity and Christian brotherhood. Their denomination's silence on the antislavery movement and foot-dragging reluctance to enter any discussion of the reform incensed them.

For their part, the Unitarian advocates of philosophical

171

antislavery as moderates did not pressure their denomination to declare publicly against slavery, and it is unlikely that, had Channing accepted the presidency of the American Unitarian Association, he would have led the body in an antislavery resolution. It is significant that the American Unitarian Association—unlike the British and Foreign Unitarian Association—excluded his antislavery writings in the denomination's series of tracts. The antislavery witness of Channing at denominational meetings came after his death, when it was recalled by either Garrisonians or political abolitionists. The contribution by the advocates of philosophical antislavery at denominational meetings was minimal.

The Unitarian political abolitionists, as moderates also, did not at first confront the conservatives who led their denomination. But after the Fugitive Slave Law, they shared and sometimes led the criticism of the denomination's conservative leadership.[1]

A. THE DREADFUL COWARDS OF THE BOSTON PULPITS

Among the Garrisonians there existed the general feeling that the demonic had gripped the churches of New England and prevented them from doing the Lord's work. Maria Weston Chapman and her husband had been drawn to William Ellery Channing because of his liberal theology and deep spirituality. But, as members of his congregation, they were appalled at his seesaw-attitude toward the abolitionists and they condemned his antislavery message as pablum for slaveholders. They objected to his apparent prejudice against color. At the time May was fighting for Miss Crandall's school, Channing boasted of the colored school he had helped to found, a school that soon became incorporated into the Boston public school system. This prejudice explains in part the Chapmans' antipathy for Channing. Mrs. Chapman, for example, claims that her husband's last words, when he went to the West Indies to die, were "Don't rest until the coloured school [i.e., Channing's] is broken up."

Mrs. Chapman's temper was aroused because Channing coupled every statement he made in favor of abolitionists with one against them. He knew the Mays, Chapmans, Sewalls, Lorings, and Quincy, and he told Mrs. Chapman, "I *entreat* you to confine your principles to your own breasts." He blamed the abolitionists for admitting blacks into their societies, for sending their publications to the South, for arousing the community, for going to the young, and he accused them of desiring (quite wrongly in light of their nonviolent stance) the slaves' vengeance upon their masters. His vacillation in talking about the abolitionists took the form of beginning every sentence with "I doubt" or "I fear."[2] Channing was a "tender-spirited, saintly sort of man," Mrs. Chapman said sarcastically, "to whom evil not before his eye (and they were not sharp eyes) was a mere abstraction." She acknowledged that his poor health had something to do with it. Actually, Mrs. Chapman would have been less likely to attack Channing had he chosen silence. But she objected to his critical remarks. He would not desist from charging that her antislavery work was dangerous to the country's health, especially in the South. "Remember," he warned her, "the Southern mothers with their infants in their arm!" "I do remember them," Mrs. Chapman shot back, "but without distinction of colour!"[3]

Mrs. Chapman's clashes with Channing resounded through the Garrisonian community and everyone knew that she would never fail "to 'heave a brick' [at him] when she had a chance."[4] Granted that Mrs. Chapman's attacks on Channing as an individual must be considered as a part of her personal vendetta against him, her dissatisfaction with the vapid nature of their denomination was shared by the bulk of the Unitarian Garrisonians. Ellis Gray Loring in his gentle way argued with Channing over his treatment of the radical abolitionists.[5] Moreover, Loring found little in Unitarian preaching to inspire him. His crisp opinion of one Unitarian sermon could be typical of most—"dull enough I suppose." Deborah Weston voiced similar displeasure over the sermons of Boston's finest preachers— Ezra Stiles Gannett and Francis Parkman. Commenting on a sermon by the latter, she remarked, "I was completely exhausted listening to his villany [sic]." Mrs. Child had found inspiration in the ministry of John Gorham Palfrey and in the presence of Daniel Webster at Brattle Street Church. Once she accepted abolitionist doctrine, the fount of inspiration dried up. Unitarianism had satisfied "her reason and her heart," but at present the church's lack of reforming zeal gave her great disappointment. Francis Jackson, a member of Hollis Street Church, wrestled with his church's leadership over the pro-slavery (from a Garrisonian point of view) and anti-abolitionist preaching of guest minister Thomas Russell Sullivan, and the refusal of the standing committee of the congregation to permit the reading of antislavery meeting announcements. Jackson was furious. As a Christian, he told the standing committee, I refuse "to submit to such an arbitrary exercise of mere human power."[6]

The inability of the Unitarian denomination to please these abolitionist sectarians caused a reshuffling of congregational allegiances among the Unitarian laymen. Loring abandoned Channing in going over, with his wife, to James Freeman Clarke's "free church" at Indiana Place. Francis Jackson eventually joined another free church, Theodore Parker's Twenty-Eighth Congregational Society. Mrs. Child left the Unitarians, flirted with Swedenborgianism, and then came back, under the influence of Edmund Sears, at a time when antislavery had become respectable and acceptable to a wider group of Unitarians. Bowditch quit, only later to return. The Chapmans and the Weston sisters drifted; Mrs. Chapman moved into Theodore Parker's orbit, and her sisters gravitated to John Pierpont's preaching for as long as he lasted in Boston. Anne Warren Weston desired to continue to labor "for the purification of the New England churches," but Maria Weston Chapman, although she maintained her Unitarian circle of friends, grew more caustic, condemning Unitarians generally as cowards, and proclaiming that the Unitarian environment of Harvard and Cambridge, Massachusetts, was never a good atmosphere for "the salvation of *a* nation," let alone America.[7]

Whenever Samuel May, Jr. had a Sunday free while general agent of the Massachusetts Antislavery Society, he attended Theodore Parker's church. He did not agree with Parker's theology, but he felt at home in Parker's society. Garrison and many of his friends periodically attended there, and Parker was far above the "dreadful cowards" who generally filled the Boston pulpits.[8] May had been a "birthright Unitarian" and had grown up thinking that the denomination's ministers were nearly impeccable men who fought fearlessly for "the truth and the right." But the "defection and decline of the early Unitarian spirit" saddened May. He saw during the 1840s that a "bigotry, narrowness, and worldliness" had crept into the Unitarian fellowship.[9] They preached once or twice a year on slavery, if at all, and professed to be its great enemies. But they attacked the Garrisonians at the same time as they attacked slavery, and their people were "quieted" rather than "quickened" on the issue.[10] May was especially censorious of George E. Ellis, Francis Parkman, George Putnam, Orville Dewey, Ezra Stiles Gannett, and Ephraim Peabody, all powerful conservatives in his denomination. His attempts with Francis Jackson to embarrass the ministry of Peabody bordered on slander.[11]

Unlike the Garrisonians, the political abolitionists as

moderates tried to avoid confrontation with the conservative leadership of their denomination. They changed their
minds when faced by the conflict over the Fugitive Slave
Law. Clarke, finding himself in between two opposing
camps, the *"Ultra-abolitionists"* and the *"Ultra-Let-Alone-ists,"*
said that he preferred the former. The one group was
generous, the other selfish.[12]

Unhappily, the latter group contained many Unitarians,
remarked Clarke, including men whom he respected as the
denomination's "wisest and best men." Samuel A. Eliot, a
member of King's Chapel, the oldest Unitarian church in
America, was one of the three northern Whigs who voted
for the Fugitive Slave Law. Judge Benjamin R. Curtis, also
of King's Chapel, gave the first legal opinion in Massachusetts in favor of the Law's constitutionality. George
Ticknor Curtis, another member of King's Chapel, issued
the first warrant for the arrest of fugitives in November
1850, a second warrant for the seizure of Shadrach in
February 1851, and a third warrant, which returned Sims
to slavery, in April 1851. Edward G. Loring, yet another
member of King's Chapel, issued the warrant that returned
Anthony Burns to slavery. The *Daily Advertiser*, edited by
Unitarian Nathan Hale, praised the passage of the Fugitive
Slave Law as a "measure long neglected and necessary for
quieting agitation." Unitarian Daniel Webster, of course,
had traveled about the country in an effort "to sell" the Law
to the American people.

To counteract, Clarke said, the revolt of conscientious
men against the Law, a group of moral teachers—he cited
conservative Unitarian minister, William Parsons Lunt, as
an example—arose called "Lower Law Doctors." They
taught that no higher law existed than an Act of Congress.
Their teaching was "equivalent to practical atheism." They
gave the impression, he said, that God sat on his throne "in
the distant heaven," had abandoned interest in human
affairs, and had delegated his authority to "Nicholas in

Russia, to Louis Napoleon in France, to the Imperial Parliament in England, and to Congress in the United States." Clarke charged that the "Lower Law Doctors" had a demonic influence upon the nation:

> They have introduced heresies and novelties of the most pernicious kind. . . . They have apostacized from the fundamental truths of the Gospel. . . . Unconsciously perhaps, they are teachers of a practical atheism—teaching men to live without God, in the world. We charge them with corrupting morality in its foundation.[13]

Clarke would be the first antislavery champion who had the temerity to throw down the gauntlet and challenge his "Ultra-Let-Alone-ist" denomination on the issue of antislavery. Since the American Unitarian Association's inception in 1825, the denomination had chosen not to issue an antislavery statement, and when Clarke, the young knight who had just returned from the land where the beast of slavery dwelt, raised the issue at the annual meeting of the A.U.A. in 1841, no action was taken. Then Garrisonian Samuel May, Jr., tried in 1842 without success. Next, in 1843, Garrisonian John Parkman, the "chaplain" to John P. Hale, tried to challenge the Unitarians but was ignored. Thereafter, with greater frequency, young antislavery challengers, and older fighters like John Pierpont and Samuel Willard, confronted their denomination at each annual meeting.[14]

Yet, while one may record the work and words of individual antislavery reformers at the annual meeting of the A.U.A. and later at the Autumnal Conventions and Ministerial Conferences, it is not possible to define precisely the denomination's position on antislavery. The Tappanite organization, the American and Foreign Antislavery Society, was aware of this problem when it undertook to describe and evaluate the positions of the many American denominations on slavery. "It is difficult," the Society's

Annual Report said in 1853, "to ascertain the position of [the Unitarian] denomination on the great question of American Slavery, because it possesses so few of the characteristics of a 'denomination' and has no adequate method of giving a denominational expression of sentiment." The Unitarian denominational meetings were not composed of delegates elected by the church's individual societies, but were free assemblies of Unitarian ministers and laymen who individually chose to attend. Giving due credit to the valiant Unitarian ministers who were antislavery reformers, the report judged that the denomination occupied "on the whole, rather a neutral position." Ministers who did speak out against slavery risked dismissal because of the "influence of the pro-slavery and conservative element," which existed "more or less in almost every Unitarian congregation." These "leading, wealthy and prominent Unitarians" supported Daniel Webster, the "fallen statesman," and tried to prevent their ministers from preaching on slavery, and from "exerting any influence upon their congregations, or the public sentiment, against [the] God-defying and Heaven-daring iniquity of our land." These conservatives also barred the American Unitarian Association from publishing any tracts or books on antislavery. The "Conservatives and moneyed men" controlled the meetings of the A.U.A., and were forcing an exodus of antislavery and "reformatory" Unitarians from participation in the annual meetings.[15]

Antislavery opinion of the Unitarian denomination's contribution to the antislavery movement was uniformly negative. In 1837, when Samuel J. May tried to describe for a fellow Garrisonian the attitudes of Unitarian ministers on antislavery, he gave a hodgepodge list of men who expressed interest in the cause but were afraid to participate; who spoke out timidly and then recanted; who were silent or "vehemently opposed"; or who were "not opposed, but not in favor." Those who were antislavery reformers suffered.

In the same year, Harriet Martineau, an English Unitarian converted to radical abolitionism while on a visit to America, gave her opinion of the Unitarian denomination:

> As a body they must, though disapproving slavery be ranked as the enemies of the abolitionists. Some have pleaded to me that it is a distasteful subject. . . . Some say that their pulpits are the property of their people, who are not therefore to have their minds disturbed by what they hear thence. . . . Some think the subject not spiritual enough. The greater number excused themselves on the ground . . . that the duty of the clergy is to decide on how much truth the people can bear, and to administer it accordingly.

Four years later, Garrisonian Stephen A. Foster included the Unitarian denomination in his book *The Brotherhood of Thieves; or, a True Picture of the American Church and Clergy*. . . . Despite the loose organization of the denomination, he remarked, the Unitarians still had an "ecclesiastical existence and their influence however trifling has given no anti-slavery cause any assistance. They have joined the oppressors." They were the "enemies of truth and freedom." Finally, in 1852 political abolitionist William Goodell declared that although there were "earnest and active" Unitarian antislavery reformers, he had heard of no "thorough anti-slavery churches of that sect, or of the withdrawal of ministers and laymen for re-organization, on account of the slave question."[16]

A few years after emancipation had been achieved, Samuel J. May recorded his recollections of the antislavery movement. With the advantage of hindsight, the saintly May stated proudly that the Unitarians had given to the antislavery cause more men and women reformers than "any other denomination in proportion to our numbers, if not more without that comparison." But once he passed from the honor roll of those individual Unitarians who had significantly contributed to the antislavery drive, he could, with no pride whatsoever, narrate the "discreditable account" of the "pro-slavery conduct of the Unitarian denomination." May declared:

> The Unitarians as a body dealt with the question of slavery in any but an impartial, courageous, and Christian way. Continually in their public meetings the question was staved off and driven out, because of technical, formal verbal difficulties which were of no real importance. . . . We had a right to expect from Unitarians a steadfast and unqualified protest against . . . American slavery. And considering their position as a body not entangled with any proslavery alliances, not hampered by any ecclesiastical organization, it does seem to me that they were *preeminently guilty* in reference to the enslavement of the millions in our land with its attendant wrongs, cruelties, horrors. They, of all other sects, ought to have spoken boldly. But they did not.

He thought this moral guilt of the Unitarians should be a sober warning to future generations. It showed that even the Unitarians, as a denomination, had been "corrupted and morally paralyzed" by the nation's subservience to slaveholders; "even the Unitarians to whose avowed faith in the paternity of God, the brotherhood of all mankind, and the divinity of human nature, the enslavement of men should have been especially abhorrent."[17]

B. THE INDICTMENT

The loose congregational polity of the Unitarians made it possible, if not easy, for May and his antislavery colleagues to bring the denomination to protest against slavery. All they had to do was to obtain a majority vote at the annual meetings that would result in an antislavery resolution. The loose congregational polity of the Unitarians made it possible for May and his antislavery colleagues to educate their congregations in antislavery and not to suffer interference from the leaders of the denomination. That it was so difficult to get the annual meetings of the denomination to issue an antislavery resolution and to get Unitarian congregations to permit even the discussion of slavery within their church walls was evidence, at least, of Unitarian reluctance to deal with the great moral problem of the age. Whether it was evidence of a "corrupted and morally paralyzed" denomination, as May would have "future generations" believe, depended largely upon just how important one considered slavery as a moral problem.

In any event, evidence has been recorded in previous chapters of the reluctance of many Unitarian congregations to deal with the problem of slavery, and the insistence of powerful cliques within many congregations that their ministers not touch it. As an antislavery preacher, Samuel May, Jr., admitted that he had as much chance "gaining admittance to the *principal* pulpits of the denomination" as being able "to preach in Westminster Abbey."[18] Mention has been made of the difficulties that Follen, Samuel J. May, Simmons, Pierpont, Higginson, Samuel May, Jr., and Furness had with their congregations over their antislavery preaching. Usually the crux of the difficulty was discussed in terms of politics and the pulpit, but it was likely that the issue of "colorphobia" lay at the base of much of the dissension. Garrisonian Thomas Treadwell Stone (1801–1895) had upset his congregation, the First Church in Salem, by supporting a Negro's attempt to hire a pew. Because of his abolitionism Stone eventually was dismissed.[19] Samuel J. May's South Scituate congregation complained that "he was always preaching for the niggers," and May's inability to stomach the ignominy of the congregation's Negro pew had forced his resignation.[20]

Other ministers who clashed with their congregations over the slavery question included John Parkman of Dover,

New Hampshire; Rufus Stebbins of Meadville, Pennsylvania; Octavius Brooks Frothingham of Salem, Massachusetts; James C. Parsons of Waltham, Massachusetts; Augustus H. Conant of Geneva and Rockford, Illinois (his antislavery preaching troubled both congregations); Horatio Stebbins of Portland, Maine; John Weiss of Watertown, Massachusetts; Samuel Longfellow of Brooklyn, New York; Moncure Daniel Conway of Washington, D.C.; Linus Hall Shaw of Sudbury, Massachusetts; William C. Tenney of Kennebunk, Maine; and W. G. Babcock of Luneburg, Massachusetts.[21]

Some of these ministers resigned voluntarily, some were asked to resign, some stood firm and watched the decimation of their congregations, a few successfully weathered the conflict with but minor defections from their flock. We have seen that similar difficulties occurred in Unitarian congregations even when antislavery preaching was not the issue, as the result of a request by a local antislavery society to use a Unitarian church for their meeting. Although many Unitarian congregations had been long accustomed to allow reform societies to use their buildings, the antislavery societies were invariably refused, whether the request was made in Nashua, New Hampshire (rejected by a large majority of the congregation); Providence, Rhode Island; or Groveland, Massachusetts, where a request was promptly rejected, even though the town's Unitarian church had previously been used by "comic singers, striped pigs, and the like."[22]

The Garrisonians complained that the Unitarian press was parsimonious in reporting their activities and censorious in printing their resolutions and announcements. They had evidence to support their accusations. Samuel J. May's sermon on Prejudice was expurgated of all references to slavery when the American Unitarian Association printed it as a tract. Henry Ware, Jr., performed the role of censor.

The year was 1830 and May remarked that a few years later Ware would not have done it nor May allowed it: "But we were all in bondage then." A count of the articles on slavery in the *Christian Register*, the main journalistic voice of American Unitarianism, between January 1, 1831, and December 28, 1839, reveals more evidence of partiality. Among the letters to the editor, announcements of meetings, editorials, feature articles, and reprints from other newspapers and journals on the topic of slavery, approximately seventy items were favorable to the colonization of Negroes, forty were by antislavery reformers or favorable to antislavery reform, and thirty-five were unfavorable to the antislavery movement."[23] Yet, readers in the South complained about the "abolition character" of the *Christian Register* and its bewildered editor wondered on what grounds they based their complaint. He was simply trying to provide a noncontroversial "family Unitarian paper."[24]

C. *ECCLESIA PLANTANDA* OR MISSIONS AS MUSHROOMS?—A DENOMINATION OF RESTRICTED GROWTH

The American Unitarian Association was a missionary organization devoted to the propaganda and extension of the Unitarian faith. For some fifteen to twenty years after its founding in 1825 it reached out westward and southward to grow with America. The South in particular seemed to be a productive soil for Unitarianism. Had not Thomas Jefferson predicted that Unitarianism would one day be the universal religion of America? In 1830 the A.U.A. had purveyors of tracts in Raleigh, North Carolina; Charleston, South Carolina; and Savannah and Milledgeville, Georgia. Missionary excitement and high hopes for continued growth and influence dominated its annual meetings. Our "purpose," declared Ezra Stiles Gannett at its meeting in 1832, "is to make Christians." Samuel J. May at the same gathering extolled the dissemination of Christian truth.[25] And under the A.U.A. banner, William Greenleaf Eliot went to St. Louis, Missouri; Clarke to Louisville, Kentucky; and Ephraim Peabody to Cincinnati, Ohio.

Unitarians always had a curious propensity to claim greater successes than could be supported by fact. Perhaps this was due to a denominational inferiority complex arising out of their position in the numbers game of American voluntary Christianity. The annual report of the A.U.A. in 1833 listed only two hundred Unitarian parishes in the United States. The denomination's executive committee, conceivably embarrassed by this small number, suggested that "if we include all that reject the doctrine of the trinity, and adopt most of our leading views in religion, the number of societies would probably be more than 2,000." This view of an inevitable and unaided growth of unitarianism outside of the denomination was severely criticized by James Freeman Clarke. Nurturing a hardy but dwarfed seedling of Unitarian Christianity in the stony soil of Kentucky, Clarke knew that the harvest could not be plentiful where laborers were few or unavailable. "I don't understand you," he wrote to a friend,

> when you say that Unitarianism will spread just as well without our aid—I know of no other good thing that will grow without human aid (except mushrooms, and Unitarianism has proved itself to be no mushroom). It strikes me that we should aid it *more* than we have.

The spread of Unitarianism required missionaries, and Clarke firmly believed they could win the West. "Only Unitarians," he declared, "or something equal to it under another name, *can ever bring the people of [the Mississippi] valley to God.* I bless and adore the Providence which has raised up this form of Christianity to refresh and regenerate this great and growing country."[26]

Clarke's missionary ebullience was a part of the denomination's general optimism during these early years, when Unitarianism could be considered a vital religious movement. No section of humanity was to be denied the Unitarian gospel. Dr. Follen at the annual meeting in 1834 urged evangelism among the poor in an effort to elevate them. A layman from Boston, having just returned from an extensive Southern tour, spoke of the need of tracts, funds, and missionaries for the South. At the next annual meeting William Greenleaf Eliot pleaded for aid to satisfy the religious needs of the West. And again at the meeting in 1836, Clarke and a fellow Unitarian minister told of their missionary thrust into the South, where a large congregation, "composed mostly of persons of the first respectability in the society," had been organized in Mobile, Alabama. They also declared with pride that 150 persons had applied for pews in the Unitarian church in New Orleans and could not be accommodated. "We feel as a denomination," they said, "we have much to do. We are striving to make our religion . . . more extensively embraced. . . ." The Association accepted their report as evidence that the denomination had achieved "much more of the *missionary character* than it has had in any previous year."[27]

For the A.U.A. to be preoccupied with a missionary effort directed primarily toward the South, in 1835–36, at the very time that Garrisonianism reached its greatest number of auxiliary societies, was indeed ominous. The new Unitarian seedlings in the South not only struggled to grow in a foreign soil unlikely to produce great yields, but they also suffered an antislavery blight. Too many Southerners avoided Unitarian congregations in their region as alien plants afflicted with the New England disease of antislavery.[28]

But Unitarian missionary hope could continue a bit

longer. An auspicious report on Unitarian progress was given at the annual meeting in 1837. A layman in Mobile, Alabama, had pledged $1,000 to the A.U.A. Advances had been made in the South, West, England, Transylvania, and, bless the soul of Servetus, in Geneva, Switzerland! A Unitarian minister in Augusta, Georgia, Stephen G. Bulfinch, commended the A.U.A. for being fully engaged in the missionary cause and recommended greater effort in the South. Another minister supported missions for the West. There, he declared, "not only the destiny of our *country,* but the destiny of *Unitarianism* is to be decided." For the next three annual meetings, despite the economic depression of 1837, exciting gains were noted: fourteen missionaries were in the field; several places in Georgia were excellent prospects for new Unitarian churches; the work in Alabama was "highly gratifying," especially the Unitarian ministry in Mobile; Alexandria and Jackson, Louisiana, awaited full time ministers; in fact, the West and South, it was declared at one meeting, were full of the "children of New England." In Florida, Louisiana, and along the whole course of the Mississippi River, transplanted New Englanders congregated. One minister rejoiced that the A.U.A. had become in "truth and fact" a missionary society. Had not George F. Simmons "awakened a deep interest" at Mobile, preached in New Orleans to "large audiences," and conducted services at Jackson and Clinton, Louisiana?[29]

The report for 1840, citing Simmons's triumphant work in the South coincided, ironically, with the end of American Unitarian missionary excitement. For Simmons had "awakened" more than "a deep interest" at Mobile, and at the very time the annual report was being read on May 26, 1840, Simmons was a missionary in flight. The immediate destiny of Unitarianism and of the nation had been decided in the South. It was to be one of conflict.

D. THE UNITARIAN PRIEST PASSES ON: THE MOTTE AFFAIR

The disruptive effects of antislavery agitation upon America's Protestant churches is well known. What is not so well known is that the Unitarian denomination underwent similar stress and strain in the 1840s and for all practical purposes was divided, North and South, by the end of the 1850s. Because of the denomination's minor representation in the South and its loose congregational polity, the division between Unitarian Church-North and Unitarian Church-South was not so dramatic as the divisions in the Presbyterian, Methodist, and Baptist denominations. At the sixteenth annual meeting of the A.U.A. in 1841, Clarke was present for the first time in eight years. In light of the Simmons Affair and Pierpont's trial, he surprised no one when he told the assembly that "differences of opinion are now springing up in our own ranks."[30]

Diplomatically (as was his style as a political antislavery reformer) he called upon his hearers to remember the antislavery work of Dr. Channing. Emotionally, he told them to try to hear the voice of Channing speaking from the past, "at a time when it was not considered respectable" to speak for the slave. He praised the work of John Quincy Adams in Congress for the "cause of the helpless African." For his own part, Clarke was determined to go forward for reform, "for Liberty, for Progress, for a more practical, more simple, less formal Christianity."[31] But he proposed no resolutions against slavery, nor did anyone else. Nothing was said at the next annual meeting in May 1842, and when Samuel May, Jr., undiplomatically (for a Garrisonian abolitionist there was no other way) introduced resolutions against slavery at the Autumnal Meeting of that year, they were quashed.[32]

The advocates of antislavery were about to receive aid

from an unexpected source—the South. A few months after the autumnal meeting in 1842, Unitarians in the North saw the South for the second time within three years reject and expel one of their missionaries. In December 1842 the Executive Committee of the A.U.A., in response to a request for a minister by the Unitarian congregation in Savannah, Georgia, sent southward the Reverend Mellish I. Motte (1801–1881). A former Episcopal minister in the South who had converted to Unitarianism, Motte had excellent credentials for service in Savannah. Moreover, his mediocre mind and innocuous personality contrasted favorably with the gifted and courageous Simmons. His salary was to be partially paid by the A.U.A.[33]

Before Motte arrived in Savannah, the Unitarian Society there had already found him unacceptable. "Unfortunately, [his] reputation," a committee report from the congregation later declared, "had preceded him and although he may have been born a Southern Man, it was but too evident that he abjured Southern principles. There were those in the City, not of our Society, who knew him as an open and avowed Abolitionist. . . ." Motte was nothing of the kind, and he tried to convince the Savannah congregation of this when he arrived. True, he had preached on prejudice once, but had only alluded to racial prejudice. However, he did not and would not preach on antislavery: "I should consider it madness to preach on the subject of [slavery] at the South," he told them. After he returned to the North, poor innocent Motte defended his conduct in a letter to the *Christian Register*. "I had no wish," he whimpered, "to cause trouble among them."[34]

The Savannah congregation had refused Motte a chance to preach. They had believed rumors rather than accepting his own personal testimony. They had packed him off to the North without even ensuring that he had enough funds to sustain him. The Northern reaction to the treatment of

Motte was explosive. The General Secretary of the A.U.A. sent a curt response when the Savannah congregation renewed their plea for a minister: "Our Association declines having anything further to do with the supply of your pulpit." Angry letters were printed in the *Christian Register*. An editorial protest appeared in the conservative *Monthly Miscellany*. Garrisonian John Parkman in Dover, New Hampshire, began to formulate a protest for the A.U.A. annual meeting on May 24, 1843, only a few weeks away.[35]

When Parkman attended the meeting, he chose to speak after the usual stirring report on Unitarian missionary success had been given. He praised, perhaps somewhat sarcastically, the "new degree of zeal and spiritual life" of the Unitarian denomination. But what about the church's "philanthropic spirit?" He feared that this was sometimes in inverse proportion to a denomination's "earnest missionary spirit." If a fugitive slave visited the annual meetings of the Baptists, Methodists, Congregationalists, Presbyterians, and other "great Orthodox" churches, he would find them discussing missions but not slavery. And if he visited the Unitarians, in view of the recent outrage in Savannah, how guilty would he find them? The American church cried for more missionary zeal, said Parkman, but ignored the groans of the slave. "Humanity, in the person of the slave, 'stripped' of everything, save the ability to suffer and to *work*;—lies bleeding—the Christian priest passes on; he is on his way to a great missionary meeting. . . ."

Parkman invoked the name of Channing. He told his fellow Unitarians to rally public sentiment against slavery. He felt that, although few in numbers, the Unitarians could be influential. He pointed to the fine example of the Friends. The Unitarian denomination, he said, had few churches in the South, and did not practice excommunication; however it could join to funds sent to Southern congregations "a solemn protest against the sin of slavery."

It could refuse to support a pro-slavery minister. Parkman offered resolutions to effect these two proposals.[36]

Parkman's presentation gave courage to others, and William Henry Channing, nephew of Dr. Channing, spoke eloquently in support of the resolutions. He urged the Unitarians to be a "church of Humanity," a church "wedded with society, in indissoluble union." The denomination had been called a "conservative body," but he believed that the "only true conservatism was growth." The resolutions tested Unitarian principles of the fatherhood of God and the brotherhood of man. If the denomination could not condemn slavery, then Unitarianism was an "empty profession."[37]

Dr. Nathaniel Bowditch sat in the audience engrossed in the debate. Once the late evening session was concluded, he hastened over to Anne Weston's house. His sharp knock awakened her. To avoid disturbing the rest of the house he took her into the basement. In great excitement he told her how the Unitarian meeting had discussed support for Southern congregations, how John Parkman had introduced two resolutions, and how William Henry Channing had made a "glorious speech" that predicted the end of Unitarianism if it did not enter heartily into all the reforms of the day. Clarke had also pushed for the resolutions, but then Ezra Stiles Gannett had moved for adjournment "after they had sung the Doxology." While Anne Weston shook with fear that he would awaken the whole house, Bowditch got up and whined in imitation of Gannett. The support for adjournment had been carried by approximately 80 to 40. A minister, Bowditch declared, then told the meeting that the Association should never meet again.[38]

The American Unitarian Association could not be moved to condemn slavery publicly this time, but the antislavery reformers would try again, and once more they would have help from "unexpected" sources—Great Britain.

E. THE BRITISH INTERVENTION: A TRANSATLANTIC APPEAL FOR LIBERTY FOR ALL

The Scottish Christian Unitarian Association had made protests against slavery in 1837 and 1840, but these were not addressed to, and were probably not known by, fellow American Unitarians.[39] In 1843 Samuel May, Jr., traveled abroad and won several British Unitarians to Garrisonianism. He spoke on abolitionism before the Western Unitarian Association assembled in Taunton, England, and later in a letter from Geneva, Switzerland, he urged the British Unitarians to put pressure upon their American coreligionists.[40]

The Irish Unitarians responded speedily. They were a small group and rabid Garrisonians. Following their annual meeting in May 1843, they addressed a letter to American Unitarians that proclaimed the incompatibility of slavery with Christianity "(or Unitarianism, which was but another name for Christianity)"; condemned the "vile treatment" of Simmons and Motte in the South; and praised "liberty for all, for the black man as well as the white man." The English Unitarians responded more slowly. A few leading ministers, including Dr. James Martineau, the brother of Harriet, objected that they were too far from the scene of action and that they had problems in England to solve. But eventually a letter was drafted, signed by nearly two hundred Unitarian ministers in Great Britain and Ireland, dated December 1, 1843, and sent to America. It urged American Unitarians as a body to rebuke the "foulest of wrongs."[41]

Some American Unitarians shrugged off the letter as an "impertinence." Like Martineau they believed that the British should tend their own hearth. Soon the letter was recognized as the work of Samuel May, Jr., and conservatives in the denomination were disturbed. "They heard you spoke of them with severity," Clarke wrote to May, "and instigated the British letter." A special meeting at the Berry Street Vestry had been called to discuss the letter, and Clarke warned May to be "forewarned and forearmed."[42]

On February 29 about fifty Unitarian ministers gathered at the Berry Street Vestry. May was chosen as secretary of the meeting. It was moved that the British letter should be answered. May then read the letter he had addressed to British Unitarians from Switzerland. An intense debate broke out, but eventually it was proposed and accepted that a committee be established to reply to the British Unitarians. Once the reply was written, accepted, and printed, it was sent to every Unitarian clergyman in the United States for approval. A parchment copy was prepared for the annual A.U.A. meeting in May and the final signatures added to it. Apart from consevative ministers like Samuel Barrett, Chandler Robbins, Andrew Preston Peabody, Rufus Ellis, and John H. Morison, few members of the Unitarian clerical establishment signed it, and the total of 130 signatures was disappointing.[43]

Despite the mild tone of this reply, a group of prominent Unitarian ministers felt obliged to send their own letter to Britain. They claimed that they did not dissent from the "general principles" of the first letter, which had simply explained why American Unitarians could not do more, that states' rights precluded direct political action, that their

> only appeal is to the consciences and hearts of our brethren whose misfortune it has been to inherit, by whose guilt it will be, if, without strong and earnest struggles they consent to uphold, an institution which, from the dreadful wrong it inflicts on master and slave, must be unblessed of God and a curse to man.
>
> We ask for ourselves, and we ask for them, the counsel and sympathy of all Christian men.

But the conservatives wanted to say more. They therefore wrote a second letter and circulated it for additional signatures. Dated September 30, 1844, their letter reached Great Britain three months after the arrival of the first one.[44]

The conservatives agreed with their British brethren on the immorality of slavery, but disputed the "serious charge" that they had been "unfaithful stewards." They urged the British to instruct themselves on the relationship between the federal and state governments of America. Because they did not favor the abolitionists they did not therefore favor slavery. Indeed, they shared in the general New England feeling of opposition to slavery. They added:

> We know no Unitarian pulpit in the northern States in which, and no Unitarian preacher by whom, all Christian condemnation of slavery might not be freely uttered, without suspicion that he was likely to assume the appearance, or share the fate of a martyr.

In view of the Hollis Street Controversy of a few years before, this was either amnesic or mendacious. The conservatives admitted that they did not speak often upon slavery "because our hearers have no connection with it, except so far as they are citizens of the United States, acknowledging allegiance to its Constitution." They made passing reference to the "mass of sin and misery" in England and then absolved themselves of the evils of Southern slaveholding. The peculiar institution was as far removed from the sphere of influence of a Northern Unitarian minister as it was from the influence of a British Unitarian minister. The conservatives were doing their best to end slavery. "We know you will pardon us for saying," they told their British brethren, "that of what we can or ought to do, we must of necessity be the most competent judges." Among the ten conservatives who signed the letter were Ephraim Peabody,

Samuel K. Lothrop, George Putnam, Francis Parkman, Nathaniel L. Frothingham, and Orville Dewey.[45]

Having gained a victory in getting his fellow ministers to reply to the British letter, an encouraged Samuel May, Jr., reintroduced resolutions similar to John Parkman's at the annual meeting of the A.U.A. in May 1844, which proposed that assistance to Southern ministers should be accompanied by a protest against slavery. Because of the lateness of the hour, May accepted the motion that his resolutions be dealt with at an adjourned meeting the following day.[46]

The Unitarian ministers crowded into the Berry Street Vestry the next day. May explained his resolutions and a heated discussion ensued. Some criticized the wording of the resolutions and questioned whether instructions could be addressed to the executive committee of the A.U.A. at all. This was a significant point. The structure of the A.U.A. was democratic enough to provide for the election of its officers (except the long list of vice-presidents who were appointed), but the determination of denominational policy was another matter. It was doubtful that an executive committee would want the obligation of carrying out an antislavery program. The argument over the resolutions dropped at one point to the level of personal attack and May was roughly treated. He was denounced for the interference from the British Unitarians. Again no vote upon the resolutions was taken and again the meeting was adjourned.[47]

A temporary deadlock occurred during the third attempt to deal with May's resolutions. Various amendments were offered and tabled. William Lloyd Garrison's presence as an observer was an added distraction at the meeting. Finally May was allowed to offer a different set of resolutions. The first declared that gifts by the A.U.A. to Southern congregations should not be construed as condoning slavery and that congregations in the South that received aid should "bear faithful testimony against slavery." The second declared that the first should be sent to every Unitarian group in the South aided by the Association.[48]

The response to May's new resolutions was mixed. One minister wanted no action by the A.U.A. on the question of slavery. First, resolutions against slavery would lose "our influence at the South." Second, they would "convert the Association into an Abolition Society." Third, it would be a "dastardly proceeding" for Northern Unitarians to show hostility toward slavery and not be in the South to suffer the consequences of their declarations. Fourth, such resolutions were outside the jurisdiction of the A.U.A. It was a Unitarian society and nothing else. Stephen Greenleaf Bulfinch, who had the experience of serving a church in the South, thought that some resolutions with proper amendment could be beneficial. But Ezra Stiles Gannett disagreed. He said that the Association had not been created to deal with slavery, that the passage of May's resolutions implied an antislavery creed for Unitarians; and that such action only made matters worse for the slaves—ten years of antislavery agitation had only increased the severity of their bondage. He worried that the Association would be identified with the Garrisonians he condemned vehemently. Turning to Garrison, seated in the back of the room, he said that there was no need to go South to rebuke an evil, for right in their presence was "a hellish spirit alive and active."[49] The Reverend William P. Lunt, a social, political, and theological conservative from Quincy, Massachusetts, and normally a "reticent," "undemonstrative," and "meditative" man, was so amused by Gannett's remark that he demonstrated his approval by stamping his feet, "flatly, loudly and repeatedly on the floor, in applause."[50]

A Unitarian layman, Stephen C. Phillips of Salem, then gave a long speech in disapproval of the resolutions. But the questions raised by the Motte affair had to be acted upon, and Phillips wanted the A.U.A. to use the opportunity to declare itself against slavery. It had been silent far too long. After his speech, the meeting was adjourned.[51]

The next day the last discussion on the resolutions was

held. As a substitution for May's resolutions, Phillips offered a preamble and six resolutions of his own. His preamble retold the story of the Motte affair. His resolutions declared, first, that the affair required deliberation by the A.U.A. on slavery; second, that the A.U.A. had to "speak the truth in love" to the Savannah congregation; third, that the Association perceived that slavery subverted the "fundamental principle of Christian Brotherhood"; fourth, that everyone should work to end slavery; fifth, that no clergyman should be rejected because of his antislavery views; and last, that the Association commended these resolutions to the Savannah society.[52]

The intense and long discussion now in its third day had frayed tempers and heightened the acrimony between the opposing parties. Lunt once again opposed any action by the Association, and vehemently denounced the Garrisonians. When he labeled them "Revolutionists" and charged them with endeavoring to subvert and destroy Christianity, several people in the hall loudly shouted their dissent. Samuel May of Leicester met Lunt's charges with an appeal to the memory of Channing, and declared that the abolitionists "desired to expose a false and corrupt church, as they believed it to be, not the Church of Christ, and still less Christianity itself, in which they gloried as the basis and impelling principle of their movement." A layman than confused the delegates with a long, rambling, and convoluted speech that was so inconsistent that he was asked whether the Association should take as his final opinion "his antislavery views or his pro-slavery views." His speech and answer lent some comic relief to the strained atmosphere. Antislavery resolutions were very difficult to draw up, he answered, and he "would never be able to draw up any expression of his personal views on slavery that would satisfy himself!"

Gannett claimed to have "private information" on the Motte affair, and was solicitous for the welfare of the

Savannah congregation. The Association had done *them* harm! The passage of the resolutions would be an even worse blow to the Savannah congregation, and injurious of the great principle of liberty of conscience. In a turnabout from his position the day before, Bulfinch opposed the resolutions and advocated an amendment that would at least assure the Savannah congregation of the Association's continued sympathy. The Association should declare its opposition to any talk of insurrectionary movements in the South, and to sending a missionary there who would "preach insurrectionary doctrines." Bulfinch was particularly anxious lest the resolutions should precipitate "some violent and tumultuous action at the South." He had a child in Savannah. Pierpont interjected the remark that a child should not be abandoned to a society wherein the "complete gospel" could not be preached. Bulfinch should heed the words of Scripture, "Out of Egypt I have called my Son." The motion for Bulfinch's amendment was at first accepted and then rescinded. Two resolutions to censure the abolitionists were defeated. Finally the resolutions of Phillips were passed 40 to 14.[53]

After three days of struggle, the antislavery reformers had won a victory. To be sure, the resolutions passed were moderate—Samuel May, Jr., called them "feeble"—but they had been obtained in the face of the most determined resistance.[54] Francis Parkman had openly proclaimed that "no letter or resolution on the subject of slavery shall ever go forth from the Unitarian Association while he was a member of it."[55] Unitarians who thought like Parkman, said Samuel May, Jr., to Mrs. Chapman, were a "millstone about the neck of Unitarianism, so far as its utterance of the true and powerful word on Slavery is concerned."[56] Now an utterance against slavery had gone forth. Albert Fearing, a very wealthy and influential Unitarian layman, accused the abolitionists of inviting Garrison in order to sway the deliberations of the A.U.A.[57] His accusation was unfounded. Without a doubt, Garrison's silent presence had nothing to do with the passage of the resolutions. The antislavery reformers, with the Garrisonians in the vanguard, had won a fair fight and they now looked forward to additional victories.

George Armstrong, who had headed the signatories of the Irish Address, sent his congratulations to May. To be sure, he admitted that the resolutions were a sort of "*abstract* denunciation" of slavery and in no way an "echo" to the "ardent" British Address. Yet the Association had been impelled by May and his Garrisonian colleagues to "take a great step forward, and [it] has now put a solemn and official record, as a body—representative of the purest of all Christian forms of faith—its protection against the fell pro-slavery system in your Western world."[58]

F. THE AMERICAN REACTION: THE UNITARIAN PROTEST AGAINST SLAVERY OF 1845

The British Unitarians did not relax their pressure on their American coreligionists after they received the American antislavery statement. Francis Parkman found while visiting his English Unitarian colleagues that it was crucial whether an American could answer yes to the question, "Are you an Abolitionist?" If one answered no, it was assumed he was pro-slavery.[59]

With such pressures at home and from abroad it was no surprise that the annual meeting of the A.U.A. precipitated another round of antislavery haggling reminiscent of the year before. The meeting also revealed that the missionary hope of the Association still lingered. The Unitarian Church in Charleston under Samuel Gilman was praised as an example of the denomination's missionary outreach. There were 150 communicants in the society, fifty of whom were "people of color." A new society had just sprung up in Georgia like an almost "natural growth"—a mushroom perhaps. Mention was also made of a very warm letter from Theodore Clapp, minister to the New Orleans Unitarian congregation, in which he said, "I esteem it an honor to be ranked among the glorious fraternity of Unitarian clergymen in the United States." He boasted an average attendance of 1,000 people—"all anti-trinitarian," and declared:

> The cause is truly flourishing. Intelligent men all over the State, when they visit New Orleans, come to our church. Indeed, in a very few years, all the vast majority of Protestants throughout Louisiana will be Unitarian.[60]

Segregated from the ordinary business meeting of the A.U.A. was a special gathering, openly called several days before, "to consider the subject of clerical duties and responsibilities in relation to the American slavery." Obviously this conclave was called and packed by Unitarian antislavery reformers. Parker came and found the antislavery forces well organized. John Parkman served as secretary and Dr. Willard gave the opening prayer. An attempt was made to clear the hall of laymen, and it was so voted, but they refused to go. Then Bulfinch spoke in behalf of colonization and thought the North misunderstood conditions of slavery in the South. Still, he deplored the moral cruelty of slavery and hoped that Unitarians would speak out. John Pierpont gave a stirring address, which was acknowledged by cheers and tremendous applause. The antislavery composition of the audience was undisguised. Three days of meetings were held.[61]

No one present denied that slavery was unchristian and an evil, but there were many different opinions regarding the "duty or propriety of agitation and associated action on this subject." Gannett, one of the few anti-abolitionists to attend the meeting, stated forcefully his position. He did not object to private discussion of the slavery question, he even believed that slavery could be mentioned in the pulpit, but he strongly objected to and protested against "all public debate on it, and especially any and all associated action against it." One word summed up a Unitarian minister's duty regarding slavery: "SILENCE." Slavery was distant from them; their interference would make it worse. Their views were well known in the South, he said, so why should they express them?

> Slavery is *almost* altogether wrong; in principle it is atrocious; and Christianity, in its progress through the world will undoubtedly subvert slavery. Nevertheless Christianity and slavery may dwell together in peace, at least temporarily. Among the Christian saints on earth, no doubt there are Christian slaveholders.

In contrast to the "Christian slaveholders" were the abolitionists. Gannett complained about the mischievous consequences of the antislavery movement. He saw slavery defended by both Northern and Southern ministers, who would never have defended it had not the abolitionists engendered so many "prejudices." This backlash had produced harsh laws and had stifled the emancipation movement in Virginia. The abolitionists had insidiously harmed the church and created a climate of distrust toward clergymen. They had caused a deterioration of moral sentiment. They had contributed to the disruption of the Baptist, Methodist, and Presbyterian Churches. Their hostility toward the Union and their attempt to dissolve it were threats to the peace and hopes not only of America, but of the world. Gannett spoke as a lonely witness to a hostile crowd. With a vote of 44 to 7 an antislavery resolution was adopted:

> *Resolved*, That we consider Slavery to be utterly opposed to the principles and spirit of Christianity, and that as

ministers of the Gospel we feel it our duty to protest against it in the name of Christ, and to do all we may to create public opinion to secure the overthrow of the institution.

Of greater importance than the resolution was the appointment of a committee of twelve to prepare and circulate for signatures a Unitarian Protest against American Slavery.[62]

In view of the previous public apathy of the denomination regarding antislavery, the Unitarian Protest against slavery was an exceptional document. Its irenic tone represented the conciliatory disposition of its author, political abolitionist James Freeman Clarke. The document declared that a group of "violent and lawless men" had made it impossible to speak freely the "whole counsel of God" in the South. Thus, truth on slavery must come from the North. Unitarian clergymen should be "foremost" in opposition to slavery, for they have contended for "individual liberty, perfect righteousness, and human brotherhood" and slavery violated all these things. As believers in religious liberty, Unitarians could not exclude slaveholders from their Christian fellowship, but while leaving to God the guilt or innocence of the individual slaveholder, Unitarians had to pronounce the system "unchristian and inhuman." Reliance on political measures had failed; only trust in the "power of Truth" remained. In conclusion, all men, North and South, were asked to put forth "their full energy, and in the most efficient modes, to show decidedly their sympathy with the Slave, and their abhorrence of the system of oppression of which he is made the victim."[63]

The "Protest" was circulated and 173 Unitarian ministers signed it. Conspicuously absent were the signatures of the leaders of the denomination, Francis Parkman, Nathaniel L. Frothingham, Ezra Stiles Gannett, Orville Dewey, Francis Kirkland Lothrop, George E. Ellis, Samuel Barrett, William Parsons Lunt, George Putnam, W. B. O. Peabody,

Ephraim Peabody, John Henry Morison, Edward Everett Hale, Henry W. Bellows, and William Greenleaf Eliot. Putnam at first signed it and then reneged. He had talked to the "Boston men," said one Garrisonian. Of the 170 who did sign, 127 ministers served churches in Massachusetts, twenty-six were from other New England states, and twenty outside New England. "The Protest," said the *Christian Register*, exhibited

> unequivocally and distinctly the sentiments of the numerous and most enlightened body of clergy whose names are attached to it, *as well as of many other ministers of the denomination who may be disinclined to act conjointly, or do not feel called upon to act at all, in any prescribed way, on the subject.*[64]

As with most controversial documents, both signers and nonsigners of the Unitarian Protest were vulnerable to sharp criticism. Jason Whitman, a signer of the document, received an abusive anonymous letter from the South, which called the signers "madmen." Southern Unitarianism was "low enough in the world's estimation" without the additional burden of the Protest. Whitman's reply, published as a pamphlet, denied that the Protest would "strike a deathblow to Unitarianism at the South." It was simply a "calm, solemn and earnest, but affectionate assertion of the truth, addressed, not to the slave, to excite his discontent, but to the reason and the conscience of the master."

Henry W. Bellows, a nonsigner, received a reproach from George F. Simmons. Hardly any of the names on the Protest, he grumbled, were of Unitarian ministers who were widely known. "Now how does this happen?" he asked, as if cross-examining Bellows. "Have you not those antislavery convictions expressed in the Protest? or are you biased and fettered by your relations to the people you influence?" For him to suggest that Bellows was muzzled by expediency showed his intense frustration with the lack of antislavery leadership by the denomination's ministerial elite. "The absence of your names does rather shame us," Simmons moaned; "we feel a little mortified to find ourselves ranked and filed without captains or generals. . . ." Theodore Parker shared Simmons's frustration and growled in a letter to Charles Sumner, "The fact that no minister of any *famous church* signed the Antislavery Protest—is to me proof of their deep degradation—the crowning act of their infamy!"[65]

G. "LESS LAUDATION" THAN USUAL: DENOMINATIONAL INTROSPECTION

Samuel May, Jr., wrote to the English Unitarian Garrisonian John Bishop Estlin in March of 1846, to thank him for prodding American Unitarians on to greater efforts against slavery. The denomination needed looking after, he said, by all who loved "true Unitarianism at home and abroad." May continued to share news with his British friends of any proslavery conduct—real or imagined—of the denomination. With alacrity English, Scotch, and Irish Unitarian Garrisonians responded. In the remaining years of the 1840s they placed heavy pressure upon the American Unitarian denomination to increase and to strengthen its antislavery pronouncements, and to encourage individual Unitarian ministers to be true to the Gospel of Abolitionism.[66]

A sample of this pressure was the "Address of the Irish Unitarian Christian Society" published in the *Christian Register* in March 1846. It expressed the Society's disappointment that American Unitarians did so little "as a body" against slavery, for this was "far from consistent with the high and holy vocation of Unitarian Christianity!" If there was not a "positive Pro-Slavery sentiment prevalent" among American Unitarians, there was

> at least an unmanly, and as appears to us, an unchristian, inclination to discourage the labors of those who demand, and who are striving to obtain equal civil rights for all alike, be their color or their complexion what it may.

It thanked the American Unitarians for the "Protest Against Slavery," and proclaimed the ideal that "Every Unitarian should be known as an abolitionist."[67]

Samuel May, Jr., wrote again to Estlin in May, about his anxiety over the war with Mexico. The war had preoccupied his thinking of late and he denounced America for beginning it. At the A.U.A. annual meeting the same month, the war and the Irish Address were undoubtedly on the minds of many, and it was May who proposed the selection of a committee to respond to the letter. His resolution was at first passed but then reconsidered when the objection was raised that the Address was directed not to the A.U.A. in particular, but American Unitarianism in general, and therefore the Association should be reluctant to respond. Later a "large number of gentlemen" chose an ad hoc committee (which represented a wide spectrum of antislavery opinion in the persons of Samuel May, Jr., Clarke, Simmons, John A. Andrew, and others) to reply independently to the Address.[68]

In the main business sessions of this A.U.A. annual meeting, the antislavery reformers were vocal; they urged their brethren to speak openly on slavery. First Clarke resolved that the denomination in its future action adhere to *"Christian Freedom and Progress."* Then John A. Andrew called upon Unitarians to feel and to manifest an "earnest interest in all social reforms and philanthropic movements." He reminded them of the "toils of the slave" and asked them to measure their churches against the "practical religion of Jesus." In view of the Unitarian motto, "Liberty,

Holiness, and Love," how did they excuse their imperfect performance?

> Have we maintained, he asked, with unshakened front the rights of man, . . . ? Have we not wavered and conformed to this world. . . ? As a branch of the Christian vine, the Unitarian body cannot defend itself for not bracing itself up, as the champion of the weak and the enslaved,—the antagonist of the hard tyranny it sees today, and has always seen. What Jesus would have done, I pray you, . . . have we not neglected?

Had not Dr. Channing said that no church in America had taken "less interest in the slavery question," or was "more inclined to conservatism" than their denomination? Channing now spoke to them from the dead to question their "unfaithfulness to the cause of the American slave." If he now looked upon them from his grave, they should make him happy by taking part in the fatal battle between freedom and slavery. They needed courage, preached Andrew, "to risk Unitarianism in that encounter."

He was followed by William Henry Channing, who praised his brethren for using "less laudation" of themselves "than usual." They talked of liberty, but frequently "acted and thought like bigots." They neither displayed the love of Jesus nor faith in the dignity of man. Many of them treated "all earnestness in reform" as either "foolish visionariness or dangerous radicalism." "My brethren," he cried, "we have the reputation of being, next to the Episcopalians, the most conservative denomination. And verily I think it must be granted, that judged by the light of our principles, we have been a backward, timid, inefficient body." There were some present who had abused Dr. Channing for his views on slavery, and had called him a "fanatic and a Jacobin." Now those who still remained aloof from the great reform movements of the day "should rally behind the principles of Dr. Channing, especially in one important area: "Look at slavery, and our nation's shame," he said; "we must carry out your holiness in love."[69]

At the Ministerial Conference that met to discuss the "relation of Christianity and Christian Ministers to Reforms," Theodore Parker proposed three resolutions attacking the "sin of Slavery" and the Mexican War. After some debate they were accepted with only one dissenting vote. On the following day the committee on the Irish Address issued its report, Samuel May, Jr., was very pleased. The annual meeting was never before so interesting, he wrote to Estlin. It had been the "freest, most practical, most truly Christian." He had "rarely attended *any* meeting (Antislavery or any other) so spirit-stirring or so hopeful." A member of the Hopedale Community, William H. Fish, who observed the Unitarian proceedings, was less enthusiastic. He reasoned that there ought to have been a "strong and emphatic protest against slavery and war" declared during the *main* business sessions of the A.U.A. rather than by an ad hoc committee at a special meeting. He expected more from Unitarians on reform— not exactly radical abolitionism, but at least a greater dedication to antislavery work. However, if they hated and opposed "extravagant reformers" more than tyranny, then, he declared, the "sooner they come to nought the better it will be for the world." He thought there was a greater possibility of enlisting Unitarians in the cause of universal reform than any other sectarian group. He expressed the "*hope* that the denomination, as a unit, will yet stand on the highest Christian ground."[70]

Both the enthusiasm of May and the hope of Fish were dampened by the official Unitarian gatherings of the next three years. The radical abolitionists temporarily floundered. The current tide of respectability for a moderate antislavery position ironically calmed the ripples caused by their agitation. A Garrisonian alluded to this at the Autumnal Convention in October. The time had arrived, he said when "nobody pretends to be anything but an anti-slavery man"; yet no respect should be given to antislavery conformists who at the same time were censorious of abolitionists.

Henry W. Bellows took immediate exception to this view. He was unwilling to have it publicized that Unitarian clergymen were "cramped in their pulpits by the tyranny of their congregations." True, some might be "restrained" or "checked" by their congregation's opinions from preaching extravagant views, but this was a "natural and providential restriction," which God had "imposed to secure wisdom and moderation." He quoted Dewey to support his view: "Moderation [was] the martyrdom of our day." The preaching of reforms had been exaggerated. There was no longer any martyrdom possible for abolitionists, he said sarcastically, for "heroism had become cheap." He condemned the "curses and imprecations" he had heard from New York abolitionists, and decried such "imbecility and ineffectiveness." He advocated no special sympathy for the abolitionists. Their "independent" course on slavery was really only an "intemperate" course. They were fully capable of taking care of themselves. Clarke met Bellows's argument by recalling the interview between Samuel J. May and Dr. Channing. The lesson May taught the good doctor was valid for Bellows. "If brother B. does not like the way the cause is managed," declared Clarke, "let him take it up and do it better."[71]

Samuel May, Jr., offered three resolutions on slavery at the annual meeting of the A.U.A. in May 1847. His first resolution was the familiar Garrisonian axiom that slavery was sin, but the second and more intriguing was "that no slaveholder ought to be elected to any office or agency in this Association." This resolution was primarily aimed at Dr. Joshua B. Whitridge (1789–1865), a member of the Charleston Unitarian congregation, a slaveholder, and an honorary vice-president of the A.U.A. May's first resolution was adopted with but one dissenting vote, but his second resolution—he had already abandoned his third resolution to expedite passage of the first two—was tabled. This action was justified, said May's opponents, because the Association—in a timely act of diplomacy—had abolished the entire board of honorary Vice-presidents in a new constitution adopted that year. May found no satisfaction in this empty victory. There was no guarantee, for example, that other offices in the denomination might not someday be filled by a slaveowner.[72]

At the Ministerial Conference the same week, resolutions by Clarke and Parker were blocked. Their proposals were tabled when it was argued that the Conference was not an association for passing resolutions, but a ministerial gathering for discussion. The Conference finally discussed the question of authority in matters of admittance to holy communion and church membership. Parker felt that his resolutions against "murder and robbery of the United States upon Mexico" were far more important than talk about "ecclesiastical procedures" or "ministerial mechanics." He noted cynically in his journal, "Unitarians are merely sectarian, and not at all human. So let it go."[73]

Antislavery reformers were further discouraged by the paralysis that gripped the Unitarian Autumnal Convention in Salem, Massachusetts, in October 1847. Two political abolitionists worked in tandem, in an effort to get the denomination to implement a useful political tool—the petition. Clarke introduced a resolution "for a friend," requesting the convention to petition Congress to end the Mexican War. Pierpont delivered a rousing oration to complement the resolution. His theme was the "application of truth to practical life and humane reform"—especially antislavery. The graphic address showed Pierpont's crusading oratory at its best. "There comes," he cried,

a poor panting slave, hunted by hounds— . . . Let such as bear the name of a Unitarian minister take hold and help him. It is part of his work for he is a redeemer of his fellowmen. Jesus came to set at liberty the captive, and the minister is in his stead.

Confront State Street in Boston, he declared; tell the merchant in Boston that safety rested only in the right. When anyone intoned "Our country right or wrong," inform him, "This is *atheism.*"

Bellows stood up to rebut Pierpont. Why did some ministers refuse to join reformers in their work, he asked. "Because reform is disconnected from Christ." Our first work was to convert individual men and so change them by the Gospel that they did the right. "Reformers reverse the true order. They [work] to reform society, instead of making men citizens of heaven." He was disturbed over the possible division of the denomination into a "reformatory and a spiritual party."

Gannett protested the resolution. It could end Unitarian conventions altogether. It could cause Unitarians to become an "*exclusive* body." The denomination had done enough for reform. Finally Dr. Francis Parkman, "to preserve harmony," moved that the resolution be tabled, and despite Clarke's pleas, it was. Any successful action would have to be obtained independently of the regular denominational meetings. Therefore a special assembly drew up a memorial and circulated it for signatures. It declared the Mexican War a "violation of the Will of God" and called for "peace now." The Unitarians' own John P. Hale presented the memorial to the Senate.[74]

The Mexican-American War ended the next spring, but slavery continued. The frustrations of the antislavery forces increased as meeting after meeting of the denomination passed without strong action against slavery. If only the denominations in America would do their duty, wrote Congressman Palfrey to the Unitarian Festival Committee in the spring of 1848, the downfall of slavery would be certain. And in the fall, Thomas Treadwell Stone urged the

Autumnal Convention "to try harder," and with a concentrated effort slavery would quickly end. But no new resolutions or action emerged from either meeting.[75]

Not even a heavy attack upon the denomination by the British Unitarians gained results. Following the Irish Address of 1846, the British Unitarians sustained a constant barrage against American Unitarian denominational inaction, and particularly against several prominent ministers: Francis Parkman, Ezra Stiles Gannett, Orville Dewey, and George E. Ellis. The trans-Atlantic correspondence became rather heated.[76] Although Garrisonian Samuel May, Jr., instigated *most* of the British attacks, Dr. Parkman maintained that he caused them *all*. Because of this lack of spontaneity, and because the British Unitarian Garrisonians did not represent a majority of their church's leaders, their harassment did not make a heavy impact upon the A.U.A.[77] The major contribution of the "non-intercourse and embargo" measures proposed by the British Unitarians lay more in boosting the flagging morale of Garrisonian abolitionists than in defeating the power of their opponents.[78]

Garrisonian abolitionist morale sorely needed assistance. What radical abolitionist could not lose heart when he found it impossible to transform a denomination of mostly "active business men" into a group of active reformers? Or be chagrined over Albert Fearing's prating on at the Autumnal Convention in 1849 about the wealth of Boston being estimated at $200,000,000 and the Unitarian share being half that figure?[79] The executive committee of the A.U.A. reported in 1850 that although Unitarian congregations were not more numerous than they were twenty years ago, the influence of Unitarian opinions was "perceptible throughout the land."[80] The Garrisonians and political abolitionists could file a similar report for their last ten years of agitation. To be sure, their adherents were not very numerous either, but their views were "perceptible throughout the land." They were still determined to have them perceptible in their denomination.

H. "ALLEGED DIVISIONS AMONG US": THE FEAR OF SCHISM

Following the Autumnal Meeting of 1850, the *Christian Inquirer* published an editorial entitled "Our Future. Alleged Divisions Among Us." The editorial tried to refute allegations that sharp divisions existed among Unitarian clergymen over "practical reforms." Schism was a very real issue for America's religious leaders. They had looked on with fear and sadness at the ruptures that had occurred in the Baptist, Methodist, and Presbyterian denominations. Three years before, the *Christian Register* had proudly observed that while these denominations had split on the slavery issue, the Unitarians could "scarcely be said to differ on the question of slavery." This statement was not true then and the editorial in the *Inquirer* was not true now. Denominational harmony did *not* exist and sharp divisions in the denomination were not only present, but they were deepening.[81]

"Bitter fighting"—in the words of Samuel May, Jr.,—broke out at the Autumnal Convention in Springfield in October 1850. The disturbance was not generated by young, hot-blooded radicals, but by two old, seasoned, antislavery warriors—sixty-five-year-old John Pierpont and seventy-four-year-old Samuel Willard. Near the conclusion of the first and rather dull day of the convention, Pierpont moved that the Association present its view on the Fugitive Slave Law, which had just been passed. He compared contemporary dedicated Christians with the persecuted Christians of old: if either obeyed Christ's law to help the poor and oppressed, they could be imprisoned. Rather than frame his own resolution, he wished the convention would indicate a Christian minister's duty toward the fugitive slave. Immediately a motion was made to table Pierpont's resolution. Gannett seconded it, declaring that it was "entirely foreign to the objectives" of the Association. The motion was carried when Dr. Parkman broke a tie vote.[82]

That night Willard could not sleep, his mind tormented by thoughts that the denomination had betrayed the fugitive slave. In the morning he vowed to bring Pierpont's resolution again before the convention. As one of the vice-presidents of the convention, he sat on the speaker's platform near Dr. Parkman, a friend from his days at Harvard. From the platform he appealed for a reconsideration of the resolution. His blindness and advanced age gave his plea a special warmth and authority. If the denomination failed to act, he declared, it would be considered a pro-slavery body. It must condemn the Fugitive Slave Law. For himself death was near and he wanted to leave no doubts as to his stand on divine law versus human law. He welcomed persecution and death rather than to betray a fugitive slave. He begged the Association to reconsider Pierpont's motion. When he sat down, many of his audience were in tears.

Dr. Parkman then rose, his feelings and conscience obviously moved by his friend's remarks, and he explained why he had voted to table the resolution. The "harmony of the Convention," he said, should not be disturbed. He advocated the protection of fugitives and he claimed to have a "little nook" in his "humble mansion" in Boston for any fugitive slave who might come to him. He agreed to a reconsideration of the resolution.[83]

Gannett led the "very vehement" attempt to squelch the resolution a second time. "Strongly and emphatically" he protested. His "imperative duty," he said, was to plead for the resolution's complete exclusion. The extreme abolitionists will say we have not gone far enough, others will say we went too far. The issue was foreign to the purposes of the convention. Are we to be called upon, he asked, to discuss "Prof. Agassiz's theory of the origin of the human race, or the theory of the unity of mankind?" He protested any attempt to force the subject of slavery upon their proceedings. Then Simmons made the irenic but familiar proposal to deal with the resolution at a special meeting. However, the motion to table Willard's motion was defeated by a vote of 50 to 53.

The Convention then proceeded to pass Willard's motion by a small majority and to record both its "profound sorrow and detestation" of the imfamous Bill and its commitment to work for its repeal. Gannett angrily objected to the resolution, but Pierpont countered that failure to pass it would be atheism: If they did not recognize, he declared, the supremacy of the divine law, they were "practical atheists." He agreed that, although the Association's general objectives were theological, still the Fugitive Slave Law fell within its jurisdiction. For as a theological question it lay

but two links off from the first great question in theology; namely, "Is there a God?—For, if there is a God, He, as God, must be and is the Supreme Lawgiver of the Universe; and; if so, his laws are paramount to all others, and all others must give place to His. If—to begin at the other end of the chain—there is no higher law than the laws of Congress, then there is no higher Law-giving power than Congress, and if there is no higher Lawgiver *than Congress then there is no God* and that is bald, stark naked *Atheism*. Then, secondly, as to the practical professional duty of ministers—if the laws of God are paramount to or higher than the highest laws of man—it appears to me, that it is our part of the duty of our profession to *say so from our pulpits*: i.e., to say when the laws of Congress or any other legislative body, conflict with, or run counter to the laws of God they must not be obeyed by Christian men, come what may come, as the consequence of our refusal to obey.

After some further discussion a vote was called and the resolution was adopted.[84]

Garrisonian Samuel J. May reported that following the Autumnal Convention "quite a number of the prominent ministers of the [Unitarian] denomination" backed compliance with the Fugitive Slave Law, and he cited three: William Parsons Lunt, Ezra Stiles Gannett, and Orville Dewey. He was disturbed over the allegations that Dewey had publicly said, once in the fall of 1850 and again in the winter of 1851, that he would rather send his mother into slavery than sacrifice the Union. He conceded that Dewey might have said brother, not mother; what bothered him was the "immoral and demoralizing" view that the "God-given rights of man ought to be violated, outraged, rather than overturn or seriously endanger a human institution called a government." He saw the North subjugated by the "slave-holding oligarchy." Sensitive to slavery's perversion of his own denomination, he wanted it to exhibit to the world a "truly Christian" stand on the Fugitive Slave Law. Therefore he presented at the A.U.A. annual meeting in May 1851 one of the most highly charged personal indictments against a church's leading ministers and laymen in American denominational history. As the Fugitive Slave Law had invaded the security of Boston, named men and women slaves, and brought the vivid reality of slavery into its midst, May's smoldering indignation descended upon the relative safety of an A.U.A. business meeting, named preeminent men as "unsound" and "practical infidels," and brought the vivid reality of radical abolitionism into its midst.

In his preamble and resolution May named the Unitarians whose conduct regarding the Fugitive Slave Law had stained their reputations: Daniel Webster and Samuel A. Eliot, who assisted its passage in Congress; President Fillmore, who signed it into law; Edward Everett and Jared Sparks, presidents of Harvard College and Harvard Divinity School, who approved Webster's sale of the Law to the

American public; and Dewey, a past president, and Gannett, the current president of the A.U.A., who advocated obedience to the Law. He also alluded to several (unnamed) "distinguished, titled ministers of our denomination in and around Boston," who also preached compliance. He called upon the A.U.A. to condemn the Law in a "most public and emphatic manner," and "to comfort and aid" as many fugitive slaves as it could. Theodore Parker, with undoubtedly a certain amount of hell-born glee and personal satisfaction, seconded May's preamble and resolution. But it lost by a vote of twenty-seven to twenty-two, a very close vote in light of the uncompromising tone of May's document.[85]

May had another chance to air his preamble and resolution the following day. At the Ministerial Conference (composed of clerical members of the A.U.A.) he again introduced his document. At first no action was taken and the meeting was adjourned, but when the Conference reassembled, debate on the document commenced. The Reverend Samuel Osgood of New York City defended Orville Dewey as never having said that he would send his mother into slavery. Deliberate misrepresentations of his words and views had driven Dewey to tears. He only feared disunion. Osgood then criticized Theodore Parker's attack on the Fugitive Slave Law, and Parker and a few others who were present began to laugh. Gannett opposed the document and blasted Parker's laughter as an "indecorum that was painful" and "unpardonable." He defended his parishioner George T. Curtis, who had assisted the return of Thomas Sims. He believed that violation of the Fugitive Slave Law would lead to disobedience of all law and to disunion. The Reverend George E. Ellis opposed the Law, and also the adoption of any resolution against it. If the Conference passed a resolution on the question, his love of individual freedom would drive him from the Conference.[86]

Parker spoke. He appreciated Ellis's solicitude for the

right of individual opinion. He wished the members of the
A.U.A. had always held that view, especially in regard to
himself. Gannett's arguments for obedience to the Fugitive
Slave Law, he said, were worthless. The value of human law
was only to conserve the "great eternal law of God." New
England's loyalty to such laws was assured, but the Fugitive
Slave Law contradicted the "acknowledged precepts of the
Christian religion, universally acknowledged." Gannett
need not worry that disobedience to the Law would lead to
disobedience to all law.

> Disobedience to the fugitive slave law is one of the
> strongest guarantees for the observance of any *just* law.
> You cannot trust a people who will keep law, *because it is
> law*; nor need we distrust a people that will only keep a
> law when it is just. The fugitive slave law itself, if obeyed,
> will do more to overturn the power of human law, than all
> disobedience to it—the most complete.

As to Gannett's fear that disobedience would dissolve the
Union, Parker felt this to be a "vain and deceitful"
argument. The Union was not threatened, and if it were, he
would rather see the Union splintered into territories the
size of Suffolk County, Massachusetts, than have one
fugitive returned to slavery.

Many Northerners had treated slavery as an abstraction,
but the Fugitive Slave Law had now made it a "most
concrete thing." Public opinion on slavery in Boston and
among members of the Ministerial Conference, exclaimed
Parker, favored "slavery and this wicked law!" Kidnappers
worshiped in Boston Unitarian churches. Parker had to
protect the fugitive slaves of his congregation—the "crown
of [his] apostleship, the seal of [his] ministry—from these
kidnappers, especially those of Gannett's congregation.
From his pulpit, Gannett justified the Fugitive Slave Law
and demanded compliance. "Yes," declared Parker, "calling on his church members to kidnap mine, and sell them
into bondage for ever."[87]

May's document was then accepted as a proposal for discussion and entered upon the records. Debate was then terminated by general consent and the ministers returned to their homes and churches. The battle over slavery at the denomination's public meetings never again reached the level of excitement created by Pierpont and Willard in 1850, and May and Parker in 1851.

In regard to the Fugitive Slave Law, an editor of the *Christian Register* had declared his desire for "perfect order and silence everywhere preserved." But the "philanthropic side" of the Unitarian body had disturbed "perfect order and silence." May's resolution, said an editorial in the *Christian Inquirer*, had "brought the extravagance of certain ultraists to a definite point, and proved how vainly they sought to invade the good sense and just feeling of the denomination by their follies and personalities." The Garrisonian abolitionists, despite the energy they expended, could not win their denomination to their cause. Following the exhausting Ministerial Conference of 1851, May complained that the "Unitarians as a body" still were not "redeemed from the moral thraldom" that gripped America as a whole. They still failed to have a "heartfelt abhorrence of slavery and the Fugitive Slave Law," Alas, said May, they could even invite Fillmore, the signer of the hated Law, to the Unitarian Festival and not elicit a single objection.[88]

The debate over May's resolution had repercussions in England. Unitarian Garrisonians there inspired a number of special meetings and pronouncements in condemnation of the Fugitive Slave Law. But they had as much trouble convincing their own British and Foreign Unitarian Association, as a body, that it should condemn the Fugitive Slave Law, as in convincing the A.U.A. that it should do their bidding. James Martineau, who objected to his radical countrymen's work, believed that there were "natural limits" to an English Unitarian's "right of supervision over the moral and spiritual affairs of the world." Samuel May,

Jr., bewailed the inability of his English friends to gather sufficient support to speak for the entire Unitarian body in England. The B.F.U.A. seemed caught up, he wrote in a letter to Mary Carpenter, in the same "time-serving spirit" long characteristic of the A.U.A. The American Association, he said,

> is a lifeless soulless thing—having but a name to live. On every point of true and vital religion, it is absolutely without the shadow of influence. . . . What men does it send forth, what publications, which are arousing, and quickening, the men of this nation to repentance and bringing them to the service of God? Their whole operations are cold, formal, technical.[89]

I. REAL DIVISION AMONG THEM: THE REALITY OF SCHISM

With Samuel May, Jr., no longer present at the annual meetings—he had withdrawn from the Unitarian ministry in 1847—and Theodore Parker boycotting them, and with the death of Francis Parkman in 1852, the potentiality for a clash on antislavery lessened. Although Samuel J. May, John Pierpont, and James Freeman Clarke continued to present effectively antislavery views, the major clashes within the A.U.A. were over. In fact, the meetings in May and October 1852 passed by with "perfect order and silence everywhere preserved." One radical abolitionist did sense the possibility of disturbances at the annual meeting of 1853, and feared there would be a *"drawing of lines"* and the *"working of the old rusty guillotine,"* but his intuition proved false. There was only a confession of astonishment by the Executive Committee at the limits of the denomination's growth, which they blamed on the "excessive radicalism" of fellow travelers in their midst. Implicit in the Executive Committee's statement was a rejection of that "radicalism and irreverence of some who have nominally stood within our own circle, and who have been considered by the public as representing our household of faith."[90]

In any event, worship was the main topic of discussion at the annual meeting of 1853, especially litanies and communion. Parker read about the proceedings in the *Christian Register* and mocked them in a letter to Samuel J. May. He ridiculed communion as a "crumb of Baker's bread" and a "sip of grocer's wine." Who cared who took communion, scoffed Parker:

> Dear me—what a world it is. Drunkenness all around us; covetousness eating the heart out of society, the Fugitive Slave Bill making it incumbent on a man to send back his own mother to bondage; ministers with kidnappers members of their Churches—discussing a litany and the terms of admission to the Lord's Supper. . . . What politician, what Philanthropist, what Merchant (of any *heart* at all) what Man of Science cares a pin for all this Humbug?[91]

The antislavery forces saw "perfect order" continued at the autumnal convention of 1853. Some looked upon the meeting, vacuous of reform, as the death knell of Unitarianism. "The organization appears to me," lamented Higginson, "aimless, hopeless, powerless, and dead." Pierpont blamed his own absence for the innocuous meeting: "It was impossible for me to be there," he told Higginson, "and *so*, it seems things went on very *quietly* and well, according to the programme."[92]

Few antislavery reformers attended the next annual meeting in 1854. The rendition of Anthony Burns occupied their time and their thoughts, for during the anniversary week Burns was arrested, tried, and returned to slavery. With the antislavery partisans away, it appeared that the A.U.A. was going to ignore the excitement, but young Harvard Divinity School student James H. Fowler forced their attention. He was one of seven students about to graduate from the Divinity School and the only one to confess abolitionism. A Garrisonian, he had become alienated from the Unitarian officialdom, who objected strenuously to his theological idiosyncracies—he had written an enthusiastic testimony to spiritualism—not to mention his abolitionist activities. "They avowedly declare their intention," he wrote to Higginson, "to do all they can to prevent my preaching." He had been denied pulpit assignments for the past several Sundays. Twice he would be thrown into jail for antislavery agitation, and few invitations to supply pulpits in Boston would be forthcoming.[93]

Fowler attended the Unitarian Collation in Faneuil Hall. The Collation or Festival was the entertainment portion of the annual meetings, and this particular one was an "immense assemblage of ladies and gentlemen including clergy and their wives." A state of "merriment" prevailed as the mayor of Boston and other dignitaries delivered witty speeches. Fowler had dutifully made his appearance and then had left to go to an antislavery rally on the Burns crisis. But suddenly "his step was arrested . . . by some strange infatuation." Some "irresistible impulse" turned the young religious abolitionist back to the Collation. There, amid the festivity and mirth, "he made his witness." Having received permission to speak, the seminarian directed the attention of the assembled merrymakers to the contrast between their pleasure and Burns's pain. There was a time to weep, as well as a time to laugh. For his own part he could not push from his mind the "dark subject and question that now agitate [d their] whole community." He could not be light-hearted when a free and innocent man languished in jail. He was disappointed that the word *Liberty* had not been uttered at their meeting; that no one had mentioned Burns's incarceration. Fowler became "choked up and had difficulty expressing what he wanted to say," but he managed to continue. God wanted them to be concerned

about the captive and set him free. "I am studying for the
Unitarian ministry," he said, "and I want to know the
sentiment of this assembly. If you are not going to express
support for Liberty and humanity, I shall go elsewhere."
He then offered a pledge:

> The American Captive—whether in Massachusetts, or in
> South Carolina, or in any State, or on any soil over which
> the flag of our nation waves,—may the chains fall from
> his limbs, and may he be *free*, as Christ demanded at our
> hands that he *should* be.

Fowler received "warm and continuous applause."[94]
Three days later Clarke watched from the law offices of
John A. Andrew as "cavalry, artillery, marines and police, a
thousand strong" escorted "one trembling colored man to
the vessel which was to carry him to slavery." He heard the
curses poured upon the soldiers and saw their embarrass-
ment over the chants of "Kidnappers! Kidnappers!"

John Parkman had lodged with Dr. Gannett during the
annual meeting. All week long he had been annoyed by
Gannett's "indifferent and unfeeling" attitude toward
Burns. "What an ado about a mere single incident of
slavery? What good is going to come of all this excitement?
What is one man set against the continuance and safety of
the Union?" Gannett ranted. Then Parkman saw Burns
returned to slavery and he ran home to tell Gannett. "Is it
true he has been surrendered?" he asked. "Yes," replied
Parkman. Crushed, Gannett slumped into a chair and
began to sob, "O God, forgive this guilty nation! What will
become of us? What dreadful judgments are in store for
us?" Parkman confessed that he met no one who was more
deeply moved by the rendition of Burns than Gannett.[95] It
was easier to proclaim abstract principles than to endure
intense and immediate ethical problems. The South could
ill afford to disturb so severely the consciences of sympathetic and moderate men like Gannett.

The remaining annual meetings of the A.U.A. in the 1850s came and went with little of the lively emotion and excitement that had gone on before. The denomination patiently endured the energy and the enthusiasm of the antislavery reformers who remained within the A.U.A. It even became receptive, as antislavery feeling mounted generally throughout the North, to antislavery resolutions. When Samuel J. May offered a resolution at the Autumnal Convention in Montreal in 1854, contrasting the treatment of fugitive slaves in the United States with that in Canada, it was passed without a dissenting vote.[96]

Moreover, an amicable debate on the relationship between religion and politics took place at the Autumnal Convention at Bangor, Maine, in 1856. Clarke as Chairman of the Committee of Arrangements had chosen the topic, and John Pierpont, was a vice-president of the A.U.A., lectured on it. His main point was that the mission of Caesar, as the embodiment of the state,

> is to protect his every subject in the enjoyment of his every right. While he is doing that work, he is a recognized *power*, UNDER the government of God. He is one of the powers that "are ordained of God." When not thus employed, he is not a recognized power—is not a power "ordained of God;" and is of no more authority over the conscience or the conduct of the subject, than any other man in the State or out of it.

One minister felt an "inward dissent and unwillingness to embrace" Pierpont's view. They all believed in the "higher law," he said, and whoever did not was a "blasphemer." What really was at question in "preaching politics" in their day was preaching on Slavery. But how far should one go? He favored preaching on it, but thought most reformers preached on it in a manner "very imtemperate and injurious to the cause." One could better discourage slavery indirectly. Act "discreetly and faithfully," he advised.

The meeting concluded on a high level of good feeling.

"We left the Conference," said a participant, "with the feeling that in interest and spirit the Convention was more distinguished than our average Autumnal meetings."[97]

Why this era of good feeling in the A.U.A. on the question of antislavery? There were several reasons. The Fugitive Slave Law and the rendition of Burns had shaken many who had chosen to remain silent. The vitriolic resolution of Samuel J. May in 1851 was the peak of Garrisonian frustration and exertion in the A.U.A. Several abolitionists had left the Association and some elderly anti-abolitionists had died. The gory reports from Kansas by Unitarian missionary Ephraim Nute, including the shocking story of his brother-in-law being scalped, ignited the New England wrath of most of the denomination's ministers. Thus, resolutions could be presented at the annual meeting in 1856 condemning the "outrage" in Kansas and the "barbarity of the slave-power" upon Charles Sumner, and be carried unanimously.[98]

And it was about this time that the Western Unitarian Conference, which had been formed in 1852 and had yet to pass an antislavery resolution, dealt with the controversy. The issue arose when the Conference met in Alton, Illinois, in 1857. The occasion was the Dred Scott Decision, and the resolutions were put forward by a new member of the Conference, Moncure Daniel Conway (1832–1907). Born and raised in Virginia, he was well acquainted with slavery. In the 1850s he had made a theological pilgrimage from Methodism to Emersonian Unitarianism, and an antislavery pilgrimage from a kind of philosophical abolitionism to vacillating Garrisonianism. After a short, controversial ministry at the Unitarian Church in Washington, D.C., he went to the First Congregational Church (Unitarian) in Cincinnati, Ohio. He represented the Cincinnati church at the Conference.[99]

Conway's resolutions condemned the Dred Scott decision as but "one of a series of deliberate assaults on religious and civil freedom in America," and proclaimed the "duty of

Christians everywhere, in and out of the pulpit, to discuss freely and fully before the people this crime against man, and therefore against God." When he pressed for their adoption, he encountered the Reverend William Greenleaf Eliot, a distinguished Unitarian conservative, who came with a large entourage from St. Louis. But he matched well Eliot's "iron inflexibility." The debate wore on and Eliot began to chafe under the lengthy discussion, which he felt was "wasted" time. The argument of the St. Louis delegation was the familiar one to render unto Caesar the things that were Caesar's. Clarke, who as an observer had kept silent, now burst out:

> I do not think the African race belongs to Caesar. I think it belongs to God. My reason for taking an interest, as a Christian, in Slavery, is just this—that Caesar has got hold of something which belongs to God, and Caesar ought to give it up.

Evidently the Conference agreed with Clarke, and in face of a threat of a walkout by Eliot, passed a mild set of resolutions as a substitute for Conway's. Eliot and his twenty-two delegates immediately withdrew. He never returned to the Conference that he had helped to found. For many years it ceased to meet.[100]

The withdrawal of the St. Louis delegation from the Conference, wrote an observer, had thus made "another church rupture, and a Unitarian Church North, and another South." Eliot observed after the meeting that the "Unitarian Church of the United States was divided." In lamenting the appearance of a "Unitarian Church North" and a "Unitarian Church South," he put the blame upon the abolitionists:

> The slavery agitation has made another inroad upon the order and well being of American society—and the call upon every National man is become . . . to thrust back this

spirit of a fanatical age, which emanating from those "believing themselves wiser than their fathers," the founders of this government, will, unchecked, dismember a great government, without eradicating the evil of which they complain.

But, for the most part, the blame for the "Alton Schism" was placed squarely upon Eliot himself and he felt obliged to defend his conduct in a sermon on social reform and in letters to the Unitarian press.[101]

Given the resilience of the Unitarian denominational polity to schism and the small number of congregations included within it, the reality of a split between those congregations of the North and those of the South has been ignored. But the schism at Alton and the disintegration of churches in the South in the late 1850s hardly enabled the denomination to call itself a national church. As early as 1839 a member of the church in Mobile had written that the "truth is . . . that *Southern* and *Northern* Unitarianism are to be hereafter separated. There is so little sympathy for us of the *South* by the Unitarians of the *North*! Our southern members all say this and what good grounds they have for saying so!!" Twenty years later another member of the same congregation, Herbert C. Peabody, wrote, "The Unitarian cause drags. . . . The curse of Abolition and Puritan Preaching hangs over us and will not down." The Boston Unitarians had forgotten them. He felt "perfect *contempt* for *them* and *their religion* as *now administered*." His solution was to look to their English friends, men like Martineau and others who might help them build a church. The English after all had built King's Chapel in Boston. "The *stones* came from George's subjects," he recalled, "why not . . . *Iron* from Victoria's!—in honor of the *women* of the *South*!!" The congregation could repay in cotton. After Samuel Gilman died early in 1858, the Charleston congregation found it impossible to get a minister. Unitarian sympathizers in Virginia were repelled by the "fanatical" zeal of abolitionists in the denomination. The Unitarian Church in Baltimore had divided into two churches over the slavery issue, destroying nearly thirty years of work by George Washington Burnap. He died suddenly in 1859, apparently crushed by the ruin of his life's ministry.[102] In the wreck of Southern Unitarianism the antislavery reformers had certainly played a part. In this sense they had triumphed in their twenty-five-year clash with those ministers and laymen in their denomination who had hoped to build missions in the South, and had sought to keep the denomination free of controversial and destructive issues.

In another sense they lost the battle for freedom in the Unitarian denomination. Perhaps they never realized their failure. An Englishman saw it. In 1859 Philip Pearsall Carpenter, an English antislavery reformer, visited Boston and was invited to the Unitarian festival. He declined, citing among his reasons that he would have to speak against slavery being on "slave-catchers' hunting ground." Therefore he attended the festival as a spectator. He watched from the gallery as 2,000 "well-dressed people" sat at ten wide tables "covered with flowers and fruits and pretty eatables" in the largest hall in New England. He had never seen an "eating-display" so beautiful before; but he noted that while the waiters were "coloured," there was none of the "proscribed race among the guests." He soon went away, "sad and dispirited."[103] He had viewed blacks waiting upon a white church.

But what happened when a white church had the opportunity to wait upon a black? This opportunity actually occurred at the Autumnal Convention in New Bedford in 1860. A Reverend Mr. Jackson, the "colored minister of New Bedford," intruded upon the Convention to testify to his conversion to Unitarianism. Since he was perhaps the "only colored Unitarian minister" (and indeed the *first* black Unitarian minister in America), he requested their kind and patient attention. After he had stated the needs of his church, the Unitarians took a collection, which totaled $49. A few dollars were added to this amount and Mr. Jackson was sent on his way. No discussion, no welcome, no expression of praise and satisfaction was uttered, that the Unitarian gospel had reached the "colored." In truth, the antislavery forces had lost the battle, perhaps because many of them had never begun to wage it.

The same Autumnal Convention accepted the long reply of Clarke and Samuel J. May to an address on slavery by the Western Unitarian Christian Union in England. The address had been irenic and warm, and the two men replied in kind, although they did gently reproach the English Unitarians about the assistance English cotton interests had given to Southern slavery. What was so remarkable was simply that here in 1860, after such a long, fatiguing agitation of the slavery question in the denomination, political abolitionist Clarke and Garrisonian May could now be entrusted to respond for it on the topic of slavery, and, having their work accepted, could be so directed to sign their letter as representing the sentiments of the Convention.[104]

Epilogue

This final coming together of the two patterns of the antislavery movement had occurred in the denomination as it had in the country at large. The religious and political abolitionists had worked together. The Mays and the Garrisonians had provided the most explosive of the resolutions that failed, and Clarke and the political abolitionists, the most diplomatic and literary of those that passed. Both groups educated their denomination in antislavery, just as they had taught their nation.

The styles of the representatives of the various antislavery patterns were different and each style made its contribution to antislavery discussion and action in the Unitarian denomination. Channing and the advocates of philosophical antislavery gave the movement prestige, authority, and reasonableness. The Mays and their fellow Garrisonians gave the movement religious passion, enthusiasm, and energy. Clarke and the political abolitionists the Union and victory over slavery.

As the Unitarian denomination should be ashamed of its antislavery conduct as a religious body, so it should be justly proud of the men and women who as individuals chose love of freedom over thoughts of expediency. The brilliance of their example makes the patterns of antislavery attitudes framed by the Unitarian denomination beautiful to behold.

Notes

NOTES TO CHAPTER 1

1. Max Farrand, *The Framing of the Constitution of the United States* (New Haven and London: Yale University Press, 1965 [1st ed., 1913]), pp. 110, 233–34, 240, 248.

2. Merrill Jensen, *The New Nation: A History of the United States During the Confederation, 1781–1789* (New York: Vintage Books, 1950), pp. 134–36; Louis Filler, *The Crusade Against Slavery, 1830–1860* (New York: Harper and Row, 1963), pp. 11–12.

3. Alice Dana Adams, *The Neglected Period of Anti-Slavery in America, 1808–1831*, (Gloucester, Mass.: Peter Smith, 1964 [1st ed., 1908]), pp. 48–49, 53.

4. Stanley M. Elkins, *Slavery: A Problem in American Institutional and Intellectual Life* (New York: Grosset and Dunlap, 1964), pp. 209–10.

5. Dwight Lowell Dumond, *Antislavery Origins of the Civil War in the United States* (Ann Arbor, Mich.: University of Michigan Press, 1960 [1st ed., 1939]), p. 6.

6. Elkins, pp. 210–11.

7. Leon Litwack, *North of Slavery: The Negro in the Free States, 1790–1860* (Chicago and London: University of Chicago Press, 1969), pp. 15, 97.

8. Filler, p. 20; George Dangerfield, *The Awakening of American Nationalism 1815–1828* (New York: Harper and Row, 1965), p. 138; Dwight Lowell Dumond, *Antislavery: The Crusade for Freedom in America* (New York: W. W. Norton and Co., 1966), pp. 128–29.

9. Gilbert Hobbs Barnes, *The Antislavery Impulse 1830–1844* (New York: Harcourt, Brace, and World, Inc., 1964[1st ed., 1933]), p. 27.

10. *Liberator,* 1 January 1831.

11. Truman Nelson, ed., *Documents of Upheaval: Selections from William Lloyd Garrison's The Liberator, 1831–1865* (New York: Hill and Wang, 1969), pp. ix, 2; John L. Thomas, *The Liberator: William Lloyd Garrison* (Boston: Little, Brown, and Co., 1963), p. 131; August Meier and Elliott M. Rudwick, *From Plantation to Ghetto: An Interpretive History of the American Negroes* (New York: Hill and Wang, 1968), p. 102.

12. Thomas, pp. 121, 123, 134, 138–40; Oliver Johnson, *William Lloyd Garrison and His Times* (Miami, Fla.: Mnemosyne Publishing Co., 1969), pp. 99, 112–13; Filler, pp. 52–53; John L. Thomas, ed., *Slavery Attacked: The Abolitionist Crusade* (Englewood Cliffs, N. J.: Prentice-Hall, 1965), p. 6; Albert Bushnell Hart, *Slavery and Abolition, 1831–1841* (New York: New American Library, 1969 [1st ed., 1906]), pp. 219–20; "Constitution [of the] New England Anti-Slavery Society," Louis Ruchames, ed., *The Abolitionists: A Collection of Their Writings* (New York: G. P. Putnam's Sons, 1963), p. 33; Meier and Rudwick, pp. 97–98; William Lloyd Garrison, *Thoughts on African Colonization,* With a preface by William Katz (New York: Arno Press and the New York Times, 1969 [1st ed., 1832]), pp. xii, xiii, 1.

13. Garrison, pp. 2, 39, 61, 68, 74, 78, 95, 111, 124, 134, 151.

14. Thomas, *Liberator,* pp. 144, 148–49, 154.

15. Ruchames, p. 16.

16. George M. Fredrickson, ed., *Great Lives Observed: William Lloyd Garrison* (Englewood Cliffs, N.J.: Prentice-Hall, 1968), p. 2.

17. Garrison, p. xx.

18. Ruchames, pp. 18–19; Filler, pp. 61–62; Thomas, *Liberator,* pp. 154, 157–63; Quarles, pp. 20–21; Samuel J. May, *Some Recollections of Our Anti-Slavery Conflict* (Miami, Fla.: Mnemosyne Publishing Co., 1969 [1st ed., 1869]), pp. 72–78.

19. Bertram Wyatt-Brown, *Lewis Tappan and the Evangelical War Against Slavery* (Cleveland, Ohio: Press of Case Western Reserve University, 1969), pp. 102–4.

20. Quoted by Barnes, p. 49.

21. Dumond, *Antislavery,* pp. 177–78; May, pp. 85–91; Johnson, p. 152; "The American Anti-Slavery Society Declares Its Sentiments," William H. Pease and Jane H. Pease, eds., *The Antislavery Argument* (Indianapolis, Ind.: Bobbs-Merrill Co., 1965), pp. 68, 69.

22. May, p. 88.

23. Ibid., pp. 84, 89.

24. Filler, pp. 64–65; Dumond, *Antislavery,* pp. 211–13; Litwack, pp. 126–31; Johnson, p. 125; May, pp. 39–72; Nelson, pp. 64–69.

25. Thomas, *Liberator,* p. 205.

26. Fredrickson, pp. 38–46; Nelson, pp. 87–91.

27. Quoted by Thomas, *Liberator*, p. 204.

28. Alma Lutz, *Crusade for Freedom: Women of the Antislavery Movement* (Boston: Beacon Press, 1968), 56–58.

29. May, pp. 153, 162–67; Johnson, pp. 207–9.

30. Filler, pp. 78–79; May, pp. 221–25; Dumond, *Antislavery*, pp. 221, 223–26; Nelson, pp. 131–32; Carleton Mabee, *Black Freedom: The Nonviolent Abolitionists from 1830 Through the Civil War* (London: Macmillan Co., 1970), p. 42.

31. Dumond, *Antislavery*, p. 226; Hart, p. 249.

32. Wendell Philips Garrison and Francis Jackson Garrison, *William Lloyd Garrison, 1805–1879. The Story of His Life Told by His Children* (New York: The Century Co., 1885), 1:462–63, 469; Thomas, *Liberator*, pp. 195–96.

33. Quoted by Hart, pp. 197–98.

34. Mabee, p. 13.

35. Quoted by Barnes, p. 93.

36. Ruchames, p. 187.

37. Quoted by Wyatt-Brown, p. 189; Filler, pp. 130–32; May, pp. 97–98, 238–48. For a good discussion of the "woman question," see Aileen S. Kraditor's *Means and Ends in American Abolitionism: Garrison and His Critics on Strategy and Tactics, 1834–1850* (New York: Pantheon Books, 1969), pp. 39–77.

38. Quoted by Lutz, p. 156.

39. Wyatt-Brown, pp. 197–98.

40. Dumond, *Antislavery*, pp. 296–97; Quarles, p. 168; Dumond, *Antislavery, Origins*, pp. 91–92.

41. Dumond, *Antislavery*, p. 297.

42. Pease and Pease, p. 1v; Hart, pp. 317–18; Richard H. Sewell, *John P. Hale and the Politics of Abolition* (Cambridge: Harvard University Press, 1965), p. 35.

43. Quoted by Filler, pp. 141, 153.

44. Sewell, pp. 47–51; Dumond, *Antislavery Origins*, p. 94; May, p. 210.

45. Kraditor, pp. 178–81; Quarles, p. 186.

46. Mabee, p. 244; Peter Brock, *Radical Pacifists in Antebellum America* (Princeton, N.J.: Princeton University Press, 1968), pp. 79, 85, 87; Thomas, *Slavery Attacked*, pp. 115, 126; Pease and Pease, pp. 343–70; Kraditor, pp. 208–12; Nelson, p. 200. Staughton Lynd argues that the Garrisonian "abolitionists were right in seeing the American Revolution as a revolution betrayed" because of the pro-slavery nature of the Constitution, Cf. Lynd, "The Abolitionist Critique of the United States Constitution," *The Antislavery Vanguard: New Essays on the Abolitionists,* Martin Duberman, ed. (Princeton, N.J.: Princeton University Press, 1965), p. 239.

47. Nelson, pp. 202–5; Fredrickson, pp. 52–55; Kraditor, pp. 200–204.

48. Nelson, p. 206; Thomas, *Slavery Attacked*, p. 93.

49. Litwack, pp. 248–49; Larry Gara, *The Liberty Line: The Legend of the Underground Railroad* (Lexington, Ky.: University of Kentucky Press, 1961), p. 38; Quarles, pp. 199–200.

50. May, pp. 348, 407–8; Filler, p. 200.

51. Quarles, pp. 203–6; Henry Steele Commager, *Theodore Parker* (Boston: Beacon Press, 1967 [1st ed., 1936]), pp. 214–15, 219–20; Mabee, pp. 302–3.

52. Quarles, p. 206; Commager, p. 222; Leonard W. Levy, "Sims' Case: The Fugitive Slave in Boston in 1851," *Journal of Negro History* 35 (1950): 39–74.

53. Quarles, pp. 209–11; May, pp. 373–84; Mabee, pp. 307.

54. Commager, pp. 236–41; Tilden G. Edelstein, *Strange Enthusiasm: A Life of Thomas Wentworth Higginson* (New Haven, Conn.: Yale University Press, 1968), pp. 158–61; Harold Schwartz, "Fugitive Slave Days in Boston," *New England Quarterly* 27 (1954): 191–212.

55. Jean Holloway, *Edward Everett Hale: A Biography* (Austin, Tex.: University of Texas Press, 1956), pp. 104; Edelstein, pp. 182–84.

56. Arthur M. Schlesinger, Jr., *The Age of Jackson* (Boston: Little, Brown and Co., 1945), p. 479.

57. Staughton Lynd, *Intellectual Origins of American Radicalism* (New York: Vintage Press Books, 1969), p. 149; Mabee, pp. 320–21.

58. Kenneth M. Stampp, *And the War Came: The North and the Secession Crisis, 1860–1861* (Chicago: University of Chicago Press, 1968), p. 250.

59. William H. Pease and Jane H. Peace, "Freedom and Peace: A Nineteenth Century Dilemma," *Midwest Quarterly* 9 (1967): 39.

60. Benjamin Quarles, *Lincoln and the Negro* (New York: Oxford University Press, 1962), pp. 71, 127–29; John Hope Franklin, *The Emancipation Proclamation* (Garden City, N.Y.: Anchor Books, 1965), pp. 17–18, 43–45; James M. McPherson, *The Struggle for Equality: Abolitionists and the Negro in the Civil War and Reconstruction* (Princeton, N.J.: University Press, 1968), p. 197.

61. McPherson, pp. 260, 271–72.

62. Ibid., pp. 126–27, 299; Pease and Pease, *Antislavery Argument*, p. 484.

Notes to Chapter 2

1. Thomas J. Mumford, *Memoir of Samuel Joseph May* (Boston: Roberts Brothers, 1873), pp. 5–9. Only my mother did I love more than Edward, wrote May. See Samuel J. May, *A Brief Account of His Ministry, Given in a Discourse, Preached to the Church of the Messiah, in Syracuse, N. Y., September 15th, 1867* (Syracuse, N. Y.: Masters and Lee, 1867), p. 6.

2. Mumford, pp. 10–12.

3. Thomas, p. 5. David Brion Davis has detailed the religious origins and overtones of the concept of immediate emancipation. To some reformers, there developed the idea of slavery as "an embodiment of worldly sin," and emancipation could be achieved only through a "subjective act of purification and a casting off of sin." See his "The Emergence of Immediatism in British and American Antislavery Thought," *Mississippi Valley Historical Review* 49 (September 1962): 212. Anne C. Loveland has explored the direct relationship of evangelicalism and the immediacy concept of the radical abolitionists. See her "Evangelicalism

and 'Immediate Emancipation' in American Antislavery Thought," *Journal of Southern History* 32 (May 1966): 172–88. "Mr. Garrison had learned the doctrine of immediatism from Dr. [Lyman] Beecher himself," wrote Oliver Johnson. See his *William Lloyd Garrison and His Times; or Sketches of the Antislavery Movement* (Miami, Fla.: Mnemosyne Publishing Co., 1969 [1st ed., 1881]), p. 45. Christianity had accepted slavery as an institution and thus the chronological jump to slavery as sin was a long one—some two thousand years. See David Brion Davis, "Slavery and Sin: The Cultural Background," *The Antislavery Vanguard: New Essays on the Abolitionists,* Martin Duberman, ed. (Princeton, N. J.: Princeton University Press, 1965), pp. 3–31.

    4. Elizur Wright, "William Lloyd Garrison," *Unity* 3 (16 June 1879): 120.

    5. "A Nineteenth Century Religion," *Unitarian Review* 32 (1889): 260, 261, 263. Cf. also John W. Chadwick, "The Garrison Memoir," ibid., pp. 506–79.

    6. Thomas Wentworth Higginson, "Anti-Slavery Days," *Outlook* 9 (3 September 1898): 47.

    7. Samuel J. May, *Some Recollections of Our Antislavery Conflict,* (Miami, Fla.: Mnemosyne Publishing Co., 1969 [1st ed., 1869]), pp. 17–19.

    8. Johnson, p. 208.

    9. Samuel A. Eliot, ed., "Samuel J. May. 1797–1871," *Heralds of a Liberal Faith* (Boston: American Unitarian Association, 1910), 4:248.

    10. W. Freeman Galpin, "Samuel J. May: 'God's Chore Boy,' " *New York History* 21 (April 1940): 139–50; Allen Johnson and Dumas Malone, eds., *Dictionary of American Biography* (New York: Charles Scribner's Sons, 1928–1958), 12:448. Hereafter cited as *DAB*; Parker quoted by Joseph May, *Samuel J. May: A Memorial Study* (Boston: Geo. H. Ellis, 1898), p. 9.

    11. *The May Memorial Church, An Account of its Dedication, together with a Brief Sketch of the Origin and Progress of the Unitarian Congregational Society of Syracuse,* (n.p.: Columbia Press, n.d.), p. 51; Garrison and Garrison, *William Lloyd Garrison . . . Life,* 1:217.

    12. Mumford, pp. 76, 80, 102–3, 105–13; May, *Recollections,* 39–72; William H. Pease and Jane H. Pease, "Freedom and Peace: A Nineteenth Century Dilemma," *Midwest Quarterly* 9 (October 1967): 24. For the intrigue behind May's departures from the Brooklyn Unitarian Church, his antislavery agency, and the South Scituate ministry, see the B.D. thesis, a careful and sensitive work, of Edward W. Ohrenstein, "Samuel J. May: Unitarian Minister and Social Radical" (Chicago: Meadville Theological School, 1937), pp. 25, 33–34, 41–43; Galpin, p. 143; and Anne Warren Weston to Deborah Weston, Groton, 13 July 1843, Weston Papers, Boston Public Library. The Library will be indicated hereafter by its Library of Congress symbol, MB. Cf. also, S. R. Calthrop, et al., eds., *In Memoriam: Samuel Joseph May* (Syracuse, N. Y.: The Journal Office, 1871); William H. Pease and Jane H. Pease, "Samuel J. May: Civil Libertarian," *Cornell Library Journal* (Autumn 1967), pp. 7–25. The Peases are writing a full-length biography of May. I regret the failure of my several attempts to see the manuscript biography of May by W. Freeman Galpin, "God's Chore Boy: Samuel Joseph May" (Syracuse Univer-

sity Library, n.d.) as cited by Louis Filler in his *The Crusade Against Slavery 1830–1860* (New York: Harper Torchbooks, 1963), p. 294.

13. Mumford, pp. 69–71; May, *Recollections,* pp. 19, 20; Samuel J. May to Henry W. Bellows, Syracuse, 20 December 1847, Bellows Papers, Massachusetts Historical Society. Hereafter cited as MBHi.

14. William H. Pease and Jane H. Pease, "The Role of Women in the Anti-slavery Movement," *Canadian Historical Association. Historical Papers Presented at the Annual Meeting held at Ottawa, June 7–10, 1967,* pp. 172, 174; Harriet Martineau, "The Martyr Age of the United States," *London and Westminster Review* 32 (December 1938): 18; Margaret Munsterberg, "The Weston Sisters and the 'Boston Mob,'" *Boston Public Library Quarterly* 9 (October 1957): 183–84; Garrison and Garrison, 2:49.

15. Johnson, p. 207.

16. Higginson, pp. 54–55.

17. John Jay Chapman, *Memories and Milestones* (New York: Moffat, Yard, and Co., 1915), p. 215.

18. Garrison and Garrison, 2:49; Maria Weston Chapman to [Fanny Garrison Villard?], n.p., [1870?], Autograph file, Houghton Library, Harvard University. Hereafter cited as MH.

19. Martineau, p. 18.

20. Chapman, p. 211.

21. Martineau, p. 18; Harriet Martineau, *Harriet Martineau's Autobiography,* Maria Weston Chapman, ed. (Boston: James R. Osgood and Co., 1877) 1:349; Higginson, pp. 47, 52, 54. Anne Warren Weston took exception to Martineau's estimation of Maria's "extraordinary beauty." Anne objected: "This is news to me, but thank fortune the statement can't be charged to Miss M. as lies. She has a right to her opinion." Quoted by Margaret Munsterberg, "The Weston Sisters and 'The Boston Controversy,'" *Boston Public Library Quarterly* 10 (January 1958): 45. There is a photograph of Mrs. Chapman in the Weston Papers of the Boston Public Library. It agrees with Miss Martineau's description.

22. Chapman, p. 212; Garrison and Garrison, 2:49.

23. Quoted by Pease and Pease, "Role of Women," p. 175.

24. Samuel Sillen, *Women Against Slavery* (New York: Masses and Mainstream, 1955), pp. 42–43; Helene G. Baer, *The Heart is Like Heaven* (Philadelphia: University of Pennsylvania Press, 1964), p. 40; Ethel K. Ware, "Lydia Maria Child and Anti-Slavery," *Boston Public Library Quarterly* 3 (October 1951): 253, 254; Pease and Pease, "Role of Women," p. 169.

25. Quoted by Ware, p. 256.

26. May, *Recollections,* pp. 97–100; Johnson, pp. 139–40; Milton Meltzer, *Tongue of Flame: The Life of Lydia Maria Child* (New York: Thomas Y. Crowell Co., 1965), pp. 38, 43, 44; George Washington Spindler, *Karl Follen: A Biographical Study* (Chicago: University of Chicago Press, 1917), p. 193; Thomas Wentworth Higginson to John Gorham Palfrey, Newport, R. I., 20 February 1868, John Gorham Palfrey Papers, MH. Cf. also Lloyd C. Taylor, Jr., " 'Reader I Beseech

You' A Study of Lydia Maria Child's 'Appeal,' " *Negro History Bulletin* 20 (December 1956): 53–55.

27. Cf. Lydia Maria Child, *The Evils of Slavery, and the Cure of Slavery. The First Proved by the Opinion of Southerners Themselves, the Last Shown by Historical Evidence* (Newburyport: C. Whipple, 1836); *Anti-Slavery Catechism* (Newburyport: Charles Whipple, 1836).

28. David Lee Child, *The Despotism of Freedom: or, The Tyranny and Cruelty of American Republican Slavemasters, Shown to be the Worst in the World; in a Speech Delivered at the First Anniversary of the New England Anti-Slavery Society, 1833* (Boston: Boston Young Men's Anti-Slavery Association, 1833); *Oration in Honor of Universal Emancipation in the British Empire, delivered at South Reading, August first* (Boston, 1834); *The Culture of the Beet, and Manufacture of Beet Sugar* (Boston: Weeks, Jordan and Co., 1840).

29. Parker Pillsbury, *Acts of the Anti-Slavery Apostles* (Boston: Cupples, Upham, and Co., 1884), p. 272; Weston quoted by Munsterberg, "Weston Sisters and 'The Boston Mob,' " p. 189.

30. Spindler, pp. 20, 35, 41, 55, 76. For the quote of Follen, cf. p. 36; Cf. also Richard Pregizer, *Die Politischen Ideen des Karl Follen* (Tuebingen: I.C.B. Mohr, 1912); Heinrich Schneider, "Karl Follen: A Re-Appraisal and Some New Biographical Materials," *Society for the History of the Germans in Maryland* 30 (1959): 73–86; Herman Haupt, "Follenbriefe," *Deutsch-Amerikanische Geschichtsblaetter* 14 (1914): 7–83.

31. Elizabeth Bancroft Schlesinger, "Two Early Harvard Wives: Eliza Farrar and Eliza Follen," *New England Quarterly* 38 (June 1965): 157–59; Spindler, p. 155; Eliza Cabot Follen, ed., *The Works of Charles Follen, with a Memoir of his Life* (Boston: Hilliard, Gray, and Co., 1842), 1:172–74, 256, 265. Mrs. Follen republished the memoir of volume one as an independent volume. See *The Life of Charles Follen* (Boston: Thomas H. Webb and Co., 1844); William Sprague, ed., *Annals of the American Unitarian Pulpit* (New York: Robert Carter and Bros., 1865), p. 541.

32. Schlesinger, pp. 160–61; Follen, 1:216, 275–77, 420–21, 475–78, 516; Eliot, pp. 286–87; Sprague, pp. 543–44; Spindler, p. 93.

33. Follen, 1:340–41, 378–80; May, *Recollections*, pp. 253–56; Charles Follen, "The Cause of Freedom in Our Country," *Quarterly Antislavery Magazine* (October 1836), pp. 61ff; Eliza Follen's novels and short stories frequently expressed religious philosophy and pious themes. In *The Skeptic*, for example, chapters labeled "Reason the Defense of Faith," and "Women should reason on Religion" flavored such more concrete themes as "Should Jane marry Ralph?" See *The Skeptic* (Boston and Cambridge: James Munroe and Company, 1850). Cf. also Eliza L. Follen, *Sketches of Married Life* (Boston: Hilliard, Gray, and Co., 1838), and *Words of Truth* (Cambridge, 1832); Eliza L. Follen, "The Three Little Kittens (A Cat's Tale, with Additions)" in volume 13 of Mrs. Follen's Twilight Stories, entitled *Little Songs* (Boston: Whittemore, Niles, and Hall, 1854); for more on the Follens see Evart A. Duyckinck and George L. Duyckinck, eds., "Charles Follen"

and "Mrs. Eliza Follen," *Cyclopedia of American Literature,* 2:242–45; Charles Hudson, *History of the Town of Lexington* (Boston: Wiggin and Lunt, 1868); Dieter Cunz, "Karl Follen: In Commemoration of the Hundredth Anniversary of His Death," *American-German Review* 7 (October 1940): 25–27, 32; Cora Holinger, "Charles Follen, A Sketch of His Life in New England," *American-German Review* 14 (June 1948): 20–22.

34. Quoted by Johnson, p. 88. See also pp. 86–87.

35. Lydia Maria Child to Henrietta Sargent, South Natick, 13 November 1836, *Letters of Lydia Maria Child,* With a biographical Introduction by John G. Whittier (Boston: Houghton, Mifflin, and Co., 1883), p. 24.

36. Galpin, p. 143.

37. Samuel J. May, *The Right of Colored People to Education, Vindicated, Letters to Andrew T. Judson, Esq. and Others in Canterbury, Demonstrating with Them on Their Unjust and Unjustifiable Procedure Relative to Miss Crandall and Her School for Colored Females* (Brooklyn: Advertiser Press, 1833), p. 6; Charles Follen, "Speech before the Anti-Slavery Society," *Works,* 1:633.

38. Lydia Maria Child to Louisa Loring, Northampton, 28 June 1840, Loring Family Papers, MCR; Maria Weston Chapman, *"How Can I Help to Abolish Slavery?" or, Counsels to the Newly Converted,* Antislavery Tracts, no. 14 (New York: American Antislavery Society, n.d.), p. 6; Follen, "Sermon . . . delivered on Thanksgiving," *Works,* 2:196.

39. Follen, "Address to the People of the United States on the Subject of Slavery," *Works,* 5:219; Child, *Anti-Slavery Catechism,* p. 3; Samuel J. May, "Resolution [of] Rev. Samuel J. May" [Title supplied] *First Annual Report of the American Anti-Slavery Society with Speeches Delivered at the Anniversary Meeting. . . . on the Sixth of May, 1834 . . .* (New York: Don and Butterfield, 1834), p. 20; Maria Weston Chapman to Louisa Loring, Boston, 7 November [n.d.], Loring Family Papers, MCR.

40. Chapman, "How Can I Help?", p. 8.

41. Susan C. Cabot, *What Have We, As Individuals To Do With Slavery?* Antislavery Tracts, no. 15 (New York: Anti-Slavery Society, n.d.), p. 6; May, "Resolution [of] Rev. Samuel J. May," pp. 20–21; May, *Right of Colored People,* p. 24.

42. Follen, "Address to the People," *Works,* 5:213, 217; May, *Right of Colored People,* p. 13; May, "Resolution [of] Rev. Samuel J. May," p.20; May, *A Discourse on Slavery in the United States, Delivered in Brooklyn, July 3, 1831* (Boston: Garrison and Knapp, 1832), p. 16.

43. May, *Right of Colored People,* p. 6; Samuel J. May, "Success of the Abolitionists," *Christian Register* 14 (4 July 1834): 187; Vincent Y. Bowditch, *Life and Correspondence* 1:127–28; Cabot, p. 6.

44. Child, *Anti-Slavery Catechism,* p. 32; Child, *An Appeal,* p. 132; Follen, "Address to the People," *Works,* 5:198; *Constitution of the Salem Female Anti-Slavery Society,* 1834, broadside, Salem Female Charitable Society Papers, James Duncan Phillips Library, Essex Institute. Hereafter cited as MSE.

45. Follen, "Address to the People," *Works*, 5:224; Child, *An Appeal*, p. 133.

46. Higginson, p. 47; Samuel J. May, *A Brief Account of His Ministry, Given in a Discourse, Preached to the Church of the Messiah, in Syracuse, N. Y., September 15th, 1867* (Syracuse, N. Y.: Masters and Lee, 1867), p. 41; Follen, *Works*, 1:384.

47. Lydia Maria Child to Theodore Weld, Wayland, 10 July 1880, Weld-Grimké Papers, William L. Clements Library, University of Michigan. Hereafter cited as Mi-UC; Deborah Weston to Anne Weston, n.p., 10 June 1836, Weston Papers, MB; Anne G. Chapman to Deborah Weston, n.p., 23 December 1836, Weston Papers, MB; Samuel J. May to Maria Weston Chapman, South Scituate, 27 December 1836, Weston Papers, MB; Lydia Maria Child to Louisa Loring, Northampton, 3 June 1838, Loring Family Papers, MCR.

48. Lillie B. Chase, "From Generation to Generation," *Atlantic Monthly* 64 (August 1889): 174; Manuscript Fragment, n.p., n.d., Loring Papers, MCR.

49. Chapman, "How Can I Help?" pp. 5, 7, 8; Clarke quoted by Samuel May, *Old Anti-Slavery Days, Proceedings of the Commemorative Meeting Held by the Danvers Historical Society, at the Town Hall, Danvers, April 26, 1893, with Introduction, Letters and Sketches*, (Danvers: Danvers Mirror Print, 1893), p. 17.

50. *The Second Annual Report of the Board of Managers of the New England Antislavery Society, Presented January 15, 1834* (Boston: Garrison and Knapp, 1833), p. 7; Samuel J. May to William Lloyd Garrison, South Scituate, 15 June 1839, Antislavery Letters, MB; Alma Lutz, *Crusade for Freedom: Women of the Antislavery Movement* (Boston: Beacon Press, 1968), p. 22.

51. Eliza Lee Cabot Follen, *Anti-Slavery Hymns and Songs*, Anti-Slavery Tracts, no. 12 (New York: American Anti-Slavery Society, n.d.); Maria Weston Chapman, compiler, *Songs of the Free, and Hymns* (Boston: Isaac Knapp, 1836).

52. Follen, *Anti-Slavery Hymns*, p. 8.

53. Eliza Lee Follen, *Hymns, Songs, and Fables for Young People* (Boston: William Crosby and H. P. Nichols, 1847), pp. iii-iv, 69–71. Samuel J. May, with some success, tried to reach children with the message of "his Gospel of Universal Freedom." One of his Sunday School children remembered at Lincoln's Emancipation Proclamation the antislavery message May had given him twenty years before. See Mumford, p. 165; Bowditch taught abolition to his Sunday School class with such determination that he was stopped by his scholars' parents, who accused him of being "too sectarian"! See Bowditch, *Life and Correspondence*, 1:119, 121–23; One six-year old pored over a children's antislavery catechism that outlined the cardinal points of Garrisonianism. She mastered it so well that she could easily parrot radical abolitionism to anyone who might inquire. See Wyman, p. 172.

54. [Mary Willard, ed.] *Life of Rev. Samuel Willard, D.D., A.A.S. of Deerfield, Mass.* (Boston: Geo. H. Ellis, 1892), p. 181.

55. James Freeman Clarke, "Anti-Slavery in Boston. Chronology. Topics," James Freeman Clarke Papers, MH; Wendell Glick, "Thoreau and Radical Abolitonism: A Study of the Native Background of Thoreau's Social Philosophy," Ph.D. dissertation, Northwestern University, 1950, pp. 169–70; Samuel J. May to

Maria Weston Chapman, South Scituate, 27 December 1836, Weston Papers, MB.

56. Lydia Maria Child to E. Carpenter, West Boylston, [Mass.], 9 May 1836, *Letters of Lydia Maria Child,* p. 19.

57. Quoted by Martineau, "Martyr Age," pp. 19–20.

58. Ibid., p. 20.

59. Lydia Maria Child to Ellis Gray Loring, Northampton, 10 July 1838, Loring Family Papers, MCR; Meltzer, p. 65; Anne Warren Weston to Deborah Weston, Boston, 19 November 1836, Weston Papers, MB.

60. Maria Weston Chapman to Louisa Loring, n.p., 10 June n.y., Loring Family Papers, MCR; Maria Weston Chapman to Catherine and Henrietta [Sargent], n.p., 24 March n.y., Maria Weston Chapman Papers, MCR.

61. Maria Weston Chapman to [Samuel May, Jr.?], Boston, 13 April 1839, Maria Weston Chapman Papers, MCR; "Statistics of the Antislavery Fair" [title supplied], Caroline Weston Notes, May Papers, MB.

62. Caroline Weston to Samuel May, Jr., Weymouth, 21 October 1871, May Papers, MB.

63. Lydia Maria Child to Angelina Grimké Weld, Wayland, 4 February 1874, Lydia Maria Child Papers, MiU-C.

64. *Old-Anti-Slavery Days, Danvers Historical Society,* p. 92.

65. See nos. 12, 32 above; Garrison and Garrison, 2:49; Chapman, *Memories and Milestones,* p. 218; Bowditch, *Life and Correspondence,* 1:101–2; Charles J. Bowen, "Extract from a Sermon preached on 1st Sunday after Mr. Loring's Death . . . at Kingston, Mass.", MS fragment, Loring Family Papers, MCR; Higginson, p. 55; Lutz, pp. 24–25; May, *Recollections,* pp. 94, 100.

66. May, *Recollections,* p. 94.

67. Ellis Gray Loring to Harriet Martineau, Boston, 22 March 1840, Loring's Letterbook, MH.

68. Loring, "Diary," See the entry for March 31, 1840, Loring Family Papers, MCR; May, *Recollections,* pp. 257–59.

69. Ellis Gray Loring to William Ellery Channing, Boston, 26 February 1840, Loring to Harriet Martineau, Boston, 22 March 1840, Loring's Letterbook, MH; William E. Channing, *A Discourse Occasioned by the Death of the Rev. Dr. Follen* (Cambridge: Metcalf, Torrey and Ballou, 1840).

70. May, *Recollections,* p. 259; Samuel J. May, *A Discourse on the Life and Character of the Rev. Charles Follen, LL.D., Who Perished, January 13, 1840. . . . Delivered Before the Massachusetts Anti-Slavery Society, in the Marlborough Chapel, Boston, April 17, 1840* (Boston: Henry L. Devereux, 1840), pp. 4–5, 15–16, 23–24.

71. Spindler, p. 220.

72. Samuel J. May, "Success of the Abolitionists," p. 187; Leonard L. Richards, *"Gentlemen of Property and Standing": Anti-Abolition Mobs in Jacksonian America* (New York: Oxford University Press, 1970), pp. 75–76.

73. May, *Recollections,* pp. 233–34; Lydia Maria Child to Ellis Gray Loring, in a postscript in a letter to Louisa Loring, Northampton, 30 April 1839, Loring Family Papers, MCR.

74. Samuel J. May, "Non-Resistance," *Monthly Miscellany of Religion and Letters* 2 (October 1839): 23.

75. Henry I. Bowditch to Henry G. Chapman, n.p., n.d., Weston Papers, MB.

76. Samuel J. May to William Lloyd Garrison, South Scituate, 18 December 1837, Antislavery Papers, MB.

77. Lutz, pp. 147–48; Pease and Pease, "Freedom and Peace," p. 28; Lydia Maria Child to Abby Kelly [sic], Northampton, 1 October 1838, Abigail Kelley Foster Papers, American Antiquarian Society.

78. *Third Annual Report of the Board of Managers of the New England Anti-Slavery Society, Presented January 21, 1835* (Boston: Garrison and Knapp, 1835), pp. 3, 16; Francis Jackson to Mr. Buckingham, n.p., 8 December 1837, Antislavery Letters, MB; Samuel May, Jr. to George T. Davis, Leicester, 29 June 1840, May Papers, MB.

79. Johnson, pp. 306–12; Conrad Wright, "The Minister as Reformer," *The Liberal Christians* (Boston: Beacon Press, 1970), p. 64; Ellis Gray Loring to [H.B.] Stanton, Boston, 14 October 1837, Loring to Lydia Maria Child, Boston, 29 April 1841, Loring's Letterbook, MH; Samuel J. May to Maria Weston Chapman, South Scituate, 3 December 1841, Weston Papers, MB, Lydia Maria Child to Louisa Loring, Northampton, 28 June 1840, Loring Family Papers, MCR; Child to Francis George Shaw, Northampton, 24 October 1840, Lydia Maria Child Papers; MH; Lutz, pp. 188–89.

80. Chapman quoted by Munsterberg, "Weston Sisters and 'The Boston Controversy,' " p. 50; Samuel J. May to William Lloyd Garrison, South Scituate, 1 May 1839, May to Garrison, South Scituate, 15 June 1839, Antislavery Letters, MB; Mrs. Child quoted by Garrison and Garrison, 3:34–35.

NOTES TO CHAPTER 3

1. William E. Channing, *A Discourse Occasioned by the Death of the Rev. Dr. Follen* (Cambridge: Metcalf, Torry, and Ballou, 1840). For the texts of Channing's published works in this chapter the following volume has been used: *The Works of William E. Channing, D.D.* (Boston: American Unitarian Association, 1878). The appropriate pages will be indicated from this single volume. For the references from Channing's eulogy of Follen in the above opening paragraph, see *Works*, pp. 609, 610.

2. William E. Channing to Lucy Aikin, Boston, 10 May 1839, Channing Papers, Houghton Library, Harvard University. Hereafter cited as MH. The letter is also in *Correspondence of William Ellery Channing, D.D., and Lucy Aikin, From 1826 to 1842*, Anna Letitia Le Breton, ed. (London: Williams and Norgate, 1874), pp. 340–44.

3. Channing, *Works*, pp. 147–48, 149.

4. William E. Channing to Joseph Blanco White, Boston, 29 July 1836, *The Life of the Rev. Joseph Blanco White, Written by Himself; with Portions of His Correspondence*, John Hamilton Thom, ed. (London: John Chapman, 1845), 2:251–52.

5. William E. Channing to Lydia Maria Child, Boston, 12 March 1842, *Memoir of William Ellery Channing, with Extracts from his Correspondence and Manuscripts,* William Henry Channing, ed. (Boston: Wm. Crosby and H. P. Nichols, 1848), 3:4.

6. Samuel J. May, *Some Recollections of Our Antislavery Conflict* (Miami, Fla.: Mnemosyne Publishing Co., 1969 [1st ed., 1869]), p. 170.

7. Maria Weston Chapman, "Memorials," *Harriet Martineau's Autobiography* (Boston: James R. Osgood & Co., 1877), 2:273.

8. William E. Channing to Lucy Aikin, Boston, August 1834, Channing Papers, MH. Cf. same in *Channing-Aikin Correspondence,* pp. 222–26.

9. John L. Thomas, *The Liberator: William Lloyd Garrison* (Boston: Little, Brown & Co., 1963), p. 56.

10. Conrad Wright, Introduction to *Three Prophets of Religious Liberalism: Channing-Emerson-Parker* (Boston: Beacon Press, 1961), p. 6.

11. Charles Richard Denton, "American Unitarians, 1830–1865: A Study of Religious Opinions on War, Slavery, and Union," Ph.D. dissertation, Michigan State University, 1969, p. 176.

12. Cyrus A. Bartol, "Channing and Garrison. A Question of Words and of Verbal Virtue," *Unitarian Review and Religious Magazine* 25 (1886): 145. Hereafter the *Review* will be cited as *UR.*

13. Caroline H. Dall, "Dr. Channing and Miss Aikin," *UR* (1874): 384.

14. Arthur W. Brown, *Always Young for Liberty: A Biography of William Ellery Channing* (Syracuse: Syracuse University Press, 1956), pp. 8, 37, 222–23.

15. *Memoir,* 3:136.

16. William E. Channing to Joseph Tuckerman, St. Croix, 20 January 1831, ibid., pp. 140–41.

17. William E. Channing to Mrs. C. Codman, St. Croix, 4 February 1831, ibid., p. 142.

18. William E. Channing to Jane E. Roscoe, St. Croix, 10 March 1831, The Clifton Waller Barrett Library of the Alderman Library, University of Virginia. A Major portion of the letter is also in *Memoir,* 3:142–46.

19. William Ellery Channing, "Sermon delivered at Federal Street Church, June, 1831, upon return from St. Croix" [title supplied], MS sermon, William Ellery Channing Papers, Meadville Theological School. Hereafter cited as ICM. Portions of this sermon are in *Memoir,* 3:148–50.

20. *Memoir,* 3:153.

21. William E. Channing to Lucy Aikin, Boston, 28 December 1833, MH. Cf. same in *Channing-Aikin Correspondence,* pp. 190–94.

22. Lydia Maria Child, *Letters of Lydia Maria Child.* With a Biographical Introduction by John G. Whittier (Boston: Houghton, Mifflin, & Co., 1883), pp. 48–49. A scrapbook of Channing contains more clippings of abolitionist writings of Mrs. Child than any other person. See "Scrapbook about 1841 by Rev. W. E. Channing on Anti-Slavery, etc." Rhode Island Historical Society. Cited Hereafter as RHi.

23. Wendell Phillips Garrison and Francis Jackson Garrison, *William Lloyd Garrison, 1805–1879. The Story of His Life Told by His Children* (New York: The Century Co., 1885–1889), 1:464–65.

24. E. S. Abdy, *Journal of a Residence and Tour in the United States of North America, from April, 1833 to October, 1834* (London: John Murray, 1835), 3:217–25, 227–33.

25. May, pp. 172–75. Cf. also *Memoir*, 3:156–58. Concerning Channing's domination of conversations in his home, Frederic Henry Hedge wrote, "There was no gossip at Dr. Channing's; the conversation, if you could call it conversation, was always on some high theme. But in truth it was not conversation; it was simply a monologue by Dr. Channing himself. . . . He did not pay the slightest attention to anything you said. If you asked a question, he very probably did not answer it; he went on talking on the thing which interested him." Quoted by Edward Everett Hale, ed., *James Freeman Clarke: Autobiography, Diary and Correspondence* (Boston: Houghton, Mifflin, and Co., 1891), p. 142.

26. William E. Channing, "Mobs," sermon delivered at the Federal Street Church, October 1834, ICM. Portions of this sermon are in *Memoir*, 3:162–64.

27. Garrison and Garrison, 1:466.

28. Abdy, 3:236. Abdy, orthodox and an abolitionist, obviously exaggerated his talk with Channing. He charged, for example, that the Unitarians on slavery were less liberal than the Pope. See ibid., 238–39. Channing would not have been likely to have been moved by Abdy's boisterous attack. Harriet Martineau claimed that Abdy's interview had a considerable effect upon Channing. See her "Martyr Age of the United States," *London and Westminster Review* 32 (December 1838): 14. Thomas F. Harwood has seized upon Martineau's statement to argue that Abdy's interview should be given more credit for influencing Channing's antislavery commitment. See Harwood, "Prejudice and Antislavery: The Colloquy between William Ellery Channing and Edward Strutt Abdy, 1834," *American Quarterly* 17 (Winter 1966): 697–700. The interview is primarily valuable for insight into Channing's opinions on race.

29. *Memoir*, 3:165.

30. *Memoir*, 3:168–71. Significantly, when the centennial edition of Channing's *Memoir* was published in 1880, these statements were deleted. Cf. William Henry Channing, *The Life of William Ellery Channing, D.D.*, The Centenary Memorial Edition (Boston: American Unitarian Association, 1880). The hiatus can be noticed on pages 536–37. The Garrison sons made note of this deletion in their biography of their father. See Garrison and Garrison, 2:99.

31. William E. Channing, *Slavery* (Boston: James Munroe & Co., 1835). See *Works*, pp. 688–743.

32. George L. Chaney, "Channing's Relation to the Charities and Reforms of His Day," *UR* 13 (1880): 313; David Walker Howe, *The Unitarian Conscience: Harvard Moral Philosophy, 1805–1861* (Cambridge: Harvard University Press, 1970), p. 287.

33. *Works*, pp. 692, 697, 704–5, 707–22, 724–26, 729.

34. Ibid., pp. 731–35.

35. Denton, p. 62.

36. E. L. Bascom to Charles Briggs, Savannah, 5 May [1835], American Unitarian Association Letters, Andover-Harvard Theological Library. Hereafter cited as AUA Letters, MH-AH.

37. James Freeman Clarke, "Channing on Slavery," *Western Messenger* 1 (April 1836): 628.

38. [James T. Austin], *Remarks on Dr. Channing's Slavery By a Citizen of Massachusetts* (Boston: Russell, Shattuck, & Co., 1835), p. 11.

39. Ellis Gray Loring to W. L. Garrison, Boston, 5 December 1835, Garrison and Garrison, 2:55.

40. William L. Garrison to Henry E. Benson, Brooklyn, 10 December 1835, *The Letters of William Lloyd Garrison*, Walter M. Merrill, ed. (Cambridge: Harvard University Press, 1971), 1:574.

41. Garrison and Garrison, 3:242–43; Samuel May, Jr., to James Freeman Clarke, Leicester, 12 January 1886, May Papers, Boston Public Library; hereafter cited as MB. Channing deserved criticism for chastizing the abolitionists on the basis of secondhand information. He admitted that he had not read their books (except Mrs. Child's *Appeal*), attended their meetings, nor heard their discourses. See William E. Channing, *Slavery*, 4th edition, revised (Boston: James Munroe & Co., 1836), p. 164, and Lydia Maria Child to Louisa Loring, New York, 15 August [1835], Loring Family Papers, Schlesinger Library, Radcliffe College; hereafter cited as MCR. The celebrated meeting of Garrison and Channing at an inquiry held at the Massachusetts state legislature in 1836 was, as Garrison described it, "only an act of ordinary civility on [Channing's] part, as he did not catch my name, and did not know me personally. . . ." See May, p. 202; *Memoir*, 3:229–31; Garrison and Garrison, 3:242; Mrs. Child, who of all the abolitionists after Charles Follen was most intimate with Channing, said that he favored the "*rich* abolitionists." Possibly he avoided Garrison in deference to class prejudice. Mrs. Child also declared that his mind had been "bound around with Lilliputian cords by his wife and daughter Mary!" He not only faced opposition from his parish and wealthy and conservative friends, but from his own family. Finally, Mrs. Child said that her conversations with Channing exhausted her spirit.

My soul has suffered many a shivering ague-fit in attempting to melt or batter away, the glazing of his prejudice, false refinement, and beautiful *theories* into which the breath of life was never infused by being boldly brought into *action*. Let him pass on, and fulfill his destiny charioteered by applause and pillowed with self-respect. Amid obscurity and trial, I likewise pass on to the fulfillment of mine. In *this* world, may I never attempt to approach him, or his tribe.

See Lydia Maria Child to Louisa Loring, South Natick, 19 July 1836, Loring Family Papers, MCR; the antislavery contributions of Channing and Garrison were compared and debated when the Garrison sons published their biography of their father. See John W. Chadwick, "William Lloyd Garrison," *UR* 24 (1885): 481–502; Bartol, pp. 145–57; idem., "Correction of article on Channing and Garrison" [title supplied], *UR* 25 (1886): 267; Oliver Johnson, "Dr. Bartol on Channing and Garrison," *UR* 25 (1886): 319–28; Samuel May, "Channing and Garrison," *UR* 25 (1886): 368–70; Wendell Phillips Garrison to Samuel May, Jr., New York City, 21 January 1886, Garrison Papers, MH.

42. *Memoir*, 3:159.

43. Charles Timothy Brooks to John S. Dwight, Cambridge, 26 May 1834, Autograph File, MH.

44. William Sprague, *Annals of the American Unitarian Pulpit* (New York: Robert Carter & Bros., 1865), pp. 472, 474, 476–77, 484; Allen Johnson and Dumas Malone, eds., *Dictionary of American Biography* (New York: Charles Scribner's Sons, 1928–1958), 19:448; John Ware, *Memoir of the Life of Henry Ware, Jr.* (Boston: James Munroe & Co., 1854), 2:147. Cf. also Evert A. Duyckinck and George L. Duyckinck, eds., *Cyclopedia of American Literature* (New York: Charles Scribner, 1855), 2:173–74; Samuel A. Eliot, ed., *Heralds of a Liberal Faith* (Boston: American Unitarian Association, 1910), 2:223–38.

45. Ware, p. 154.

46. A. B. Muzzey, *Reminiscences and Memorials of Men of the Revolution and Their Families* (Boston: Estes and Lauriat, 1883), p. 296; Garrison and Garrison, 1:463.

47. Henry Ware, Jr., to Samuel J. May, Cambridge, 29 April 1834, Ware, pp. 151–52.

48. [Henry Ware, Jr.,], "Constitution of the Cambridge Anti-Slavery Society," MS notes, Slavery in the United States Collection, American Antiquarian Society.

49. Ibid. See the newspaper clipping attached to a page of the MS notes. Cf. also Muzzey, pp. 294–96.

50. Ware, p. 150.

51. Oliver C. Everett to Henry W. Bellows, Cambridge, 12 November 1835, Bellows Papers, Massachusetts Historical Society. Hereafter cited as MHi.

52. Henry Ware, Jr. to Samuel J. May, Cambridge, 15 October 1834, Ware, pp. 152–53; Garrison and Garrison, 1:462.

53. "Constitution of the Cambridge Anti-Slavery Society."

54. Ware, pp. 147–48.

55. Samuel May, Jr. to J. B. Estlin, Leicester, 30 March 1846; May, "American Unitarians," notes submitted to Mr. Estlin, in 1853, for use in the *Anti-Slavery Advocate*, May Papers, MB.

56. *Memoir*, 3:175, 177–80.

57. William E. Channing to Harriet Martineau, Newport, 28 July 1836; Channing to Follen, Newport, 5 October 1836, ibid., pp. 182, 184.

58. William Ellery Channing, *Letter of William Ellery Channing to James G. Birney* (Boston: James Munroe & Co., 1837); *Works*, pp. 743–52; John White Chadwick, *William Ellery Channing* (Boston: Houghton, Mifflin, & Co., 1903), p. 280. See also James G. Birney to Lewis Tappan, Cincinnati, 7 December 1836, Dwight L.

Dumond, ed., *Letters of James Gillespie Birney, 1831–1857* (Gloucester, Mass.: Peter Smith, 1966 [1st ed., 1938]), 1:372–373.

59. Chadwick, *Channing*, p. 281; *Works*, p. 744.

60. *Memoir*, 3:193–94; Lewis Tappan to William E. Channing, New York City, 19 June 1837, ICM; William Ellery Channing, *A Letter to the Hon. Henry Clay, on the Annexation of Texas to the United States* (Boston: J. Munroe & Co., 1837); *Works*, pp. 752–81.

61. *Works*, pp. 765, 767, 774.

62. Thomas F. Harwood, "Great Britain and American Antislavery," Ph.D. dissertation, university of Texas, 1959, p. 265. For the opinions of John Quincy Adams and Henry Clay on Channing's ideas, cf. John Quincy Adams to William Ellery Channing, Quincy, 11 August 1837; Henry Clay to Channing, Washington, 13 December 1837, RHi.

63. "The Right of Free Discussion," Boston *Morning News*, 4 December 1837, newspaper clipping, "Scrapbook [of Samuel A. Eliot], 1837–1860," Harvard University Archives.

64. William E. Channing, "To the Citizens of Boston," newspaper clipping, ibid.; *Memoir*, 3:201–6.

65. William E. Channing to Samuel E. Sewall, [Boston, 25 November 1837], Garrison Papers, MB.

66. Chadwick, *Channing*, p. 285; for Channing's address and resolutions, cf. *Memoir*, 3:207–13; Mrs. Chapman refused to praise Channing for the Lovejoy meeting. "He deserves no more credit," she said, "for moral courage than the Captain of Cavalry whose Colonel leads his horse's head to the fight. Moreover it was easier at that instant to be with Ellis Gray Loring and his friends than Gov. Everett and his." See Maria Weston Chapman, "Notes on William Ellery Channing and the Abolitionists" [title supplied], Weston Papers, MB.

67. *Memoir*, 3:218–28.

68. Lydia Maria Child to Louisa Loring, Northampton, 16 August 1838, Loring Family Papers, MCR.

69. William E. Channing, "Blessed Are the Peacemakers, 1838," MS sermon, ICM.

70. William E. Channing, *Remarks on the Slavery Question, in a Letter to Joanthan Phillips, Esq.* (Boston: James Munroe & Co., 1839); *Works*, pp. 782–820.

71. *Works*, pp. 784, 786–88, 800, 811–15.

72. George F. Simmons to Henry W. Bellows, Boston, 23 October 1840, MHi.

73. Sprague, 555–56, 558.

74. James Freeman Clarke, "George F. Simmons," *Christian Inquirer*, 22 September 1855.

75. George F. Simmons to John Gorham Palfrey, n.p., 27 May 1838, John Gorham Palfrey Papers, MH.

76. Clarke, *Christian Inquirer*, 22 September 1855; [Henry W. Bellows], "George F. Simmons," *Christian Register*, 22 September 1855; Sprague, p. 556. For additional material on Simmons, cf. *Heralds*, 2:173–74; *National Cyclopedia of*

American Biography (New York: James T. White & Co., 1897), 7:499; Joseph Palmer, *Necrology of Alumni of Harvard College 1851–1852 to 1862–1863* (Boston: John Wilson & Son, 1864), pp. 97–98.

77. [George F. Simmons], *Review of the Remarks on Dr. Channing's Slavery, by a Citizen of Massachusetts* (Boston: James Munroe & Co., 1836), pp. 46–48.

78. Sidney Smith to Henry W. Bellows, Mobile, 19 February 1839, Herbert C. Peabody to Bellows, Mobile, 22 December 1838, MHi; Samuel St. John, Jr. to Charles E. Briggs, Mobile, January 1838 [*sic*], AUA Letters, MH–AH; Sophia St. John to Bellows, Newport, 31 December 1838 and 5 January 1839 [same letter], MHi.

79. *Inquirer,* 17 May 1845; Denton, p. 83.

80. George F. Simmons, *Two Sermons on the Kind Treatment and on the Emancipation of Slaves. Preached at Mobile, On Sunday the 10th, and Sunday the 17th of May, 1840* (Boston: William Crosby & Co., 1840), pp. v, 12–13, 16.

81. Ibid., pp v–vi, 22–23, 29.

82. Ibid., pp. vi–viii.

83. George F. Simmons, *Public Spirit and Mobs. Two Sermons Delivered at Springfield, Mass., on Sunday, February 23, 1851, after the Thompson Riot* (Springfield: Merriam, Chapin, & Co., 1851); Clarke, *Christian Inquirer,* 22 September 1855.

84. Palmer, p. 98.

85. William E. Channing, *Emancipation* (Boston: E. P. Peabody, 1840); *Works,* pp. 820–53.

86. *Works,* pp. 835–38. After reading Gurney's pamphlet, Simmons believed that free Negroes could be "held in subjection" with "facility," and therefore could be safely emancipated. See George F. Simmons, "Emancipation in the West Indies," *Monthly Miscellany of Religion and Letters* 3 (November 1840): 255.

87. Ibid., pp. 841, 844.

88. Ibid., pp. 846–48.

89. *Works,* pp. 845–46. For other references to Channing's displeasure over political abolitionism, see *Memoir,* 3:187–90; Chadwick, *Channing, pp. 281–82.* The schism of 1840 as it was related to political activity confirms Channing in his anti-associational and anti-political views. See William E. Channing to Gerrit Smith, Newport, 10 August 1841, Gerrit Smith Papers, George Arents Research Library, Syracuse University. On Channing's political thought, see John E. Reinhardt, "The Evolution of William Ellery Channing's Sociopolitical Ideas," *American Literature* 26 (May 1954): 154–65.

90. Granville Hicks, "Dr. Channing and the Creole Case," *American Historical Review, 37 (1931–*32): 516–525; William E. Channing, *The Duty of the Free States, or Remarks Suggested by the Case of the Creole* (Boston: William Crosby & Co., 1842); *Works,* pp. 853–907.

91. *Works,* pp. 853–67, 871, 874, 879–80, 897.

92. Anne Warren Weston to Deborah Weston, Chauncey Place, 15 January 1842, Weston Papers, MB.

93. Chadwick, *Channing*, pp. 404–5, 412, 415.

94. Ibid., pp. 417–18; *Memoir*, 3:241; William E. Channing, *An Address Delivered at Lenox, on the First of August, 1842, the Anniversary of Emancipation, in the British West Indies* (Lenox: J. G. Stanly, 1842); *Works*, pp. 907–24.

95. *Works*, pp. 918, 920, 923–24.

96. Lucretia Mott to Maria Weston Chapman, Philadelphia, 30 November 1842, Weston Papers, MB.

97. Samuel May, Jr. to Richard D. Webb, Boston, 16 July 1847, May Papers, MB.

98. Oliver Johnson, p. 323.

99. Samuel May, Jr. to Richard D. Webb, Boston 16 July 1847, May Papers, MB; Lydia Maria Child to Francis George Shaw, New York, 12 October 1842, MH; [Theodore Parker], "Extracts from his Journal," transcription in the Franklin Sanborn Papers, MH.

100. Vestiges of "abolitionism as philosophy" continued to appear in the antislavery attitudes of a man like Ralph Waldo Emerson. Cf. James Elliot Cabot, *A Memoir of Ralph Waldo Emerson* (Boston, 1888), 2:424–431, 574–78, 587, 595; William M. Slater, "Emerson's Views of Society and Reform," *International Journal of Ethics* 13 (July 1903): 418; Majory M. Moody, "The Evolution of Emerson as an Abolitionist," *American Literature* 17 (March 1945): 1–21; James Freeman Clarke, *Events and Epochs in Religious History* (Boston: James R. Osgood & Co., 1881), p. 292; David P. Edgell, *William Ellery Channing: An Intellectual Portrait* (Boston: Beacon Press, 1955), pp. 134–36; Helene G. Baer, *The Heart is Like Heaven* (Philadelphia: University of Pennsylvania Press, 1964), pp. 98, 120, 149.

101. Garrison and Garrison, 1:462.

Notes to Chapter 4

1. James Freeman Clarke, "Channing on Slavery," *Western Messenger* 1 (April 1836): 628. Cited hereafter as *WM*. Clarke, *Autobiography, Diary and Correspondence*, Edward Everett Hale, ed. (Boston: Houghton, Mifflin, and Co., 1891), p. 51; Samuel A. Eliot, *Heralds of a Liberal Faith* (Boston: American Unitarian Association, 1910), 3:68.

2. James F. Clarke, "Duties of Masters Towards Servants. A Sermon, Preached in Louisville, Ky.," *WM* (April 1839) 6:383. For Clarke's observations upon the kindness of his slaveholding friends in Kentucky, especially Judge Speed of Louisville, see *Autobiography*, pp. 76–77, 98, 103; Clarke, *Anti-Slavery Days* (New York: R. Worthington, 1884), pp. 21–22; James F. Clarke to William H. Channing, Lexington, 8 November 1833, James Freeman Clarke Papers, Houghton Library, Harvard University. Hereafter cited as MH. See also Clarke's correspondence with his relatives from Georgia, Maria Campbell to Clarke, Newton, Massachusetts, 5 July 1836; Sarah Campbell to Clarke, Springville, Georgia, 23 February 1838; Edward F. Campbell to Clarke, Augusta, Georgia, 16 October 1854: Edward F. Campbell to Clarke, Augusta, 28 November 1854; Clarke

Papers, MH. By 1854, Clarke's opinions had changed, of course, and the letters written then reflect his new views.

3. James F. Clarke to Margaret Fuller, 13 September 1833, *The Letters of James Freeman Clarke to Margaret Fuller*, John Wesley Thomas, ed. (Hamburg: Cram, de Gruyter & Co., 1957), p. 62.

4. James F. Clarke, "Channing on Slavery," *WM* 1 (April 1836): 628; Clarke, "Reply to Criticism on Art. VI, April No.," *WM* (August 1836), 2:51, 53–54; Clarke to Samuel May, Jr., n.p., n.d., May Papers, Boston Public Library. Hereafter cited as MB. Cf. also Clarke, "The Mosaic Institution of Slavery," *WM* IV (December 1837), pp. 252–55.

5. Clarke, *WM* 2 (August 1836): 53, 58.

6. [James F. Clarke], "The Alton Murder," *WM* 4 (January 1838): 359–60; Clarke, "Mob Law," *WM* 5 (July 1838): 287.

7. [James F. Clarke], "Western Messenger and Abolitionism," *WM* 4 (September 1837): 65. See also Clarke, "Letter from T.M.," *WM* 4 (February 1838): 397–401.

8. James F. Clarke, "Colonization," *Christian Register*, 3 September 1836; Clarke, "Colonization Meetings," *WM* 2 (September 1836): 142; Clarke to William H. Channing, Louisville, 22 October 1833, Clarke Papers, MH.

9. James F. Clarke, "Abolition in Mobile," *WM* 8 (August 1840): 184, 185, 187.

10. *Autobiography, p. 72.*

11. *Derek Keith Colville, "James Freeman Clarke: A Practical Transcendentalist and His Writings," Ph.D. dissertation, Washington Univeristy, 1953, pp. 12–13, 65, 68.*

12. James F. Clarke to Anna Huidekoper, Cincinnati, 18 March 1839, *Autobiography*, p. 129; Clarke to Sarah Clarke, Meadville, 13 July 1840, Clarke Papers, MH.

13. *Autobiography*, pp. 65, 146; James F. Clarke to Sarah Clarke, Meadville, 7 January 1841, Clarke Papers, MH; Eliot, 3:170.

14. *Autobiography*, pp. 141, 248–49.

15. James F. Clarke to the Editor of the Courier, n.p., n.d., [draft of letter], Clarke Papers, MH.

16. James F. Clarke, "Thanksgiving Day, November 28, 1846," MS sermon, Clarke Papers, MH.

17. James F. Clarke, "The Ethics of the Ballot Box," *Everyday Religion* (Boston: Houghton, Mifflin, & Co., 1886), p. 436; Clarke to the Editor of the Boston *Herald*, Jamaica Plain, 2 November 1878 [draft of letter], Clarke Papers, MH; Eliot, 3:68.

18. James F. Clarke, "Slavery in the United States Delivered in Chicago, August, 1845," MS lecture; Clarke, "Thanksgiving—November 27, 1845," MS sermon, Clarke Papers, MH.

19. James F. Clarke, " 'Is it such a fast that I have chosen?' Fast Day [1842?] in Amory Hall," MS sermon, Clarke Papers, MH.

20. James F. Clarke to the Editor of the Boston *Herald*, Jamaica Plain, 2 November 1878 [draft of letter], Clarke Papers, MH.

21. John Pierpont, *Moral Rule of Political Action. A Discourse, Delivered in Hollis Street Church, Sunday, January 27, 1839* (Boston: James Munroe & Co., 1839), pp. 7–8.

22. Pierpont, pp. 18–19.

23. Abe Ravitz, "John Pierpont and the Federalist Muse in Essex County," *Essex Institute Historical Collections* 96 (April 1960): 142–147; John Pierpont, *The Anti-Slavery Poems of John Pierpont* (Boston: Oliver Johnson, 1843); Ravitz, "John Pierpont and the Slaves' Christmas," *Phylon* 21 (Winter 1960): 383–86; Eliot, 2:185–87. For additional information on Pierpont, see Allen Johnson and Dumas Malone, eds., *Dictionary of American Biography* (New York: Charles Scribner's Sons, 1928–1958), 14:586–87. Cited hereafter as *DAB*. Evert A. Duyckinck and George L. Duyckinck, eds., *Cyclopedia of American Literature* (New York: Charles Scribner, 1855) 2:72–73; [John Neal], "John Pierpont," *Atlantic Monthly* 18 (December, 1866): 649–65; Henry De Long, "John Pierpont," *Medford Historical Register* 6 (October 1903): 75–89; and esp., Ravitz, "John Pierpont: Portrait of a Nineteenth Century Reformer," Ph. D. dissertation, New York University, 1955.

24. John Pierpont to Elizur Wright, 27 January 1838, Pierpont Papers, American Antiquarian Society; Pierpont to Francis Jackson, n.p., 19 August 1838, Anti-Slavery Papers, MB; Abe C. Ravitz, "John Pierpont, Abolitionist," *Boston Public Library Quarterly* 8 (October 1956): 195. Ravitz ignores differentiation in abolitionist types and mistakenly declares that Pierpont was a "staunch Garrisonian." See ibid., pp. 195, 199, and Ravitz, "John Pierpont: Portrait," pp. 144–45.

25. John Ross Dix, *Pulpit Portraits, or Pen Pictures of Distinguished American Divines; with Sketches of Congregations and Choirs . . .* (Boston: Tappan & Whittemore, 1854), p. 199.

26. *DAB*, p. 586; Franklin Bowditch Dexter, *Biographical Sketches of the Graduates of Yale College* (New York: Henry Holt and Company, 1911), 5:693–94; Marion E. Brown, " 'To Smoking Clergymen,' " *Books at Brown* 13 (April 1951): 4. Ravitz discusses Pierpont's trial in great detail. See his "John Pierpont: Portrait," pp. 278–300.

27. "Rev. John Pierpont," *Christian Register,* 19 October 1839; "Mr. Pierpont's Letter," *Christian Register,* 9 November 1839; *Proceedings in the Controversy Between a Part of the Proprietors and the Pastors of Hollis Street Church, Boston, 1838 and 1839* (Boston: S. N. Dickinson, n.d.); Caleb Stetson to Frederic Henry Hedge, Medford, 10 September 1848, Poor Family Papers, Schlesinger Library, Radcliffe College.

28. Samuel K. Lothrop, *Proceedings of an Ecclesiastical Council, in the Case of the Proprietors of the Hollis-Street Meeting-House and the Rev. John Pierpont, their Pastor, Prepared from the Official Journal and Original Documents* (Boston: W. W. Clapp and Son, 1841), pp. 52, 383–84.

29. Theodore Parker, "Hollis Street Council," *Dial* 3 (October 1842): 220.

30. Dexter, p. 694. See also *Reply of the Friends of Rev. John Pierpont, to a*

Proposal for Dissolving the Pastoral Connexion Between Him, and the Society in Hollis Street (n.p., n.d.) and *Letter of the Boston Association of Congregational Ministers, to Rev. John Pierpont, with His Reply* (Boston: Benjamin H. Greene, 1846); Seymour Katz wrote that Pierpont had violated the "one 'principle' to which Boston's Unitarian clergy remained loyal"; he ignored the preference of the proprietors of his church. See Seymour Katz, "The Unitarian Ministers of Boston, 1790-1860," Ph.D. dissertation, Harvard University, 1961, p. 244.

31. Theodore Parker to John Pierpont, 15 October 1845, John Weiss, *Life and Correspondence of Theodore Parker* (New York: D. Appleton & Co., 1864), 1: 256-57.

32. Conrad Wright, "Introduction" to *Three Prophets of Religious Liberalsim: Channing-Emerson-Parker* (Boston: Beacon Press, 1961), pp. 36, 41-42.

33. Octavius Brooks Forthingham, *Theodore Parker: A Biography* (Boston: James R. Osgood & Co., 1876), p. 378; Louis Bonzano Weeks III, "Theodore Parker: The Minster as Revolutionary," Ph.D. dissertation, Duke University, 1970, pp. 30, 230; Weiss, 1:250; Theodore Parker, "Speech Delivered at the Anti-War Meeting in Faneuil Hall, February 4, 1847," *Collected Works of Theodore Parker*, Frances Power Cobbe, ed. (London: Truebner & Co., 1863), 4:32; "The Political Destination of America and the Signs of the Times—Delivered Before Several Literary Societies, 1848," ibid., 4:81-82; "A Letter to the Boston Association of Ministers, Touching Certain Matters of Their Theology," ibid., 12: 177-84.

34. Henry Steele Commanger, *Theodore Parker: Yankee Crusader* (Boston: Beacon Press, 1967 [1st ed., 1936]), 4; Weiss, 1:56, 178.

35. Frothingham, p. 376; Parker, "A Sermon of Slavery. Delivered January 31, 1841, Repeated June 4, 1843," *Works, 5:1-16.*

36. Parker, *Works,* 5:13. See also pp. 5, 8.

37. Edmund Quincy to Caroline Weston, Dedham, 9 February 1841, Weston Papers, MB. Samuel May, Jr., appreciated Parker's antislavery work. However, Mrs. Chapman thought him lacking in moral courage. She felt that he never led the abolitionist movement, but only kept pace with it. See May, Jr., to Richard D. Webb, Boston, 18 February 1850, May Papers, MB; Chapman, "Theodore Parker and the Abolitionists" [title supplied], MS notes, n.d., Weston Papers, MB.

38. Frothingham, pp. 377-78; John White Chadwick, *Theodore Parker: Preacher and Reformer* (Boston: Houghton, Mifflin, & Co., 1901), pp. 328-32; Parker to Charles Sumner, West Roxbury, 17 August 1845, Parker to John Gorham Palfrey, Boston, 9 December 1847; John Gorham Palfrey Papers, MH; Parker to John P. Hale, Boston, 8 March 1850, Parker to Hale, Boston, 9 March 1850, John P. Hale Papers, New Hampshire Historical Society; cf. also Parker's letters to political leaders in Weiss, 1:317, and 2: passim.

39. Theodore Parker, "Theodore Parker's Experience as a Minister, with Some Account of His Early Life, and Education for the Ministry [1859]," *Works,* 12: 308, 329-30.

40. Thomas Wentworth Higginson, *Cheerful Yesterdays* (Boston: Houghton,

Mifflin, & Co., 1898), p. 98; Mary Thacher Higginson, *Thomas Wentworth Higginson: The Story of His Life* (Boston: Houghton, Mifflin, & Co., 1914), pp. 68, 84–85.

41. Mary T. Higginson, *Thomas Wentworth Higginson* ... , pp. 38, 76, 89, 103–4; Higginson, Cheerful Yesterdays, 123–24, 126, 130; Mary Thacher Higginson, ed., *Letters and Journals of Thomas Wentworth Higginson* (Boston: Houghton, Mifflin Co., 1921), pp. 19–21; Anne Mary Wells, *Dear Preceptor: The Life and Times of Thomas Wentworth Higginson* (Boston: Houghton, Mifflin Co., 1963), p. 64; Tilden G. Edelstein, *Strange Enthusiasm: A Life of Thomas Wentworth Higginson* (New Haven: Yale University Press, 1968), pp. 85–95; Samuel Johnson to Samuel Longfellow, n.p., December, 1848 [draft of letter], Samuel Johnson Papers, James Duncan Phillips Library, Essex Institute. Hereafter cited as MSE.

42. John A. Andrew to Cyrus Woodman, n.p. [1841?], [copy of letter], John A. Andrew Papers, MH.

43. Peleg W. Chandler, *Memoir of Governor Andrew, with Personal Reminiscences,* 3d ed. (Boston: Roberts Brothers, 1881), p. 24; Andrew quoted by James Freeman Clarke, *Memorial and Biographical Sketches* (Boston: Houghton, Mifflin, & Co., 1878), pp. 11, 13.

44. Chandler, pp. 64, 87, 119; Clarke, *Sketches,* pp. 13, 15, 22; Archibald H. Grimké, "Anti-Slavery Boston," *New England Magazine,* n.s. 3 (December 1890): 458; Elias Nason, *Discourse Delivered Before the New-England Historic-Genealogical Society, Boston, April 2, 1868, on the Life and Character of the Hon. John Albion Andrew, LL.D., Late President of the Society* (Boston: New-England Historic-Genealogical Society, 1868), pp. 30, 32, 37. See also Henry Greenleaf Pearson, *The Life of John A. Andrew: Governor of Massachusetts, 1861–1865,* 2 vols. (Boston: Houghton, Mifflin, & Co., 1904); James F. Clarke, "Fragments of a MS Lecture on John Andrew" [title supplied], n.d., Clarke Papers, MH; *DAB,* 1:279–81.

45. Samuel A. Eliot, 2:150–53; *DAB,* 14:169–70; Frank Otto Gatell, "Palfrey's Vote, the Conscience Whigs, and the Election of Speaker Winthrop," *New England Quarterly* 31 (June 1958): 218–31; "Doctor Palfrey Frees His Slaves," *New England Quarterly* 34 (March 1961): 74–86; and *John Gorham Palfrey and the New England Conscience* (Cambridge: Harvard University Press, 1963), pp. 70–71, 108–19, 126–27, 224–25. Palfrey later softened his opinion of the Garrisonians. He continued to object to their disapproval of political action, but "respected" their work. On the Garrisonian side, Samuel J. May included Palfrey in his list of Unitarians who were "fellow-laborers in the antislavery cause." See Palfrey to Samuel May, Jr., Cambridge, 27 July 1849, Palfrey Papers, MH; Samuel J. May, *Some Recollections of our Antislavery Conflict* (Miami, Fla.: Mnemosyne Publishing Co., 1969 [1st ed., 1869]), p. 335.

46. Richard H. Sewell, *John P. Hale and the Politics of Abolition* (Cambridge: Harvard University Press, 1965), pp. 13, 33–35, 53–54, 82, 96, 147, 220.

47. Samuel T. Pickard, *Life and Letters of John Greenleaf Whittier,* (Boston: Houghton Mifflin, & Co., 1899), 1:286–88; Ravitz, "Pierpont: Portrait," pp. 172–74.

48. Francis H. Drake to Maria Weston Chapman, Leominster, 31 October 1843, Abby Kelley to Chapman, Seneca Falls, New York, 28 August 1843, Weston Papers, MB; Elizur Wright, Jr. to James G. Birney, Boston, 16 September 1843; Henry B. Stanton to Birney, Boston, 11 August 1845, *Letters of James Gillespie Birney, 1831–1857*, Dwight L. Dumond, ed. (Gloucester, Mass.: Peter Smith, 1966 [1st ed., 1938]), 2:760, 960.

49. John Pierpont, *A Discourse on the Covenant with Judas, Preached in Hollis-Street Church, Nov. 6, 1842* (Boston: Charles C. Little and James Brown, 1842), pp. 29, 32, 34.

50. Dexter, pp. 694–95; Parker quoted by Ravitz, "Pierpont: Portrait," p. 175. See also p. 177.

51. Quoted by Mary T. Higginson, p. 90; see also p. 89; Higginson, *Cheerful Yesterdays*, pp. 128, 132.

52. Edelstein, p. 86.

53. Ibid., pp. 100–103.

54. Thomas Wentworth Higginson, *Mr. Higginson's Address to the Voters of the Third Congressional District of Massachusetts* (Lowell: C. L. Knapp, 1850), pp. 3–7.

55. Edelstein, pp. 107, 109.

56. Frothingham, p. 377; Weiss, p. 56. Cf. n. 38 above.

57. Weiss, 1:264; Mary T. Higginson, pp. 73–74; Frothingham, p. 192; John Gorham Palfrey, [Letter to the clergy in Massachusetts] MS, n.p., November, 1845, and printed broadside of same, Boston, 3 November 1845, Palfrey Papers, MH; James Freeman Clarke, *The Annexation of Texas. A Sermon Delivered in the Masonic Temple on Fast Day* (Boston: Office of the Christian World, 1844), p. 5; Clarke's friends criticized him for backing Clay. "Are you going to do evil that good may come?" they asked. Clarke returned their question: Would they do evil, that is, assent to the annexation of Texas, in the hope some good antislavery result might be achieved? Our goal at the moment, said Clarke, was to stop annexation. See Clarke to Joshua Pollard Blanchard, n.p., n.d., Clarke Papers, MH.

58. James Freeman Clarke, "Fast Day Sermon, April, 1845. Just After the Joint Resolution for the Annexation of Texas." MS sermon, Clarke Papers, MH.

59. James Freeman Clarke, "Thanksgiving—November 27, 1845," MS sermon, Clarke Papers, MH.

60. J. F. Clarke, "Thanksgiving Day, November 28, 1846," MS sermon; "Thanksgiving Day—1847," MS sermon; "Anti-Slavery League," n.d., MS lecture; Clarke Papers, MH.

61. James Freeman Clarke, "Mexican War: Its History—Character and Probable Results. Fast Day—April 8th, 1847," MS sermon, Clarke Papers, MH; Pierpont quoted by Ravitz, "Pierpont: Portrait," p. 175.

62. Theodore Parker, "A Sermon of War, Preached at the Melodeon, on Sunday, June 7, 1846," *Works*, 4:11–12.

63. Theodore Parker, "A Sermon of the Mexican War.—Preached at the Melodeon, on Sunday, June 25, 1848," *Works*, 4:33, 35, 38–39, 58, 67, 70; although Parker believed the Mexican War was sin, he would support a war to end

slavery. See Arthur I. Ladu, "The Political Ideas of Theodore Parker," *Studies in Philology* 38 (January 1941): 121.

64. Clarke, "Mexican War—April 8th, 1847," MS sermon, Clarke Papers, MH; William H. Channing, Theodore Parker, et al., to John Gorham Palfrey, Boston, 10 December 1847 [the letter is in the handwriting of Channing], Palfrey Papers, MH; Parker to Palfrey, Boston, 19 January 1848, Palfrey Papers, MH; Thomas Wentworth Higginson to Joshua R. Giddings, Newburyport, 30 June 1848, Joshua R. Giddings Papers, Ohio Historical Society.

65. Theodore Parker, "The Public Education of the People.—An Address Delivered Before the Onondaga Teachers' Institute, at Syracuse, New York, October 4, 1849," *Works*, 7:193.

66. Theodore Parker, "A Sermon of Merchants. Preached at the Melodeon, on Sunday, November 22, 1846," *Works*, 7:18.

67. Theodore Parker, "The Administration of the Late Mr. Polk," *Massachusetts Quarterly Review* 3 (December 1849): 156–57.

68. Parker, "Sermon of Merchants," *Works*, 7:20–21.

69. Theodore Parker, "Speech at Faneuil Hall, Before the New England Anti-Slavery Convention, May 31, 1848," *Works*, 5:94–95, 97, 100.

70. Theodore Parker, "Some Thoughts of the Free Soil Party and the Election of General Taylor, December, 1848," *Works*, 4:113, 126–27, 132–34.

71. Theodore Parker, "Speech at a Meeting of the Citizens of Boston, in Faneuil Hall, March 25, 1850, to Consider the Speech of Mr. Webster," *Works*, 4:213; Parker, "Speech at the New England Anti-Slavery Convention in Boston, May 29, 1850," *Works*, 5:115; James F. Clarke to Thomas Wentworth Higginson, Boston, 16 May 1850, Thomas Wentworth Higginson Papers, MH.

72. John Langdon Sibley, "Private Journal of John Langdon Sibley of Harvard University Library, Cambridge, Mass.," 1 (1846–65): 256, Harvard University Archives; Theodore Parker, "The Function and Place of Conscience, in Relation to the Laws of Men: A Sermon for the Times. Preached at the Melodeon, on Sunday, Sept. 22, 1850," *Works*, 5:140, 148.

73. Commager, pp. 214–16; Edelstein, 105–6.

74. James F. Clarke to Rebecca H. Clarke, Meadville, 20 November 1850, Clarke Papers, MH; Clarke to Dr. Samuel Cabot, Jr., Meadville, 22 November 1850, New England Immigrant Aid Papers, 1855–1857. With Cabot-Medical Letters, Military Historical Society, Mugar Memorial Library, Boston University.

75. Theodore Parker, "The State of the Nation, Considered in a Sermon for Thanksgiving Day.—Preached at the Melodeon, November 28, 1850," *Works*, 4:255. See also pp. 252–53.

76. Parker, "State of the Nation," *Works*, 4:257–58.

NOTES TO CHAPTER 5

1. Lydia Maria Child to John Pierpont, New York, 9 March 1842, James E. Murdock Papers, Department of Archives, Louisiana State University.

2. Ellis Gray Loring to Lydia Maria Child, Boston, 29 April 1841, Loring's Letterbook, Harvard University. Hereafter cited as MH.

3. Samuel J. May to Maria Weston Chapman, South Scituate, 3 December 1841, Weston Papers, Boston Public Library. Hereafter cited as MB.

4. Quoted by Lydia Maria Child in a letter to Ellis Gray Loring, Wayland, 16 August 1857, Lydia Maria Child Papers, Schlesinger Library, Radcliffe College. Hereafter cited as MCR.

5. John J. Chapman, *Memories and Milestones* (New York: Moffat, Yard, and Co., 1915), p. 214.

6. Henrietta Sargent to Abby Kelley, Boston, 15 July 1841, Abigail Kelley Foster Papers, American Antiquarian Society. Hereafter cited as MWA.

7. Eliza Lee Follen to Abby Kelley, West Roxbury, 12 February 1845, Foster Papers, MWA.

8. William Lloyd Garrison to Louisa Loring, Boston, 30 July 1847, Loring Family Papers, MCR.

9. Quoted by Lydia Maria Child in a letter to Ellis Gray Loring, Wayland, 16 August 1857, Child Papers, MCR.

10. Nonresistants included, e.g., Garrisonians Samuel J. May, Thomas T. Stone, Maria and David Child, Ellis Gray Loring, Maria Weston Chapman, Anne Warren Weston, and Edmund Quincy. See Peter Brock, *Radical Pacifists in Atnebellum America* (Princeton: Princeton University Press, 1968), pp. 39, 43, 96, 103–7, 243; Ellis Gray Loring to Lydia Maria Child, Boston, 22 May 1841, Loring's Letterbook, MH; John Demos traces the line of nonresistance thought of the abolitionists through the ante-bellum period. See John Demos, "Antislavery Movement and the Problem of Violent Means," *New England Quarterly* 37 (December 1964).

11. Lydia Maria Child to Ellis Gray Loring, New York, 27 May 1841, Loring Family Papers, MCR; Child to Francis George Shaw, New York, 15 February 1842, Child to Shaw, New York, 15 January 1843, Child Papers, MH.

12. Samuel J. May, "The Present Duty of the United States Toward Mexico," *Christian Register,* 18 December 1847. Cf. also William H. Pease and Jane H. Pease, "Freedom and Peace: A Nineteenth Century Dilemma," *Midwest Quarterly* 9 (October 1967): 31.

13. William Lloyd Garrison to Louisa Loring, Boston, 11 January 1845, Loring Family Papers, MCR.

14. Maria Weston Chapman to James Russell Lowell, Boston, 15 September [?], James Russell Lowell Papers, MH.

15. Henrietta Sargent to Abby Kelley, Boston, 16 July 1841, Foster Papers, MWA.

16. Jane H. Pease and William H. Pease, "The Role of Women in the Antislavery Movement," *Canadian Historical Association. Historical Papers presented at the Annual Meeting held at Ottawa, June 7-10, 1967* (n.p., n.d.), p. 178; Lydia Maria Child to Louisa Loring, New York, 15 January 1847, Child Papers, MCR; Child to Louisa Loring, New York, 4 September 1846, Lydia Maria Child Papers,

William L. Clements Library, Ann Arbor, Michigan. Hereafter cited as MiU-C;
Mary Estlin to Maria Weston Chapman [Bristol, 17 September 1850], Weston
Papers, MB; Milton Meltzer, *Tongue of Flame: The Life of Lydia Maria Child* (New
York: Thomas Y. Crowell Co., 1965), pp. 112, 120; Alma Lutz, *Crusade for
Freedom: Women of the Antislavery Movement* (Boston: Beacon Press, 1968), pp.
204–5.

17. Helen G. Baer, *The Heart is Like Heaven* (Philadelphia: University of Pennsylvania Press, 1964), p. 98; Pease and Pease, "Role of Women," pp. 178–79.

18. Eliza Lee Follen to Abby Kelley, West Roxbury, 12 February 1845,
Henrietta Sargent to Abby Kelley, Boston, 16 July 1841, Foster Papers, MWA.

19. Maria Weston Chapman to James Russell Lowell, Boston, 20 October [?],
Lowell Papers, MH.

20. Eliza Lee Follen to Joseph Congdon, Esq., West Roxbury, 17 June 1846,
Eliza Lee Cabot Follen Papers, MCR.

21. Ellis Gray Loring to Anna Loring, Brookline, 22 December 1851, Loring
Family Papers, MCR.

22. Louisa Loring to Anna Loring, Boston, 2 January 1855, Loring Family
Papers, MCR; Maria Weston Chapman to Mary Estlin, n.p., January, 1858,
Chapman to Eliza Wigham, n.p., 11 February 1859 [Copy by Mary Estlin], Estlin
Papers, Dr. Williams's Library, London. Hereafter cited as LDW. Cf. also Anne
Warren Weston, "The Sixteenth National Anti-Slavery Bazaar," *Liberator*, 25
January 1850; Maria Weston Chapman, et al., "The Twenty-Third National
Anti-Slavery Bazaar," *Liberator*, 16 May 1856.

23. Thomas Wentworth Higginson, "Anti-Slavery Days," *Outlook* 60 (September 1898): 47.

24. Maria Weston Chapman to Anne Weston, n.p. [1841?], Weston Papers,
MB; Samuel May, Jr. to George T. Davis, Leicester, 29 June 1840, May Papers,
MB; Lydia Maria Child to Ellis Gray Loring, New York, 27 May 1841, Loring
Family Papers, MCR; Loring to Child, Boston, 29 April 1841, Loring's Letter-
book, MH; Vincent Y. Bowditch, *Life and Correspondence of Henry Ingersoll
Bowditch* (Boston: Houghton, Mifflin, & Co., 1902), 1:187–88; Henry Ingersoll
Bowditch to John Gorham Palfrey, Boston, 10 December 1847, Bowditch to
Palfrey, Boston, 28 February 1848, Bowditch to Palfrey, Boston, 10 January
1849, John Gorham Palfrey Papers, MH; Wendell Phillips Garrison and Francis
Jackson Garrison, *William Lloyd Garrison 1805–1879. The Story of His Life Told
by His Children* (New York: The Century Co., 1885–1889), 3:134; Letter of Loring
to editor of Boston Post, "Letters and Obituaries kept by Louisa Loring after
[her husband's] death," Loring Family Papers, MCR; Loring to Palfrey,
Boston, 27 December 1842, Loring to Palfrey, n.p., 24 March 1845, Loring to
Palfrey, Boston, 15 July 1857, Palfrey Papers, MH; Loring to Anne Weston,
Boston, 9 September 1853, Weston Papers, MB.

25. "I am disgusted with political partyism," exclaimed Samuel J. May. Still, he
wanted to go to the Liberty Party conventions to see whether anything could be
done by them to help the Negro obtain political rights. See Samuel J. May to

Maria Weston Chapman, Syracuse, 19 February 1846, Weston Papers, MB. Cf. also Samuel J. May to [Samuel May, Jr.], Buffalo, 12 August 1848, *Liberator,* 25 August 1848, Lydia Maria Child to Francis George Shaw, New York, 18 July 1844, Child Papers, MH; Elizabeth M. Geffen, *Philadelphia Unitarianism, 1796– 1861* (Philadelphia: University of Pennsylvania Press, 1961), p. 208; Geffen, "William Henry Furness, Philadelphia Antislavery Preacher," *Philadelphia Magazine of History and Biography* 82 (July 1958): 281.

26. Garrison and Garrison, 3:134–35; Samuel May, *Some Recollections of our Anti-Slavery Conflect* (Miami, Fla.: Mnemosyne Publishing Co., 1969 [1st ed., 1869]), pp. 313–21; William Henry Furness, *A Thanksgiving Discourse . . . November 27th, 1845* (n.p., n.d.), p. 20.

27. Samuel J. May to Joshua R. Giddings, Syracuse, 11 July 1848, Joshua R. Giddings Papers, Ohio Historical Society; William Henry Furness, *Two Discourses, Delivered June 25, A.M. and July 2, A.M., 1843* (Philadelphia: John Pennington, 1843), p. 21.

28. Garrison and Garrison, 3: 448–51.

29. Mumford, p. 185; John W. Chadwick, "Samuel May of Leicester," *New England Magazine* 20 (April 1899): 203, 206, 208–10; *Old Anti-Slavery Days. Proceedings of the Commemorative Meeting Held by the Danvers Historical Society, at the Town Hall, Danvers, April 26, 1893, with Introduction, Letters and Sketches* (Danvers: Danvers Mirror Print, 1893), pp. 101–2; Samuel A. Eliot, ed., *Heralds of a Liberal Faith* (Boston: American Unitarian Association, 1910), 3:235–237. Cf. also John W. Chadwick, "Rev. Samuel May," *Christian Register,* 7 April 1910; "The Rev. Samuel May," *Harvard Graduates Magazine,* 8 (March 1900): 395; Joseph Allen, *The Worcester Association and Its Antecedents* (Boston: Nichols and Noyes, 1868), pp. 376–77.

30. William Henry Furness, *A Sermon Occasioned by the Destruction of Pennsylvania Hall, and Delivered the Lord's Day Following, May 20, 1838, in the First Congregational Unitarian Church* (Philadelphia: John C. Clark, 1838), pp. 4–5; "Mr. Furness's Discourse," *Christian Register,* 14 July 1838.

31. Geffen, *Philadelphia Unitarianism,* pp. 190–91.

32. W. H. Furness, *A Sermon, Delivered May 14, 1841, on the Occasion of the National Fast Recommended by the President* (Philadelphia: John C. Clark, 1841), p. 11.

33. Geffen, "Furness," p. 270. For references to slavery in the prayers of Furness, cf. his *Domestic Worship* (Philadelphia: James Kay, Jun. & Bro., 1840), 43, 144, 222, 223, 245, 258–59.

34. Geffen, "Furness," pp. 272–78; Geffen, *Philadelphia Unitarianism,* pp. 190–96, 205–6.

35. Geffen, *Philadelphia Unitarianism,* p. 199.

36. Geffen, "Furness," p. 279.

37. William Henry Furness, *A Discourse Occasioned by the Boston Fugitive Slave Case, Delivered in the First Congregational Unitarian Church, Philadelphia, April 13, 1851* (Philadelphia: Merrihew and Thompson, 1851), pp. 9, 13. Furness recognized, said an observer, "*one revival of religion having happened since the days of the*

Apostles, and that is the one which . . . commenced twenty-five years ago, when the Anti-Slavery Society was organized!" See "Rev. William H. Furness," *Liberator,* 28 May 1858.

38. Quoted by Geffen, "Furness," pp. 278–79. Furness was "essentially a non-political man," said Elizabeth Geffen in a letter to the author, dated Annville, Pennsylvania, 28 January 1970.

39. Lydia Maria Child to Ellis Gray Loring, New York, 27 May 1841, Loring Family Papers, MCR; Chapman quoted by Geffen, "Furness," p. 278. Cf. also Lydia Maria Child to Francis George Shaw, New York, 27 May 1841, Child Papers, MH. William Still said of Furness: "Among the Abolitionists of Pennsylvania no man stands higher than Dr. Furness." See William Still, *The Underground Rail Road (Chicago: Johnson Publishing Co., 1970,* [Reprint of 1871 edition]), p. 684.

40. *Old Anti-Slavery Days,* p. 84.

41. W. H. Furness, *A Discourse, Delivered, January 5th, 1851, in the First Congregational Unitarian Church, in Philadelphia* (n.p., n.d.), p. 9.

42. Maria Weston Chapman to Henry Wadsworth Longfellow, n.p., October, 1844, Henry Wadsworth Longfellow Papers, MH.

43. Henrietta Sargent to Abby Kelley, Boston, 16 July 1841, Foster Papers, MWA.

44. Henry Ingersoll Bowditch to Maria Weston Chapman, Boston, 6 August 1843, Weston Papers, MB.

45. May defended the abolitionists' use of the Sabbath by saying that their meetings were more holy than most church services held in the United States. If the churches would preach an antislavery gospel, the Sunday meetings of the abolitionists would not be necessary. See Samuel May, Jr. to Edward Brooks Hall, Leicester, 20 October 1850 [copy of letter]; Hall to May, Providence, 22 October 1850; Hall to May, Providence, 28 October 1850; May to Hall, Leicester, 4 November 1850 [copy of letter]; May Papers, MB. Cf. also Samuel May, Jr. to J. B. Estlin, 15 December 1847, May Papers, MB; The question of holding an antislavery celebration on a Sunday was raised in 1854 when the Rescue of Jerry Day, October 1, fell on a Sunday. Samuel J. May said how better could a Sunday be used than to celebrate a good deed. See Samuel J. May to Gerrit Smith, Syracuse, 31 August 1854, Gerrit Smith Papers, Syracuse University.

46. Susan Cabot to Mary Estlin, London, 12 and 13 February [1851], Estlin Papers, LDW.

47. Mrs. Thomas J. Mumford, ed., *Life and Letters of Thomas J. Mumford, with Memorial Tributes* (Boston: George H. Ellis, 1879), p. 38.

48. Marian H. Studley, "An 'August First' in 1844," *New England Quarterly* 16 (December 1843): 567–69.

49. Samuel J. May, *Emancipation in the British W. Indies, August 1, 1834. An Address, Delivered in the First Presbyterian Church in Syracuse, on the First of August, 1845* (Syracuse: J. Barber, 1845), p. 3.

50. Studley, pp. 569, 575–76.

51. *Christian Register*, 22 July 1843. The announcement in the *Christian Register* for the antislavery picnic at Dedham in 1843 was the first major insertion for the abolitionists to be uncritically reported in this Unitarian paper. The fact that several Unitarian clergymen, e.g., Caleb Stetson, John Pierpont, Theodore Parker, Joseph Henry Allen, James Freeman Clarke, Robert C. Waterston, were to speak there, may have been one good reason to promote the picnic. See also *Christian Register*, 29 July 1843; 27 July 1844; 10 August 1844.

52. "Pic Nic at Dedham," *Child's Friend: Designed for Families and Sunday Schools* 1 (October 1843): 21–25. Mrs. Follen reprinted "Hal's" letter in a pocket-sized volume she compiled for the Anti-Slavery Fairs of 1846. Cf. Eliza Lee Follen, *The Liberty Cap* (Boston: Leonard C. Bowles, 1846).

53. Caleb Stetson, "The Child's Friend," *Christian Register*, 28 October 1843. To the *Register's* credit, the paper clearly stated that it did not approve of everything in Stetson's rebuttal. They also hoped that Mrs. Follen's magazine would have a good circulation.

54. Studley, p. 569; Henry Ingersoll Bowditch to Maria Weston Chapman, Boston, 6 August 1843, Weston Papers, MB.

55. W. Freeman Galpin, "Samuel Joseph May: 'God's Chore Boy,' " *New York History* 21 (April 1940): 144–46. For May's own account of the "Rescue of Jerry," see Samuel J. May, *Some Recollections of our Anti-Slavery Conflict* (Miami, Fl.: Mnemosyne Publishing Co., 1969), pp. 373–84. Cf. also Edward B. Ohrenstein, "Samuel Joseph May: Unitarian Minister and Social Radical," B.D. thesis, Meadville Theological School, 1937, pp. 54–58; Thomas J. Mumford, *Memoir of Samuel Joseph May* (Boston: Roberts Brothers, 1873), pp. 219–25; William H. Pease and Jane H. Pease, "Freedom and Peace: A Nineteenth Century Dilemma," *Midwest Quarterly* 9 (October 1967): 34–36.

56. Quoted by Ohrenstein, p. 58.

57. Samuel J. May to John Gorham Palfrey, Syracuse, 26 November, 1851, John Gorham Palfrey Papers, MH; May to William Henry Seward, Syracuse, 23 August 1853, May to Seward, Syracuse, 7 September 1853, May to Seward, Syracuse, 17 October 1855, William Henry Seward Collection, Rush Rhees Library, University of Rochester.

58. Bowditch, 1:222–23.

59. Ibid., pp. 226–28.

60. Lydia Maria Child to Louisa Loring, South Natick, n.d., Child Papers, MCR.

61. William Henry Furness, Christian Duty. *Three Discourses Delivered in the First Congregational Unitarian Church of Philadelphia, May 28th, June 4th, and June 11th, 1854 . . . with Reference to the Recent Execution of the Fugitive Slave Law in Boston and New York* (Philadelphia: Merrihew & Thompson's Steam Power Press, 1854), p. 22.

62. Furness, *Discourse Delivered April 13, 1851*, pp. 6, 8.

63. Lydia Maria Child to Francis George Shaw, Wayland, 3 June 1854, Child Papers, MH; Mrs. Chapman continued by mentioning her vigil by a dead loved

one. She recalled how on the following morning she stretched out her hand to the *Liberator* on the table as if to grasp a buoy before sinking. "I shall not be able to read it," she thought, "I shall care for nothing again." But she opened it and found to her "astonishment that all *that* highly sublimal part of existence was untouched by death." She related this scene to Mary Estlin, a Unitarian friend and Garrisonian comrade in England. Miss Estlin's beloved father had died and her whole life had been bound up in his. Mrs. Chapman received a short note from her that said, "He has gone so good, so perfect, so beloved. . . . You will, I know ask with fear and trembling how I feel. *The Liberator seems just as interesting to me as ever.* This will tell you all!" See Maria Weston Chapman to James Russell Lowell, n.p. [1855?], Lowell Papers, MH.

64. Lydia Maria Child to Anna Loring, Wayland, 8 June 1856, Loring Family Papers, MCR; Child to Sarah Blake (Sturgis) Shaw, Wayland, 3 August 1856, Child to Shaw, Wayland, 14 September 1856, Child to Shaw, 14 October 1856, Child Papers, MH.

65. Quoted by Mumford, p. 216.

66. Lydia Maria Child to Oliver Johnson, Wayland, 20 December 1859, MiU-C; Child to Sarah Blake (Sturgis) Shaw, Wayland, 22 December 1859, Child Papers, MH.

67. Samuel Sillen, *Women Against Slavery* (New York: Masses and Mainstream, 1955), pp. 45–46; Meltzer, p. 148.

68. Geffen, "Furness," p. 387; Maria Weston Chapman to Miss Whitelegge, n.p., 18 December 1859 [Copy by Mary Estlin], LDW.

69. William Henry Furness, *Put Up thy Sword. A Discourse Delivered Before Theodore Parker's Society, At the Music Hall, Boston, Sunday, March 11, 1860* (Boston: R. F. Wallcut, 1860), p. 14; Maria Weston Chapman to Mrs. Michell, n.p., 6 December 1859 [Copy by Mary Estlin], LDW; Samuel Johnson, "John Brown, 1859," MS Sermon, MSE; Chapman to Miss Whitelegge, n.p., 18 December 1859 [Copy by Mary Estlin], LDW; Lydia Maria Child to Sarah Blake (Sturgis) Shaw, Wayland, 28 December 1859, Child Papers, MH.

70. Maria Weston Chapman to [Harriet Beecher Stowe], Weymouth, 5 February [1858], Beecher-Stowe Papers, MCR.

71. Eliza Lee Follen, *To Mothers in the Free States*, Antislavery Tracts, no. 8 (New York: American Anti-Slavery Society, 1855), p. 3.

72. Lydia Maria Child to Sarah Blake (Sturgis) Shaw, Wayland, 3 August 1856; Child to Shaw, Wayland, 14 September 1856; Child to Shaw, Wayland, 27 October 1856; Child to Shaw, Wayland, 9 November 1856; Child Papers, MH.

73. Ohrenstein, p. 60; Lydia Maria Child to Sarah Blake (Sturgis) Shaw, Wayland, 3 August 1856; Child Papers, MH; Samuel J. May to James Freeman Clarke, Syracuse, 31 July 1856, Clarke Papers, MH.

74. Lydia Maria Child to Sarah Blake (Sturgis) Shaw, Wayland, 20 February 1857; Child to Shaw, Wayland, 20 March 1857; Child to Shaw, Wayland, 7 July 1857; Child to Shaw, 4 November 1859; Child Papers, MH.

75. Maria Weston Chapman to Mrs. Reid, n.p., 11 November 1860 [Copy by

Mary Estlin], LDW; Caleb Stetson to Samuel May, Jr., South Scituate, 27 October 1858; May Papers, MB; Samuel May, Jr. To Richard D. Webb, Leicester, 6 November 1860, May Papers, MB.

76. Samuel J. May to Maria Weston Chapman, Syracuse, 25 January, 1860, Weston Papers, MB; Chapman to Louisa Loring, n.p., [1859?], Loring Family Papers, MCR.

Notes to Chapter 6

1. James Freeman Clarke, "The Compromises and Slavery [1851?]," MS lecture, Clarke Papers, Houghton Library, Harvard University. Cited hereafter as MH.

2. John Pierpont to Susan F. Porter, Medford, 1 June 1852, Pierpont Papers, Rush Rhees Library, University of Rochester. Cited hereafter as NRU.

3. John Gorham Palfrey, "Address to the Free Soil Convention at Worcester, 1852," MS lecture, Palfrey Papers, MH.

4. James Freeman Clarke, "The Demoralization of the North by Slavery [1855]," MS lecture, Clarke Papers, MH.

5. James Freeman Clarke to [Ellis Gray Loring?], n.p., 24 April 1851 [draft of letter], Clarke Papers, MH.

6. James Freeman Clarke, "The Compromises and Slavery [1851?]," MS lecture, Clarke Papers, MH.

7. Harold Schwartz, "Fugitive Slave Days in Boston," *New England Quarterly* 27 (June 1954): 192; John T. Horton, "Millard Fillmore and the Things of God and Caesar," *Niagara Frontier* 2 (Spring 1955): 5–6; Weiss, 2:100–102.

8. Theodore Parker, "Circular," Boston, 23 December 1850 [printed letter and petition], Slavery in the United States Collection, American Antiquarian Society. Hereafter cited as MWA.

9. Theodore Parker to William H. Seward, Boston, 23 December 1855, William Henry Seward Collection, NRU.

10. James Freeman Clarke to Abiel Abbot Livermore, n.p., 11 September 1860, Clarke Papers, MH; Abe C. Ravitz, "John Pierpont: Portrait of a Nineteenth Century Reformer," Ph.D. dissertation, New York University, 1955, p. 185.

11. Orville Dewey to [James Freeman Clarke], Sheffield, 10 August 1853, Clarke Papers, MH; Ephraim Peabody to John Gorham Palfrey, Boston, 29 September 1852; Palfrey to Peabody, Cambridge, 2 October 1852, Palfrey Papers, MH.

12. Theodore Parker, "The Chief Sins of the People.—A Sermon Delivered at the Melodeon, Boston, on Fast Day, April 10, 1851," *The Collected Works of Theodore Parker*, Frances Power Cobbe, ed. (London: Truebner and Co., 1864), 7:274.

13. James Freeman Clarke to Theodore Parker, n.p., 4 October 1856, Clarke Papers, MH; Clarke, "Good Men for Public Office. VII. Vision of a Christian State," *Christian Inquirer*, 23 October 1858.

14. James Freeman Clarke, "Good Men for Public Office: What Can Be Done?" *Christian Inquirer*, 30 October 1858.

15. Theodore Parker to Charles Sumner, Boston, 26 April 1851, Sumner Papers, MH; Parker to Henry Wilson, Boston, 15 February 1855, Wilson to Parker, Senate Chamber, 28 February 1855, Parker to Wilson, Boston, 7 July 1855, John Weiss, *Life and Correspondence of Theodore Parker* (New York: D. Appleton and Co., 1864), 2:212–13.

16. Theodore Parker, "The Law of God and the Statutes of Men. A Sermon Preached at the Music Hall, in Boston, on Sunday, June 18, 1854," *Works*, 5:235–37.

17. James Freeman Clarke, "Anti-Slavery Lecture. Indiana Place, February 18, 1855," MS lecture, Clarke Papers, MH.

18. John Pierpont to G. W. Reynolds, West Medford, 25 June 1855, Pierpont Papers, MWA; David Mead, "Theodore Parker in Ohio," *Northwest Ohio Quarterly* 21 (Winter 1948–49): 20.

19. Theodore Parker to Charles Sumner, Boston, 14 June 1856, Sumner Papers, MH. This letter is also published in Weiss, 2:157–60. Cf. also Parker, "The Aspect of Freedom in America. A speech at the Mass. Anti-Slavery Celebration of Independence, at Abington, July 5, 1852," *Works*, 4:278.

20. Thomas Wentworth Higginson, *Cheerful Yesterdays* (London: Gay and Bird 1898), p. 148; Higginson quoted by Mary Thacher Higginson, *Thomas Wentworth Higginson: The Story of His Life* (Boston: Houghton, Mifflin Co., 1914), p. 142.

21. A coroner's inquest found that the guard had been stabbed. It was initially believed that he had been shot. See T. W. Higginson, pp. 155–57. Parker quoted by ibid., p. 155; John Gorham Palfrey to Ephraim Peabody, Cambridge, 6 June 1854, Palfrey Papers, MH. Cf. also Schwartz, pp. 204–6; M. T. Higginson, pp. 143–44.

22. Theodore Parker, "The New Crime Against Humanity. A Sermon Preached at the Music Hall, in Boston, on Sunday, June 4, 1854...," *Works*, 6:50. Cf. also the newspaper clippings in "The Kidnapping of Anthony Burns," scrapbook, Parker Papers, Boston Public Library. Hereafter cited as MB; M. T. Higginson, pp. 147–48; Thomas Wentworth Higginson to Robert Carter, Worcester, 11 June 1854, Higginson Papers, MH; James Hackett Fowler to Higginson, Cambridge, 30 June 1854, Burns Papers, MB. The Burns's Rendition was not, as Higginson called it, the "first act of violence." In the chronology of New England antislavery it was, but for the nation as a whole the "Christiana Riot" in Pennsylvania in 1851 was the first defense of fugitive slaves to result in bloodshed. See Benjamin Quarles, *Black Abolitionists* (New York: Oxford University Press, 1970), pp. 211–13.

23. T. W. Higginson, pp. 161–62; Theodore Parker, *The Trial of Theodore Parker, for the "Misdemeanor" of a Speech in Faneuil Hall Against Kidnapping, before the Circuit Court of the United States, at Boston, April 3, 1855 with the Defence* (Boston: Published by the Author, 1855).

24. Thomas Wentworth Higginson, *Massachusetts in Mourning. A Sermon, Preached in Worcester, on Sunday, June 4, 1854* (Boston: James Munroe and Co., 1854), pp. 4–5, 10–13, 15. Cf. *Liberator*, 16 June 1854.

25. James Freeman Clarke, *The Rendition of Anthony Burns. Its Causes and Consequences. A Discourse on Christian Politics, Delivered in Williams Hall, Boston, on Whitsunday, June 4, 1854* (Boston: Crosby, Nichols, and Co., 1854), pp. 8–9. The sermon was also published under the title "The Relation of Freedom to Slavery in America," *Christian Inquirer*, 1 July 1854.

26. Ibid., pp. 17–19.

27. Clarke, *Rendition of Anthony Burns*, pp. 21, 24, 27.

28. Parker, "New Crime Against Humanity," *Works*, 6:108.

29. James Freeman Clarke, "Clerical Defences of Slavery, Fast Day, April, 1856," MS sermon, Clarke Papers, MH.

30. James Freeman Clarke, "Lecture on Kansas—Indiana Place Chapel, February, 1856," MS lecture, Clarke Papers, MH.

31. Quoted by M. T. Higginson, p. 181. See also pp. 166–80; Tilden G. Edelstein, *Strange Enthusiasm: A Life of Thomas Wentworth Higginson* (New Haven: Yale University Press, 1968), pp. 182–83; Higginson, *Cheerful Yesterdays*, pp. 196–98.

32. Theodore Parker to Charles Sumner, Boston, 14 June 1856, Sumner Papers, MH; Parker to John P. Hale, Galesburg, Illinois, 21 October 1856, Weiss, 2:187; Frank B. Sanborn to Parker, Concord, 10 June 1856, Concord Free Public Library; Parker to Miss Hunt, n.p., 21 September 1845, Parker to Miss Hunt, n.p., 16 November 1856, Octavius Brooks Frothingham, *Theodore Parker: A Biography* (Boston: James R. Osgood and Co., 1876), pp. 438–39.

33. James Freeman Clarke to Thomas Wentworth Higginson, Jamaica Plain, 3 December 1856; Samuel Gridley Howe to Clarke, South Boston, 5 December n.y.; Clarke to Edward Everett Hale, Jamaica Plain, 10 December n.y.; Clarke, "Clothing for Kanzaz, [1856]," MS notes; Clarke Papers, MH.

34. Theodore Parker, "A New Lesson for the Day: A Sermon Preached at the Music Hall, in Boston, on Sunday, May 25, 1856," *Works*, 4:281, 293; Parker to John P. Hale, Boston, 23 August 1856, Sumner Papers, MH.

35. Parker, *Works*, 4:311.

36. Quoted by Weiss, 2:155.

37. Ibid., p. 69; Theodore Parker to Charles Sumner, Boston, 14 June 1836, Parker Papers, MH; Parker to Sumner, Burlington, Vermont, 21 May 1856, Parker Papers, MH. This letter is also in Weiss, 2:179–80.

38. Theodore Parker to William H. Seward, Boston, 6 December 1851, Parker to Seward, Boston, 11 February 1855, Parker to Seward, October, 1853, Seward Collection, NRU; Parker, "The Great Battle between Slavery and Freedom. Considered in Two Speeches, Delivered before the American Anti-Slavery Society at New York," *Works*, 6:266; Weiss, 2:190; Parker, "The Present Crisis in American Affairs: The Slave-Holders' Attempt to Wrench the Territories from the Working People, and to Spread Bondage Over All the Land. Delivered on . . . May 7, [1856]," *Works*, 6:285.

39. James Freeman Clarke to [Peter Lesley], Jamaica Plain, 19 August 1856, American Philosophical Society Library.

40. James Freeman Clarke, "Who Shall We Vote For? [1856]," MS lecture, Clarke Papers, MH.

41. Sister Thomas Catherine Brennan, "Thomas Wentworth Higginson: Reformer and Man of Letters," Ph.D. dissertation, Michigan State University, 1958, p. 257; Edelstein, p. 183; Higginson, *Cheerful Yesterdays*, p. 215; Higginson quoted by M. T. Higginson, pp. 179–80; Parker, "Present Crisis in American Affairs," *Works*, 6:272; Theodore Parker to Horace Mann, Boston, 27 June 1856, Weiss, 2:188.

42. Higginson, *Cheerful Yesterdays*, pp. 236–37; Higginson quoted by Wendell Phillips Garrison and Francis Jackson Garrison, *William Lloyd Garrison, 1805–1879. The Story of His Life Told by His Children* (New York: The Century Co., 1885–1889), 3:449.

43. Garrison and Garrison, 3:450; Thomas Wentworth Higginson to John Gorham Palfrey, Worcester, 30 December 1856, Palfrey Papers, MH; Theodore Parker to Higginson, Railroad cars from New Haven to Boston, 18 January 1857, Weiss, 2:192–94.

44. Mary Thacher Higginson, ed., *Letters and Journals of Thomas Wentworth Higginson* (Boston: Houghton, Mifflin Co., 1921), p. 77; Thomas Wentworth Higginson to John Gorham Palfrey, Worcester, 17 January 1857, Palfrey Papers, MH; M. T. Higginson, *Higginson*, p. 181; "Call for a National Convention" [Printed petitions for the call of a national convention to meet, October, 1857, to consider "the practicability, probability, and expediency of a Separation between the Free and Slave States."], Slavery in the United States Collection, MWA.

45. Edward Everett Hale, ed., *James Freeman Clarke, Autobiography, Diary and Correspondence* (Boston: Houghton, Mifflin and Co., 1891), pp. 234–35; "Letter from Rev. J. F. Clarke to the Editor of the Boston Courier," *Christian Inquirer*, 5 September 1857.

46. Higginson, *Cheerful Yesterdays*, p. 239; M. T. Higginson, *Higginson*, p. 181.

47. Parker, "Present Aspect of the Anti-Slavery Enterprise," *Works*, 6:237.

48. Theodore Parker, "The Present Aspect of Slavery in America, and the Immediate Duty of the North. A Speech Delivered in the Hall of the State House, Before the Massachusetts Anti-Slavery Convention, on Friday, January 29, 1858," *Works*, 6:319.

49. Parker, "Present Aspect of Slavery in America, . . ." *Works*, 6:321–22.

50. John Brown to Thomas Wentworth Higginson, Rochester, 2 February 1858, Higginson, *Cheerful Yesterdays*, pp. 216–17.

51. Quoted by M. T. Higginson, *Higginson*, p. 191.

52. Higginson, *Cheerful Yesterdays*, pp. 217–23; Edelstein, p. 210; Stephen B. Oates, *To Purge This Land with Blood: A Biography of John Brown* (New York: Harper and Row, 1970), p. 271, and passim.

53. Quoted by Edelstein, p. 211.

54. Higginson, *Cheerful Yesterdays*, pp. 153–54; Theodore Parker to Francis Jackson, Rome, 24 November 1859, Weiss, 2:174–75; Parker, "Present Aspect of the Anti-Slavery Enterprise," *Works*, 6:217.

55. Parker, "Present Aspect of Slavery in America," *Works*, 6:289–90.

56. Theodore Parker to Francis Jackson, Rome, 24 November 1859, Weiss, 2:176.

57. Parker, "Present Crisis in American Affairs," *Works*, 6:257.

58. Theodore Parker to Mrs. Apthorp, Frederikstad, March, 1859, Weiss, 2:287.

59. Theodore Parker to Andrew L. Russell, Santa Cruz, 23 April 1859, [copy of letter], Sanborn Papers, MH.

61. James Freeman Clarke, "Ethnology as Applied to the Slavery Question and some Remarks on the Dred Scott [Case], 1857," MS lecture, Clarke Papers, MH. Cf. also Clarke, *Present Condition of the Free Colored of the United States* (New York: American Anti-Slavery Society, 1859).

62. Clarke, "Ethnology."

63. James Freeman Clarke to [Henry Wilson], Boston, 17 April 1860, Clarke Papers, MH.

64. Theodore Parker to Francis Jackson, Rome, 24 November 1859, Weiss, 2:170.

65. Quoted by Edelstein, p. 224.

66. Quoted by Edelstein, pp. 227–28; M. T. Higginson, *Higginson*, pp. 194–95; Thomas Wentworth Higginson to his mother, Worcester, 5 November 1859, M. T. Higginson, *Letters and Journals*, p. 87. Intrigued by the subject of slave insurrection, Higginson wrote in the 1850s and 1860s several studies on this topic. In 1889 the essays appeared as a part of *Travellers and Outlaws*, and have recently been reprinted as a separate volume. See Thomas Wentworth Higginson, *Black Rebellion* (New York: Arno Press and the New York Times, 1969).

67. Quoted by James Freeman Clarke, *Memorial and Biographical Sketches* (Boston: Houghton, Mifflin, and Co., 1878), p. 21.

68. James Freeman Clarke, *Causes and Consequences of the Affair at Harper's Ferry. A Sermon Preached in the Indiana Place Chapel, on Sunday Morning, Nov. 6, 1859* (Boston: Walker, Wise, and Co., 1859), p. 4; Hale, p. 237.

69. James Freeman Clarke to Theodore Parker, Jamaica Plain, 5 October 1859, Clarke Papers, MH.

70. Hale, p. 238; Weiss, 2:73; John White Chadwick, *Theodore Parker: Preacher and Reformer* (Boston: Houghton, Mifflin, and Co., 1901), pp. 328, 334; Edelstein, pp. 239–40.

71. James Freeman Clarke, "Address made in Indiana Place Chapel—Sunday evening—Nov. 4th, 1860, on the Issues and Parties in the Coming Presidential Election," MS sermon, Clarke Papers, MH.

72. James Freeman Clarke, *Everyday Religion* (Boston: Houghton, Mifflin, and Co., 1886), p. 436.

NOTES TO CHAPTER 7

1. Samuel J. May to Jason Whitman, Brooklyn, Conn., 13 May 1834, American Unitarian Association Letters, Andover-Harvard Theological Library. Hereafter cited as MH-AH. *The Report of the British and Foreign Unitarian Association; the Proceedings of the Annual General Meeting, 1843* (London: Richard and John E. Taylor, 1843), p. 43.

2. Alma Lutz, *Crusade for Freedom: Women of the Antislavery Movement* (Boston: Beacon Press, 1968), pp. 68–69; Wendell Phillips Garrison and Francis Jackson Garrison, *William Lloyd Garrison 1805–1879. The Story of His Life Told by His Children* (New York: The Century Co., 1885–1889), 2:149; Maria Weston Chapman, "Notes on William Ellery Channing and the Abolitionists" [title supplied], Weston Papers, Boston Public Library. Cited hereafter as MB.

3. Maria Weston Chapman, "Theodore Parker and the Abolitionists" [title supplied], Weston Papers, MB.

4. Francis J. Garrison to W. C. Ford, Boston, 10 May 1900, Weston Papers, MB.

5. Ellis Gray Loring, "Diary," entry for 18 March 1838, Loring Family Papers, MCR; Loring to William Ellery Channing, Boston, 26 February 1840, Loring to Harriet Martineau, Boston, 22 March 1840, Loring's Letterbook, Houghton Library, Harvard University. Cited hereafter as MH.

6. Loring, "Diary," See entry for 25 March 1838; "Diary of Deborah Weston," See entries indicated as Sunday 5 and Sunday 11, Weston Papers, MB; Lydia Maria Child to John Gorham Palfrey, Wayland, 1 January 1865, John Gorham Palfrey Papers, MH; Child to Frances George and Sarah Blake (Sturgis) Shaw, Northampton, 17 August 1838, Lydia Maria Child Papers, MH; Francis Jackson to T. R. Sullivan, Boston, 8 April 1836; Jackson to James Boyd, Isaac Parker, and Moses Everett, Esq., Standing Committee of the Hollis Street Society, Boston, 12 October 1837; James Boyd, Moses Everett, and Isaac Parker to Jackson, Boston, 27 October 1837; Jackson to James Boyd, Everett, and Parker, Boston, 29 October 1837 [copy of reply]; Jackson to John Pierpont, Boston, 9 November 1837; Antislavery Letters, MB.

7. Ellis Gray Loring, "Diary." See entries for 19 March 1838, 22 March 1838, Loring Family Papers, MCR; William Lloyd Garrison, *The Letters of William Lloyd Garrison*, Walter Merrill, ed. (Cambridge: Harvard University Press, 1971), 1:557; Lydia Maria Child to Francis George Shaw, New York, 27 May 1841, Child to Shaw, New York, 2 August 1846, Lydia Maria Child Papers, MH; Vincent Y. Bowditch, *Life and Correspondence of Henry Ingersoll Bowditch by His Son* (Boston: Houghton, Mifflin and Co., 1902), 1:124–25; Child to Louisa Loring, New York, 11 July, n.y., Child to Ellis Gray Loring, Wayland, 3 July 1856, Child Papers, Mi-UC; Child to Sarah Blake (Sturgis) Shaw, Wayland, 25 October 1857, Child Papers, MH; Anne Warren Weston to Deborah Weston, Chauncy Place, 15 January 1842, Anne Weston to Deborah Weston, Boston, 1 January 1837, Anne Weston to Deborah Weston, 22 January 1837; "Diary of Deborah Weston." Cf. entries for 11 Sunday, 26 Sunday, 10 Sunday, and passim, Weston Papers,

MB. For an explication and defense of the religious views of Maria Weston Chapman and her sisters, see Samuel May, Jr. "Fragment of a letter," [1 July 1859?], May Papers, MB.

8. John W. Chadwick, "Samuel May of Leicester," *New England Magazine* 20 (April 1899): 208; Samuel May, Jr., to Richard D. Webb, Boston, 18 February 1850, May Papers, MB.

9. Samuel May, Jr., to Mary Carpenter, Leicester, 15 July 1851, May Papers, MB.

10. Samuel May, Jr. to George Armstrong, Geneva, Switzerland, 9 October 1843, May Papers, MB.

11. Samuel May, Jr. to Richard D. Webb, Boston, 16 July 1847, May to John Bishop Estlin, Boston, 30 September 1847, May to Estlin, Boston, 15 December 1847, May Papers, MB; Maria Weston Chapman to Carolina Weston, n.p., n.d., Weston Papers, MB.

12. James Freeman Clarke, "Introduct[ory] Lecture at Salem, Oct. 4th, 1858. 'What has the North to do with Slavery?' " MS lecture, James Freeman Clarke Papers, MH.

13. James Freeman Clarke, "Anti-Slavery Lecture. Indiana Place, Feb. 18th, 1855," MS lecture, Clarke Papers, MH.

14. [Sixteenth] *Annual Report of the American Unitarian Association* (Boston: Bowles and Dearborn, 1841), pp. 38–39; Samuel May, Jr., "Resolutions Offered at Autumnal Unitarian Conference held at Worcester, Massachusetts, 1842" [title supplied] May Papers, MB; *18th A.U.A. Annual Report, 1843*, pp. 24–28, 35–36.

15. *The Thirteenth Annual Report of the American and Foreign Anti-Slavery Society, Presented at New York, May 11, 1853* . . . (New York: American and Foreign Anti-Slavery Society, 1853), pp. 105–8.

16. Samuel J. May to Amos A. Phelps, South Scituate, 26 December 1837, Phelps Papers, MB; "Miss Martineau's Opinion of the American Clergy," *Christian Register*, 8 July 1837; Stephen S. Foster, *The Brotherhood of Thieves; or, a True Picture of the American Church and Clergy* . . . (Boston: Anti-Slavery Society, 1844), pp. 58–59; William Goodell, *Slavery and Anti-Slavery; A History of the Great Struggle in Both Hemispheres; with a View of the Slavery Question in the United States* (New York: William Harned, 1852), p. 196.

17. Samuel J. May, *Some Recollections of Our Anti-Slavery Conflict* (Miami, Fl.: Mnemosyne Publishing Co., 1969 [1st ed., 1869]), pp. 335–37.

18. Samuel May, Jr., to John Bishop Estlin, Boston, 15 April 1847, May Papers, MB.

19. Samuel Johnson to Samuel Longfellow, Salem, 26 June 1849 [draft of letter], Samuel Johnson Papers, James Duncan Phillips Library Essex Institute, Salem, Massachusetts. Hereafter cited as MSE; Samuel A. Eliot, ed., *Heralds of a Liberal Faith* (Boston: American Unitarian Association, 1910), 3:359.

20. Caleb Stetson to Samuel May, Jr., South Scituate, 27 October 1858, May Papers, MB; Anne Warren Weston to Deborah Weston, Groton, 13 July 1842,

Weston Papers, MB; Edward W. Ohrenstein, "Samuel Joseph May: Unitarian Minister and Social Radical," B.D. thesis, Meadville Theological School, 1937), pp. 41–43.

21. Richard H. Sewell, *John P. Hale and the Politics of Abolition* (Cambridge: Harvard University Press), p. 33; Earl Morse Wilbur, *A Historical Sketch of the Independent Congregational Church, Meadville, Pennsylvania, 1825–1900* (Meadville, 1902), p. 45; Edward James Young, *Tribute to Octavius Brooks Frothingham* [Reprinted from the Proceedings of the Massachusetts Historical Society, December, 1895] (Cambridge: John Wilson and Sons, 1895), p. 6; George A. Stearns, *The First Parish in Waltham: A Historical Sketch* (Boston, 1914), pp. 39–40; Harold Kenneth Shelby, "Liberal Religion in Rockford, Illinois, 1841–1943," B.D. thesis, Meadville Theological School, 1945, pp. 38, 43; Charles A. Murdock, *Horatio Stebbins: His Ministry and His Personality* (Boston: Houghton Mifflin Co., 1921), pp. 24–25; Henry Dyer Locke, *An Ancient Parish: An Historical Survey of the First Parish, Watertown, Massachusetts* (Boston: Stetson Press, 1930), p. 16; Samuel Longfellow, *Parting Words: A Discourse, Preached, Sunday, June 24, 1860, in the New Chapel, Brooklyn* (New York: John A. Gray, 1860), p. 21; Moncure Daniel Conway, *Autobiography, Memories and Experiences*, 1:242, 248. For Shaw, Tenney, and Babcock, see Charles Richard Denton, "American Unitarians, 1830–1865: A Study of Religious Opinion on War, Slavery, and the Union," Ph.D. dissertation, Michigan State University, 1969, pp. 92–93.

22. Leonard Freeman Burbank, *History of the First Unitarian Society in Dunstable New Nashua 1826–1926* (Nashua: F. E. Cole and Co., n.d.), p. 69; "The Westminster Church [Providence, Rhode Island]," newspaper clipping, Poor Family Papers, Schlesinger Library, Radcliffe College; David A. Wasson to Samuel Johnson, Groveland, 30 December 1853, MSE.

23. May, p. 24; The figures for articles on slavery were obtained by a careful reading of the *Christian Register* between the dates cited. Items invariably are missed and the margin of error can be wide. Moreover, the figures given do not take into account the length in column inches of each article. The figures at least suggest that the *Christian Register* was neither pro-slavery nor antislavery, but partial to what it considered to be a conservative solution to the problem of slavery—colonization.

24. "Slavery and the Christian Register," *Christian Register*, 22 June 1837; "Editorial Retrospect," *Christian Register*, 29 December 1838.

25. Clarence Gohdes, "Some Notes on the Unitarian Church in the Ante-Bellum South: A Contribution to the History of Southern Liberalism," *American Studies in Honor of William Kenneth Boyd*, David K. Jackson, ed. (Durham: Duke University Press, 1940), p. 327; *5th A.U.A. Annual Report, 1830*, p. 58; *7th A.U.A. Annual Report, 1832*, pp. 65, 71.

26. *8th A.U.A. Annual Report, 1833*, p. 19; James Freeman Clarke to William Henry Channing, Louisville, 4 October 1833, Clarke Papers, MH; Clarke to the editor of the *Western Messenger*, New Orleans, 22 December 1835, *Western Messenger* 1 (February 1836): 587.

27. *9th A.U.A. Annual Report, 1834*, pp. 38–39, 40, 44; *10th A.U.A. Annual Report, 1835*, pp. 47–50; *11th A.U.A. Annual Report, 1836*, pp. 19–20, 34.

28. Gohdes, p. 331.

29. *12th A.U.A. Annual Report, 1837*, pp. 13, 26, 28, 31; *13th A.U.A. Annual Report, 1835*, pp. 8, 13–15, 38–39; *14th A.U.A. Annual Report, 1839*, pp. 18–19, 34.

30. For a concise statement of the various schisms that took place in America's denominations, cf. Lowell H. Zuck, "The American Anti-Slavery Movement in the Churches before the Civil War," *Zeitschrift Fuer Religions-Und Geistesgeschichte* 17 (1965): 361–64; *16th A.U.A. Annual Meeting*, 1841, p. 40.

31. *16th A.U.A. Annual Meeting*, pp. 37–40.

32. Samuel May, Jr., "Resolutions Offered at Autumnal Unitarian Conference held at Worcester, Massachusetts, 1842" [title supplied], MS notes, May Papers, MB.

33. Denton, pp. 83–85; It was said of Motte that "he had a mental delicacy and reserve that made him shrink from putting himself forward." Edward Everett Hale remarked that his ministry in Boston was "no sensational history" and "no exciting tale." See Samuel A. Eliot, 1:259–60, 262.

34. "The Officers of the American Unitarian Association in Correspondence with the Unitarian Church at Savannah," *Christian Register*, 11 March 1843; "The A.U.A. and the Church at Savannah," *Christian Register*, 1 April 1843; "American Unitarian Association and the Unitarian Society at Savannah," *Christian Register*, 22 April 1843.

35. *Christian Register*, 11 March 1843; *Christian Register*, 18 March 1843; "The A.U.A. and the Church at Savannah," *Christian Register*, 1 April 1843; *Christian Register*, 15 April 1843; *Monthly Miscellany* (1843), p. 253. Hereafter cited as MM.

36. *18th A.U.A. Annual Report, 1843*, pp. 24–28.

37. Ibid., pp. 35–36.

38. Anne W. Weston to [?], n.p., 29 May [1843], Weston Papers, MB.

39. [George Harris], "Slavery in America," *Christian Pioneer* 18 (January 1844): 19.

40. Chadwick, p. 211; William James, *Memoir of John Bishop Estlin, Esq., F.L.S., F.R.C.S.* [from the *Christian Reformer* for August, 1855] (London: Charles Green, 1855), p. 16; May, pp. 339–40.

41. "Address of the Irish Unitarian Christian Society to Their Brethren in America," *Christian Register*, 2 September 1843; same, with editorial comment in *MM*, pp. 184–85; John James Tayler, *Letters Embracing [the] Life of John James Tayler, B.A.*, John Hamilton Thom, ed. (London: Philip Green, 1905), pp. 255–56; Russell Lant Carpenter, ed., *Memoirs of the Life and Work of Philip Pearsall Carpenter . . . Chiefly Derived from His Letters*, 2d ed. (London: C. Kegan Paul & Co., 1880), pp. 63–64; Harris, pp. 23–27; "An Address from the Unitarian Ministers of Great Britain and Ireland, to their Ministerial Brethren of the Unitarian Churches in the United States of North America," *Christian Register*, 27 January 1844; *An Address From the Undersigned Unitarian Ministers of Great Britain and Ireland, to their Ministerial Brethren of the Unitarian Churches in the United States of*

North America. December 1st, 1843 (Bristol: Philip and Evans, n.d.), [printed copy amended and corrected by George Armstrong], George Armstrong Papers, Manchester College, Oxford.

42. May, p. 338; James Freeman Clarke to Samuel May, Jr., n.p., 26 February 1844, May Papers, MB.

43. "Letter from Great Britain upon Slavery," *Monthly Religious Magazine* 1 (May 1844): 178–79, cited hereafter as MRM; "The Letter of the English Unitarian Ministers on Slavery," *Christian Register*, 20 April 1844; John H. Morison to Samuel K. Lothrop, Salem, 7 April 1844, May Papers, MB; Samuel May, "Secretary's Minutes of the Adjourned Meeting of the Unitarian Ministers to Discuss the Slavery Question, April 11, 1844" [title supplied], May Papers, MB; [George Harris], "Slavery in America," *Christian Pioneer* 18 (December 1844): 533–38; "Reply of the American Unitarian Ministers to the Address on Slavery," *Inquirer*, 11 September 1844.

44. "Letter of Some American Unitarian Ministers on Slavery," *Christian Register*, 30 November 1844; "Letter to England," *Christian Register*, 11 January 1845.

45. "Letter to England," *Christian Register*, 11 January 1845; "The American Unitarians and Slavery," *Inquirer*, 21 December 1844.

46. Samuel May, Jr., "The Annual Business Meeting of the A.U.A., May 28, 1844" [title supplied], MS notes, May Papers, MB; *19th A.U.A. Annual Report*, 1844, p. 9.

47. May's resolution did say that the "Executive Committee be instructed . . . to accompany . . . assistance [to Southern congregations] with a protest against the institution of Slavery." See Eliot, 3:233, 235; Chadwick, p. 211.

48. May, "Annual Business Meeting"; S. J. May, *Recollections*, pp. 340–41.

49. May, "Annual Business Meeting"; May, *Recollections*, p. 341. On the appearance of Samuel J. May's "Recollections" in 1869, Gannett disputed that he had said "hellish spirit," but May, Jr., who had taken notes on the meeting, confirmed that the phrase had been used by Gannett. See Ezra Stiles Gannett to Samuel J. May, Boston, 29 October 1869, Samuel J. May to Samuel May, Jr., Syracuse, 1 November [1869], Samuel May, Jr., to Samuel J. May, Leicester, 2 November 1869, May Papers, MB.

50. Eliot, 3:233, 235; Samuel May, Jr., to Samuel J. May, Leicester, 2 November 1869, May Papers, MB; May, Jr. "Reminiscences of A.U.A. Meeting on Slavery—May, 1844," MS notes, May Papers, MB.

51. May, Jr., "Annual Meeting."

52. *19th A.U.A. Annual Report, 1844*, pp. 39–42.

53. May, Jr., "Annual Business Meeting"; May, *Recollections*, pp. 342–43; May, Jr., "Reminiscences"; *MRM* 1 (June 1844): 211.

54. Samuel May, Jr., to Maria Weston Chapman, Leicester, 23 July 1844, Weston Papers, MB.

55. May, *Recollections*, p. 343; Samuel May, Jr., "American Unitarians," MS notes, May Papers, MB.

56. Samuel May, Jr., to Maria Weston Chapman, Leicester, 23 July 1844, May Papers, MB.

57. May, Jr., "Reminiscences."

58. George Armstrong to Samuel May, Jr., Clifton Vale, Bristol, 8 July 1844, Robert Henderson, *A Memoir of the Late Rev. George Armstrong*. . . . London: Edward T. Whitfield, 1859), pp. 358–59.

59. "London Inquirer—American Unitarian Association—Slavery," *Christian Register*, 4 September 1844; Francis Parkman, "Courtesy and Charity of Abolitionism," *Christian Register*, 18 October 1845.

60. *20th A.U.A. Annual Report, 1845*, p. 20.

61. An announcement of the meeting signed by the Mays, Clarke, Nathaniel Hall, A. P. Peabody [!], et al., appeared in the *Christian Register*, 10 May, 17 May, and 24 May, 1845; "Discussion of Slavery," *MRM* 2 (May 1845): 212; [Theodore Parker], "Extracts from his Journals," F. B. Sanborn Papers, MH.

62. "Clerical Meeting on Slavery," *Christian Examiner* 39 (July 1845): 135; *Christian Register*, 21 June 1845; Samuel May, Jr. "Notes on Association Meeting at Marlboro Hall, May, 1845" [title supplied], May Papers, MB; Among those on the committee of twelve were Clarke, John Parkman, May, Jr., S. J. May, Bulfinch, A. P. Peabody, and William Henry Channing. See "Meeting of Clergymen for the Discussion of Slavery," *Christian Register*, 7 June 1845.

63. [James Freeman Clarke], *American Slavery. A Protest Against American Slavery, by One Hundred and Seventy-Three Unitarian Ministers* (Boston: B. H. Greene, 1845), pp. 4–8, 12. Samuel J. May gave Caleb Stetson, John Turner Sargent, and Samuel May, Jr., as the authors of the "Protest." But in a letter to Samuel May, Jr., in 1883, Clarke corrected Samuel J. May's mistake. "I wrote," said Clarke, "the Unitarian Protest against Slavery." See May, *Recollections*, p. 344; Clarke to May, Jr., n.p., 4 February 1883, MH. To declare that political measures had failed was a puzzling remark for Clarke to make. He may have acceded here to the wishes of other members of the committee, who felt perhaps that political measures held no hope for emancipation. John Parkman objected to this negative attitude toward politics and thought the "Protest" too considerate of slaveholders. The latter emphasis he attributed to the influence of Bulfinch. See John Parkman, Jr., to Samuel May, Jr., Cape Elizabeth, 29 July 1845, May Papers, MB.

64. May, *Recollections*, p. 344; Samuel May, Jr., "Non-Subscribing Unitarian Ministers to the Protest Against Slavery, issued October, 1845," MS list, May Papers, MB; George Putnam to Caleb Stetson, Roxbury, 9 August 1845, Putnam to Stetson, Roxbury, 16 September 1845, Stetson to May, Jr., Medford, 16 October 1845, May Papers, MB; "Protest Against American Slavery by One Hundred and Seventy Unitarian Ministers" [Three more signatures were later added], *Christian Register*, 4 October 1845. Emphasis added.

65. *Letter to Rev. Jason Whitman, by a Southerner, and Mr. Whitman's Reply. Occasioned by the Protest of Unitarian Ministers Against American Slavery*, no. 18, Tract for the Times (Boston: Office of the Christian World, 1845), pp. 4, 12, 23. The tract was also published in the *Christian Register* 24 (29 November 1845); George F. Simmons to Henry W. Bellows, Waltham (on a visit), 8 November 1845,

MHi; Theodore Parker to Charles Sumner, West Roxbury, 21 March 1846, Sumner Papers, MH.

66. Samuel May, Jr., to J. B. Estlin, Leicester, 7 March 1846, May Papers, MB.

67. "Address of the Irish Unitarian Christian Society to their Brethren in America," *Christian Register*, 21 March 1846.

68. *21st A.U.A. Annual Report, 1846*, pp. 3–4; Samuel May, Jr., to J. B. Estlin, Boston, 15 December 1847, May Papers, MB; *Christian Register*, 30 May 1846.

69. *21st A.U.A. Annual Report, 1846*, pp. 23, 28–33, 38–40, 43–46.

70. "Ministerial Conference," *MRM* 3 (June 1846): 287–88; "Antislavery Meeting," p. 288; Samuel May, Jr., to J. B. Estlin, Leicester, 30 May 1846, May Papers, MB; [William Henry Fish], "Impressions of Anniversary Week," *Christian Register*, 27 June 1846.

71. "Regular Autumnal Convention of Unitarian Denomination," *Christian Inquirer*, 31 October 1846.

72. "Misapprehensions of English Unitarians," *Christian Register*, 14 August 1847; *22nd A.U.A. Annual Report, 1847*, pp. 8–9.

73. "Ministerial Conference," *MRM* 4 (May 1847): 284; [Theodore Parker], "Extracts from his Journals," Sanborn Papers, MH.

74. "Convention at Salem," MRM 4 (1847): 524–27; "Autumnal Convention at Salem," *Christian Register*, 6 November 1847; "Memorial of Unitarians," *MRM* 4 (1847): 575–76; "Hon. J. P. Hale's Speech," *Christian Register*, 5 February 1848. Clarke's "friend" was probably Samuel May, Jr., who had left the Unitarian ministry in 1847.

75. John G. Palfrey to [Unitarian Festival Committee], U.S. House of Representatives, 26 May 1848, Palfrey Papers, MH; "Autumnal Convention at New Bedford," *Christian Register*, 28 October 1848.

76. See "Mrs. Dana and Mr. Haughton," *Christian Register,* 12 September 1846; "Mr. Haughton and Mrs. Dana," *Christian Register,* 14 November 1846; "British and Foreign Unitarian Association," *Christian Register*, 10 July 1847; "Ezra S. Gannett and George Armstrong Correspondence" [title supplied], *Christian Register*, 24 July 1847; "Rev. Dr. Dewey's Letter," and "Dr. Dewey's Letter—Abolitionism," *Christian Register*, 7 August 1847; "To the Rev. Charles Briggs," and "Misapprehensions of English Unitarians," *Christian Register*, 14 August 1847; George W. Briggs, Samuel May, Jr., et al. "A Response to the Address of the Irish Unitarian Christian Society. . . ," *Christian Register*, 30 October 1847; George E. Ellis, "Correspondence Between English and American Unitarians on Slavery," *Christian Register*, 11 December 1847.

77. Samuel May, Jr., to [J. B.] Estlin, Boston, 30 September 1847, May to Estlin, Boston, 31 October 1847, May Papers, MB; Estlin to [Mrs. Maria Weston Chapman], Bristol, 2 September 1847, Weston Papers, MB; "English and American Unitarians," *Christian Register*, 28 August 1847. See also May to Richard D. Webb, Boston, 16 July 1847, May to Estlin, Boston, 15 August 1847, May to Estlin, 7 March 1848, Joseph Hutton to May, n.p., 28 March 1848, May Papers, MB.

78. "English and American Unitarians," *Christian Register*, 28 August 1847;

"Gannett and George Harris Correspondence" [title supplied], *Christian Register*, 11 September 1847; "Correspondence Between Unitarians in America, and Unitarians in England and Scotland," *Christian Register*, 11 December 1847; *Reply to the Invitation of the Friends of Unitarian Christianity in Boston to their Brethren in a Common Faith in England and Scotland* [printed petition], May Papers, MB; Samuel May, Jr., to J. B. Estlin, Boston, 15 December 1847, May Papers, MB; "Anniversary of the Irish Unitarian Christian Society," *Christian Register*, 29 July 1848.

79. "Autumnal Convention at New Bedford," *Christian Register*, 28 October 1848; "Eighth Unitarian Autumnal Convention at Portland," *Christian Register*, 20 October 1849. Richard Sykes in his study of the class structure of Unitarian parishes indicates that the Unitarians were associated with the highest quartile of income. See his "The Changing Class Structure of Unitarian Parishes in Massachusetts, 1780–1880," *Review of Religious Research* 12 (Fall 1970): 28.

80. *25th A.U.U. Annual Report, 1850*, p. 46.

81. "Our Future. Alleged Divisions Among Us," *Christian Inquirer*, 16 November 1850; "Protests Against Slavery," *Christian Register*, 17 July 1847.

82. Samuel May, Jr., "American Unitarians," MS notes, May Papers, MB; "Autumnal Convention," *MRM* 7 (November 1850): 523; "Autumnal Convention," *Christian Register*, 26 October 1850.

83. [Mary Willard, ed.], *Life of Rev. Samuel Willard, D.D., A.A.S. of Deerfield, Mass.* (Boston: Geo. H. Ellis, 1892), pp. 182–85; "Autumnal Convention," *Christian Register*, 26 October 1850; S. J. May, *Recollections*, p. 366.

84. Mary Willard, p. 185; "Autumnal Convention," *Christian Register*, 26 October 1850; "Autumnal Convention," *MRM* 7 (November 1850): 525–27; John Pierpont to Samuel May, Jr., Medford, 23 June 1853, May Papers, MB.

85. S. J. May, *Recollections*, pp. 366–70; "Slavery Discussion at the Unitarian Ministerial Conference," "Action of the American Unitarian Association on the Fugitive Slave Law," *Liberator*, 6 June 1851.

86. S. J. May, *Recollections*, pp. 370–72; Theodore Parker, "Speech at the Ministerial Conference in Boston, May 29, 1851," *Collected Works of Theodore Parker*, Frances Power Cobbe, ed. (London: Truebner and Co., 1865), 5:164–66.

87. Parker, pp. 166–71.

88. S. J. May, *Recollections*, pp. 372–73; "What Shall We Do?" *Christian Register*, 26 April 1851; "Boston Anniversaries: Ministerial Conference," and "Afterthoughts," *Christian Inquirer*, 7 June 1851.

89. For repercussions in England over May's resolution and the Fugitive Slave Bill, see, "Our Concern with Slavery" and "American Slavery," *Inquirer*, 7 June 1851; "Anti-Slavery Meeting of Unitarians." *Inquirer*, 14 June 1851; George Armstrong, "American Slavery" and [Anon.], "The American Unitarian Association and Slavery," *Inquirer*, 28 June 1851; "The Anti-Slavery Meeting," and "Northern Unitarian Association and the Fugitive Slave Bill," *Inquirer*, 12 July 1851; J. B. Estlin, "The Meeting at the Freemasons' Tavern," *Inquirer*, 19 July 1851; Russell Lant Carpenter, "The Anti-Slavery Meeting," *Inquirer*, 26 July

1851. At this point the editor of the *Inquirer* declared, "We cannot admit any further correspondence on this subject." Yet the discussion continued. See *Inquirer*, 1851, passim. See also, *American Slavery* [A broadside announcement of the meeting of the B.F.U.A. to discuss the slavery question in the United States.], Weston Papers, MB; *American Slavery. Report of a Meeting of Members of the Unitarian Body, Held at the Freemasons' Tavern, June 13th, 1851, To Deliberate on the Duty of English Unitarianism in Reference to Slavery in the United States. Rev. Dr. Hutton in the Chair.* (London: E. T. Whitfield, 1851); *Report of the Fiftieth Anniversary of the Southern Unitarian Society, Adopted At the Annual Meeting at Wareham, Doretshire, July 9, 1851,—The Rev. Hugh Hutton, A.M. in the Chair* (n.p., n.d.), pp. 4–5; "What is Thought and Said of Us in the Fatherland," *Christian Register* 30 (26 July 1851); [Joseph Hutton], "English View of Our Position Respecting Fugitive Slave Law," *Christian Register* 30 (9 August 1851). James Martineau to Sarah Howorth, Liverpool, 27 May 1851, J. Estlin Carpenter, *James Martineau Theologian and Teacher: A Study of his Life and Thought* (London: Philip Green, 1905), p. 356; Samuel May, Jr., to Mary Carpenter, Leicester, 15 July 1851, May Papers, MB; cf. also Samual May, Jr., "American Unitarians," MS notes, May Papers, MB.

90. John T. Sargent to Samuel Johnson, Boston, 19 May 1853, MSE: *28th A.U.A. Annual Report, 1853,* pp. 18, 21–22.

91. Theodore Parker to Samuel J. May, Boston, 24 October 1853, Autograph File, MH.

92. Higginson quoted by Tilden G. Edelstein, *Strange Enthusiasm: A Life of Thomas Wentworth Higginson* (New Haven: Yale University Press, 1968), p. 145; John Pierpont to Higginson, Medford, 16 November 1853, Autograph File, Wellesley College Library.

93. "The Collation," *Christian Register*, 3 June 1854; James Hackett Fowler to Thomas Wentworth Higginson, Cambridge, 30 June 1854, Burns Papers, MB; James Hackett Fowler, *New Testament "Miracles" and Modern "Miracles." The Comparative Amount of Evidence for Each. The Nature of Both. Testimony of a Hundred Witnesses. An Essay, Read Before the Middle and Senior Classes in Cambridge Divinity School* (Boston: Bela Marsh, 1854).

94. "The Collation," *Christian Register*, 3 June 1854; "Unitarian Festival in Faneuil Hall," *Christian Inquirer*, 10 June 1854.

95. James Freeman Clarke, *Anti-Slavery Days* (New York: R. Worthington 1884) pp. 172–73; William C. Gannett, *Ezra Stiles Gannett* (Boston: Roberts Bros., 1875), pp. 288–89.

96. "Convention at Montreal," *Christian Register*, 21 October 1854.

97. "The Fifteenth Autumnal Convention at Bangor, Maine," *Christian Register*, 25 October 1856; "Autumnal Convention," *Christian Inquirer*, 25 October 1856.

98. Denton, pp. 111–14; "Anniversaries," *Christian Register*, 7 June 1856; "Letter from Ephraim Nute" [title supplied], *Quarterly Journal of the American Unitarian Association* 4 (1 October 1856): 97.

99. Moncure Daniel Conway, *Autobiography Memories and Experiences* (Boston: Houghton, Mifflin, & Co., 1904), 1:28, 80, 90, 109–10, 248. See also Moncure D. Conway, *Pharisaism and Fasting. A Discourse Delivered In the Unitarian Church, Washington City, on September 30, 1855* (Washington: Buell and Blanchard, 1855); Conway, "A Fearless Preacher," *Christian Inquirer,* 16 February 1856; Conway, "The Only Path. A Sermon in the Unitarian Church at Washington Sunday Morning, February 3d," *Christian Inquirer,* 23 February 1856; Mary Elizabeth Burtis, *Moncure Conway, 1832–1907* (New Brunswick, N. J.: Rutgers University Press, 1952); Samuel Atkins Eliot, *Heralds of a Liberal Faith* (Boston: Beacon Press, 1952), 4: 104–6.

100. "[Sixth Annual] Conference of Western Unitarian Churches," *Christian Inquirer,* 30 May 1857; Conway, 1:274; Charles H. Lyttle, *Freedom Moves West: A History of the Western Unitarian Conference 1852–1952* (Boston: Beacon Press, 1952), p. 88; Shippen, p. 184.

101. [William Greenleaf Eliot], "Wide Awake." "Alton Correspondence. Unitarian Conference at Alton—Explosion upon Slavery Question," newspaper clipping, William Greenleaf Eliot Collection, Washington University Library; "Unitarian Conference at Alton," *Christian Register,* 30 May 1857; Eliot, "Social Reform," *Christian Inquirer,* 8 August 1857.

102. Samuel St. John to Henry W. Bellows, Mobile, 18 February 1839, Sophia St. John to Bellows, Newport, 7 April 1839, MHi; Herbert C. Peabody to Samuel St. John, Mobile, 20 September 1858, Peabody to St. John, Mobile, 29 October 1858, Peabody to St. John, Mobile, 15 January 1859, Herbert C. Peabody Papers, Southern Historical Collection, University of North Carolina; George H. Gibson, "Unitarian Congregations in the Ante-Bellum South," *Proceedings of the Unitarian Historical Society* 12 part 2 (1959): 66; Arthur A. Brooks, *The History of Unitarianism in the Southern Churches* (Boston: American Unitarian Association, n.d.), 7–8; *Quarterly Journal of the A.U.A.* 4 (1 April 1857): 374; George W. Burnap to Bellows, Baltimore, 22 December 1858, Burnap to Bellows, Baltimore, 7 January 1859, MHi; Eliot, *Heralds,* 3:54.

103. Russell Lant Carpenter, ed., *Memoirs of the Life and Work of Philip Pearsall Carpenter. . . . Chiefly Derived from His Letters,* 2d ed. (London: C. Kegan Paul and Co., 1880), pp. 198–99.

104. "The Nineteenth Autumnal Unitarian-Convention in New Bedford" [title supplied], *Christian Inquirer,* 20 October 1860; Samuel J. May and James F. Clarke, "Reply to the English Unitarian Address on Slavery," *Christian Register,* 27 October 1860; John Bowring, Edwin Chapman, and William James, "Letter from England," *Christian Register,* 3 November 1860.

Bibliography

A. MANUSCRIPTS

Ella Strong Denison Library, Scripps College, Claremont—
CCC-S Lydia Maria Child Papers

Meadville Theological Seminary Library—ICM
William Ellery Channing Papers

Dr. William's Library, London—LDW
Estlin Papers

Louisiana State University, Department of Archives—LU-
Archives
James E. Murdock Papers

Boston Public Library—MB
Antislavery Letters
Burns Papers
Garrison Manuscripts
May Papers
Phelps Papers
Weston Papers

Massachusetts Historical Society—MBHi
  Bellows Papers

Mugar Memorial Library, Boston University—MBU
  New England Immigrant Aid Papers

Concord Free Public Library—MCo
  Franklin B. Sanborn Papers

Schlesinger Library, Radcliffe College—MCR
  Beecher-Stowe Papers
  Eliza Lee Cabot Follen Papers
  Maria Weston Chapman Papers
  Lydia Maria Child Papers
  Loring Family Papers
  Alma Lutz Collection
  May-Goddard Papers
  Poor Family Papers

Houghton Library, Harvard University—MH
  John A. Andrew Papers
  Autograph file
  William Ellery Channing Papers
  William Henry Channing Papers
  Lydia Maria Child Papers
  James Freeman Clarke Papers
  William Lloyd Garrison Papers
  Thomas Wentworth Higginson Papers
  Loring's Letterbook
  James Russell Lowell Papers
  Charles E. Norton Papers
  John Gorham Palfrey Papers
  Franklin B. Sanborn Papers
  Charles Sumner Papers

Andover-Harvard Theological Library—MH-AH
  American Unitarian Association Letters

Harvard University Archives—MH-Archives
  College Papers
  Samuel A. Eliot Papers
  Henry Ware, Jr. Papers

James Duncan Phillips Library, Essex Institute—MSE
  Samuel Johnson Papers

Salem Female Charitable Society

American Antiquarian Society—MWA
Autograph collection
Lydia Maria Child Letters
Abigail Kelley Foster Papers
Edward Everett Hale Papers
Thomas Wentworth Higginson Papers
John Pierpont Papers
Slavery in the United States Collection

William L. Clements Library, University of Michigan—MiU-C
James G. Birney Papers
Lydia Maria Child Papers
Weld-Grimké Papers

Olin Library, Washington University—MoSW
William Greenleaf Eliot Collection

Wellesley College Library—MWelC
Autograph File

University of North Carolina Library—NcU
Herbert C. Peabody Papers

New Hampshire Historical Society—NhHi
John P. Hale Papers

Rush Rhees Library, University of Rochester—NRU
Pierpont Papers
William Henry Seward Collection

George Arents Library, Syracuse University—NSyU
Gerrit Smith Papers

William R. Perkins Library, Duke University—NcD
American Writers' Papers
Richard D. Arnold Papers
Bellows Papers
Burt Papers
James F. Clarke Papers
Moncure Daniel Conway Papers
Austin Johnson Papers

Ohio Historical Society—OHi
Joshua R. Giddings Papers

Manchester College Library, Oxford—OMC

George Armstrong Papers
Carpenter Family Papers
Lant Carpenter Papers
Valentine D. Davis Manuscripts

American Philosophical Society—PPAmP
Lesley Papers

Rhode Island Historical Society—RHi
Channing Autograph Collection

Brown University Library—RPB
Burleigh Papers
John Hay Collection

Alderman Library, University of Virginia—ViU
The Clifton Waller Barrett Library Collection

B. REPORTS AND PROCEEDINGS

Annual Reports of the American and Foreign Anti-Slavery Society Annual Reports of the American Anti-Slavery Society

Annual Reports of the American Society for Colonizing Free People of Colour of the United States

Annual Reports of the American Unitarian Association

Annual Reports of the Board of Managers of the Massachusetts Anti-Slavery Society

Annual Reports of the Board of Managers of the Massachusetts Colonization Society

Annual Reports of the Board of Managers of the New England Anti-Slavery Society

Annual Reports of the Board of Managers of the New-York State Colonization Society

Annual Reports of the Executive Committee of the Benevolent Fraternity of Churches

Proceedings of the Colonization Society of the City of New York

Reports of the Worcester County Auxiliary Colonization Society

C. NEWSPAPERS AND PERIODICALS

Abolitionist

African Repository, and Colonial Journal

Christian Examiner

Christian Inquirer

Christian Register

Colonization Herald and General Register

Inquirer

Liberator

Monthly Miscellany of Religion and Letters

Monthly Religious Magazine

Quarterly Journal of the American Unitarian Association

Unitarian Review and Religious Magazine

Western Messenger

D. CONTEMPORARY BOOKS, PAMPHLETS, LETTERS, SERMONS, BIOGRAPHIES, AND COLLECTIONS

Abdy, E. S. *Journal of a Residence and Tour in the United States of North America, from April, 1833, to October, 1834.* 3 vols. London: John Murray, 1835.

Allen, Joseph. *The Worcester Association and Its Antecedents: A History of Four Ministerial Associations: The Marlborough, the Worcester (Old), the Lancaster, and the Worcester (New) Associations.* Boston: Nichols and Noyes, 1868.

American Colonization Society, and the Colony at Liberia. Published by the Massachusetts Colonization Society. Boston: Pierce & Parker, 1831.

Barnes, Gilbert H. and Dwight L. Dumond, *Letters of Theodore Dwight Weld, Angelina Grimké Weld and Sarah Grimké 1822–1844.* Gloucester, Mass.: Peter Smith, 1965 (1st ed., 1934).

Barnes, James A. "Letters of a Massachusetts Woman Reformer to an Indiana Radical." *Indiana Magazine of History*. 26 (March 1930): 46–59.

Bearse, Austin. *Reminiscences of Fugitive-Slave Law Days in Boston.* Boston: Warren Richardson, 1880.

The Boston Slave Riot, and Trial of Anthony Burns. . . . Boston: Fetridge and Co., 1854.

Bowditch, Vincent Y. *Life and Correspondence of Henry Ingersoll Bowditch by his son.* 2 vols. Boston: Houghton, Mifflin and Co., 1902.

Bremer, Fredrika. *The Homes of the New World: Impressions of America.* 2 vols. New York: Harper and Bros., 1853.

Cabot, James Elliot. *A Memoir of Ralph Waldo Emerson.* 2 vols. Boston: 1888.

Cabot, Susan C. *What Have We, As Individuals, To Do With Slavery?* Anti-Slavery Tracts, no. 15. New York: American Anti-Slavery Society, n.d.

Calthrop, S. R.; et al., eds. *In Memoriam: Samuel Joseph May.* Syracuse, N.Y.: The Journal Office, 1871.

Carpenter, Russell Lant, ed. *Memoirs of the Life and Work of Philip Pearsall Carpenter,* . . . *Chiefly Derived from His Letters.* 2d ed. London: C. Kegan Paul and Co., 1880.

Chandler, Peleg W. *Memoir of Governor Andrew, with Personal Reminiscences.* 3d ed. Boston: Roberts Brothers, 1881.

Channing, William E. *An Address Delivered at Lenox, on the First of August, 1842, the Anniversary of Emancipation, in the British West Indies.* Lenox, Mass.: J. G. Stanly, 1842.

———. *A Discourse Occasioned by the Death of the Rev. Dr. Follen.* Cambridge: Metcalf, Torry, and Ballou, 1840.

———. *The Duty of the Free States, or Remarks Suggested by the Case of the Creole.* Boston: William Crosby and Co., 1842.

———. *Emancipation.* Boston: E. P. Peabody, 1840.

———. *Letter of William E. Channing to James G. Birney.* Boston: James Munroe and Co., 1837.

———. *A Letter to the Hon. Henry Clay, on the Annexation of Texas to the United States.* 5th ed. Boston: J. Munroe and Co., 1837.

————. *Remarks on the Slavery Question, in a Letter to Jonathan Phillips, Esq.* Boston: James Munroe and Co., 1839.

————. *Slavery.* 4th ed., rev. Boston: James Munroe and Co., 1836.

————. *The Works of William E. Channing, D.D.*, With an Introduction. Boston: American Unitarian Association, 1878.

Channing, William Henry. *The Life of William Ellery Channing, D.D.* Boston: American Unitarian Association, 1882.

————, ed. *Memoir of William Ellery Channing.* 3 vols. Boston: Wm. Crosby and H. P. Nichols, 1848.

Chapman, Maria Weston, ed. *Harriet Martineau's Autobiography* and *Memorials of Harriet Martineau.* 2 vols. Boston: James Osgood and Co., 1877.

————. *"How Can I Help to Abolish Slavery?" Or, Counsels to the Newly Converted.* Anti-Slavery Tracts, no. 14, New York: American Anti-Slavery Society, n.d.

————. *Pinda: A True Tale.* New York: American Anti-Slavery Society, 1840.

Chapman, Maria Weston, comp. *Songs of the Free, and Hymns.* Boston: Isaac Knapp, 1836.

Chase, Salmon P. "Diary and Correspondence." *Annual Report of the American Historical Association for the Year 1902.* vol. 2. Washington, D.C.: Govt. Printing Office, 1903.

Child, David Lee. *The Culture of the Beet, and Manufacture of Beet Sugar.* Boston: Weeks, Jordan and Co., 1840

————. *The Despotism of Freedom; or, The Tyranny and Cruelty of American Republican Slave-masters, Shown to be the Worst in the World; in a Speech Delivered at the First Anniversary of the New Anti-Slavery Society, 1833.* Boston: Boston Young Men's Anti-Slavery Association, 1833.

————. *Oration in Honor of Universal Emancipation in the British Empire, delivered at South Reading, August first, 1834.* Boston, 1834.

————. *Rights and Duties of the United States Relative to Slavery Under the Laws of War. No Military Power to Return Any Slave. "Contraband of war" Applicable Between the United States and Their Insurgent Enemies.* Boston: R. F. Wallcut, 1861.

————; L. Maria Child; et al. *Memorial on the Personal Liberty Law.* n.p., March, 1861.

Child, Lydia Maria. *Anti-Slavery Catechism.* Newburyport, Mass.: Charles Whipple, 1836.

————. *An Appeal in Favor of that Class of Americans Called Africans.* New York: John S. Taylor, 1836.

————. *Brief History of the Condition of Women, in Various Ages and Nations.* 2 vols., 5th ed. New York: C. S. Francis and Co., 1845.

————. *Correspondence between Lydia Maria Child and Gov. Wise and Mrs. Mason, of Virginia.* Boston: American Anti-Slavery Society, 1860.

————. *The Duty of Disobedience to the Fugitive Slave Act: An Appeal to the Legislatures of Massachusetts.* Anti-Slavery Tracts, no. 9, n. s. Boston: American Anti-Slavery Society, 1860.

————. *The Evils of Slavery, and the Cure of Slavery. The First Proved by the Opinions of Southerners Themselves, the Last Shown by Historical Evidence.* Newburyport, Mass.: C. Whipple, 1836.

————. *The Freedmen's Book.* Boston: Ticknor and Fields, 1865.

————. *Isaac T. Hooper: A True Life.* Boston: J. P. Jewett and Co., 1853.

————. *Letters of Lydia Maria Child* With a Biographical Introduction by John G. Whittier. Boston: Houghton, Mifflin and Co., 1883.

————. *The Progress of Religious Ideas, Through Successive Ages.* New York: C. S. Francis and Co., 1855.

Clarke, James Freeman. *The Annexation of Texas. A sermon Delivered in the Masonic Temple on Fast Day.* Boston: Office of the Christian World, 1844.

————. *Anti-Slavery Days.* New York: R. Worthington, 1884.

————. *Autobiography, Diary, and Correspondence.* Edited by Edward Everett Hale. Boston: Houghton, Mifflin and Co., 1891.

————. *Causes and Consequences of the Affair at Harper's Ferry. A Sermon Preached in the Indiana Place Chapel, on Sunday Morning, Nov. 6, 1859.* Boston: Walker, Wise and Co., 1859.

————. *Events and Epochs in Religious History.* Boston: James R. Osgood and Co., 1881.

————. *Everyday Religion*. Boston: Houghton, Mifflin and Co., 1886.

————. *The Hour Which Cometh, and Now Is: Sermons, Preached in Indiana-Place Chapel, Boston*. Boston: Walker, Wise, and Co., 1864.

————. *Memorial and Biographical Sketches*. Boston: Houghton Mifflin and Co., 1878.

————. *Present Condition of the Free Colored of the United States*. New York: American Anti-Slavery Society, 1859.

————. *The Rendition of Anthony Burns. Its Causes and Consequence. A Discourse on Christian Politics, Delivered in Williams Hall, Boston, on Whitsunday, June 4, 1854*. Boston: Crosby, Nichols, and Co., 1854

————. *Slavery in the United States. A Sermon Delivered in Amory Hall, on Thanksgiving Day, November 24, 1842*. Boston: Benjamin H. Greene, 1843.

Collins, John A., ed. *The Anti-Slavery Picknick: A Collection of Speeches, Poems, Dialogues, and Songs; Intended for Use in Schools and Anti-Slavery Meetings*. Boston: H. W. Williams, 1842.

Conway, Moncure D. *Autobiography Memories and Experiences*. 2 vols. Boston: Houghton, Mifflin and Co., 1904

————. *Pharisaism and Fasting. A Discourse Delivered in the Unitarian Church, Washington City, on September 30, 1855*. Washington, D.C.: Buell and Blanchard, 1855.

Craft, William. *Running a Thousand Miles for Freedom; or, the Escape of William and Ellen Craft from Slavery*. London: William Tweedle, 1860.

DeNormandie, James. *In Memory of William Henry Furness, D.D., A Sermon Preached to the First Church in Roxbury, Boston, February 2, 1896*. n.p., [1896?].

Dix, John Ross. *Pulpit Portraits, or Pen Pictures of Distinguished American Divines; with Sketches of Congregations and Choirs. . . .* Boston: Tappan and Whittemore, 1854.

Dumond, Dwight L., ed. *Letters of James Gillespie Birney 1831–1857*. 2 vols. Gloucester, Mass.: Peter Smith, 1966 (1st ed., 1938).

Dyckinck, Evert A.; and George L. Duyckinck, eds. *Cyclopaedia of American Literature*. 2 vols. New York: Charles Scribner, 1855.

Extracts From Remarks On Dr. Channing's Slavery, With Comments, By An Abolitionist. Boston: D. K. Hitchcock, 1836.

Follen, Charles. "The Cause of Freedom in Our Country." *Deutsch-Amerikanische Geschichtsblaetter*. 16 (1916): 235–47.

Follen, Eliza Lee Cabot. *Anti-Slavery Hymns and Songs*. Anti-Slavery Tracts, no. 12. New York: American Anti-Slavery Society, n.d.

———. *Hymns, Songs, and Fables for Young People*. Boston: Wm. Crosby and H. P. Nichols, 1847.

———. *Liberty Cap*. Boston: Leonard C. Bowles, 1846.

———. *The Life of Charles Follen*. Boston: Thomas H. Webb and Co., 1844.

———. *Little Songs*. Boston: Whittemore, Niles and Hall 1856.

———. *The Skeptic*. Boston: James Munroe, and Co., 1850.

———. *Sketches of Married Life*. Boston: Hilliard, Gray and Co., 1838.

———. *To Mothers in the Free States*. Anti-Slavery Tracts, no. 8. New York: American Anti-Slavery Society, 1855.

———. *Words of Truth*. Cambridge, Mass., 1832.

———, ed., *The Works of Charles Follen, with a Memoir of his Life*. 5 vols. Boston: Hilliard, Gray, and Co., 1842.

Folsom, C. F. *Henry Ingersoll Bowditch, M.D.* n.p., n.d.

Foster, Stephen S. *The Brotherhood of Thieves; or, a True Picture of the American Church and Clergy*. . . . Boston: Anti-Slavery Society, 1844.

Fowler, Henry. *The American Pulpit: Sketches, Biographical and Descriptive, of Living American Preachers*. . . . New York: J. M. Fairchild and Co., 1856.

Fowler, James Hackett. *New Testament "Miracles." The Comparative Amount of Evidence for Each. The Nature of Both. Testimony of a Hundred Witnesses. An Essay, Read Before the Middle and Senior Classes in Cambridge Divinity School*. Boston: Bela Marsh, 1854.

———. *A Sermon on the State of the Country, Delivered in the Theatre of Savannah, Ga., on Fast Day, June 1st, 1865.* Published by the Union League of Savannah, Ga., Savannah: Republican Office, 1865.

Frothingham, Octavius Brooks. *Boston Unitarianism, 1820–1850: A Study of the Life and Work of Nathaniel Langdon Frothingham.* New York: G. P. Putnam's Sons, 1890.

———. *Memoir of William Henry Channing.* Boston: Houghton, Mifflin and Co., 1886.

———. *Theodore Parker: A Biography.* Boston: James R. Osgood and Co., 1876.

Furness, William Henry. *The Blessings of Abolition. A Discourse Delivered in the First Congregational Unitarian Church Sunday, July 1, 1860.* Philadelphia: C. Sherman and Son, 1860.

———. *Christian Duty. Three Discourses Delivered in the First Congregational Unitarian Church of Philadelphia, May 28th, June 4th, and June 11th, 1854 . . . with Reference to the Recent Execution of the Fugitive Slave Law in Boston and New York.* Philadelphia: Merrihew and Thompson's Steam Power Press, 1854.

———. *A Discourse Delivered, January 5th, 1851, in the First Congregational Unitarian Church, in Philadelphia.* n.p., n.d.

———. *A Discourse Delivered on the Occasion of the National Fast September 26th, 1861 in the First Congregational Unitarian Church in Philadelphia.* Philadelphia: T. B. Pugh, 1861.

———. *A Discourse Occasioned by the Boston Fugitive Slave Case, Delivered in the First Congregational Unitarian Church, Philadelphia, April 13, 1851.* Philadelphia: Merrihew and Thompson, 1851.

———. *Discourses.* Philadelphia: G. Collins, 1855.

———. *Domestic Worship.* Philadelphia: James Kay, Jun. and Bro., 1840.

———. *The Moving Power. A Discourse Delivered in the First Congregational Unitarian Church in Philadelphia, . . . Feb. 9, 1851 after the Occurence of a Fugitive Slave Case.* Philadelphia: Merrihew and Thompson, 1851.

———. *Our Duty as Conservatives. A Discourse Delivered in the First Congregational Unitarian Church Sunday November 25, 1860,*

Occasioned by the Threatened Secession of Some of the Southern States.
Philadelphia: C. Sherman and Son, Printers, 1860.

———. *Put Up thy Sword. A Discourse Delivered Before Theodore Parker's Society, At the Music Hall, Boston, Sunday, March 11, 1860.*
Boston: R. F. Wallcut, 1860.

———. *The Right of Property in Man. A Discourse Delivered in the First Congregational Unitarian Church, Sunday, July 3, 1859.* Philadelphia: C. Sherman and Son, 1859.

———. *A Sermon, Delivered May 14, 1841, on the Occasion of the National Fast Recommended by the President.* Philadelphia: John C. Clark, 1841.

———. *A Sermon Occasioned by the Destruction of Pennsylvania Hall, and Delivered the Lord's Day Following, May 20, 1838, in the First Congregational Unitarian Church.* Philadelphia: John C. Clark, 1838.

———. *A Thanksgiving Discourse . . . Nov. 27th, 1845.* n.p., n.d.

———. *Two Discourses Occasioned by the Approaching Anniversary of the Declaration of Independence, Delivered June 25, A.M., and July 2, A.M., 1843.* Philadelphia: John Pennington: 1843.

Gannett, William C. *Ezra Stiles Gannett: Unitarian Minister in Boston, 1824–1871.* Boston: Roberts Bros., 1875.

Higginson, Thomas Wentworth. *Mr. Higginson's Address to the Voters of the Third Congressional District of Massachusetts.* Lowell, Mass.: C. L. Knapp, 1850.

Hudson, Charles. *History of the Town of Lexington. . . .* Boston: Wiggin and Lunt, 1868.

Johnson, Oliver. *W. L. Garrison and His Times,* Miami, Fla.: Mnemosyne Publishing Co., 1969 (1st ed., 1881).

Knight, Frederick I.; et al. *Henry Ingersoll Bowditch, M.D..* n.p., n.d.

LeBreton, Anna Lelita, ed. *Correspondence of William Ellery Channing, D.D., and Lucy Aikin, From 1826 to 1842.* Boston: Roberts, 1874.

Letter of the Boston Association of Congregational Ministers, to Rev. John Pierpont, with His Reply. Boston: Benjamin Greene, 1846.

Longfellow, Samuel. *Parting Words: A Discourse, Preached, Sunday,*

June 24, 1860, in the New Chapel, Brooklyn. New York: John A. Gray, 1860.

Martineau, Harriet. *The Martyr Age of the United States of America*. Newcastle Upon Tyne: Finlay and Charlton, 1840.

May, Joseph. *Samuel Joseph May: A Memorial Study*. Boston: Geo. H. Ellis, 1898.

May, Jr., Samuel. *Catalogue of Anti-slavery Publications in America*. [New York, 1863].

———. *The Fugitive Slave Law and Its Victims*. Anti-Slavery Tracts, no. 15, n.s. New York: American Anti-Slavery Society, 1861.

May, Samuel J. *A Brief Account of His Ministry. Given in a Discourse, Preached to the Church of the Messiah, in Syracuse, N.Y., September 15th, 1867*. Syracuse, N.Y.: Masters and Lee, Book and Job Printers, 1867.

———. *A Discourse on Slavery in the United States, Delivered in Brooklyn, July 3, 1831*. Boston: Garrison and Knapp, 1832.

———. *A Discourse on the Life and Character of the Rev. Charles Follen, LL.D. Who Perished, Jan. 13, 1840, . . . Delivered Before the Massachusetts Anti-Slavery Society, in the Marlborough Chapel, Boston, April 17, 1840*. Boston: Henry L. Devereux, 1840.

———. *Emancipation in the British W. Indies, August 1, 1834. An Address, Delivered in the First Presbyterian Church in Syracuse, on the First of August, 1845*. Syracuse, N.Y.: J. Barber, 1845.

———. *The Right of Colored People to Education, Vindicated. Letters to Andrew T. Judson, Esq. and Others in Cantebury, Remonstrating with Them on Their Unjust and Unjustifiable Procedure Relative to Miss Crandall and Her School for Colored Females*, Brooklyn: Advertiser Press, 1833.

———. *Some Recollections of Our Antislavery Conflict*. Miami, Fla.: Mnemosyne Publishing Co., 1969 (1st ed., 1869).

Mumford, Thomas; George B. Emerson, and Samuel May. *Memoir of Samuel Joseph May*. Boston: Roberts Brothers, 1873.

Mumford, Mrs. Thomas, ed. *Life and Letters of Thomas J. Mumford, with Memorial Tributes*. Boston: George H. Ellis, 1879.

Muzzey, A. B. *Reminiscences and Memorials of Men of the Revolution and Their Families*. Boston: Estes and Lauriat, 1883.

Nason, Elias. *Discourse Delivered Before the New-England Historic-Genealogical Society, Boston, April 2, 1868, on the Life and Character of the Hon. John Albion Andrew, LL.D., Late President of the Society.* Boston: New-England Historic-Genealogical Society, 1868.

[Neal, John]. "John Pierpont," *Atlantic Monthly* 18 (December 1866): 649–65.

Old Anti-Slavery Days. Proceedings of the Commemorative Meeting Held by the Danvers Historical Society, at the Town Hall, Danvers, April 26, 1893, with Introduction, Letters, and Sketches. Danvers, Mass: Danvers Mirror Print, 1893.

Palfrey, John G. *A Letter to a Friend.* Cambridge, Mass.: Metcalf and Co., 1850.

Palmer, Joseph. *Necrology of Alumni of Harvard College 1851–52 to 1862–63.* Boston: John Wilson and Son, 1864.

Parker, Theodore. "The Administration of the Late Mr. Polk." *Massachusetts Quarterly Review* 3 (December 1849): 118–57.

———. *The Chief Sins of the People: A Sermon Delivered at the Melodeon, Boston, on Fast-Day, April 10, 1851.* Boston: Benjamin H. Greene, 1851.

———. *The Collected Works of Theodore Parker. . . .* Edited by Francis Power Cobbe. 12 vols. London: Truebner and Co., 1865.

———. *A Discourse Occasioned by the Death of Daniel Webster, Preached at the Melodeon on Sunday, October 31, 1852.* Boston: Benjamin B. Mussey and Co., 1853.

———. *The Great Battle Between Slavery and Freedom, Considered in Two Speeches Delivered Before the American Antislavery Society, at New York, May 7, 1856.* Boston: Benjamin H. Greene, 1856.

———. "Hollis Street Council," *Dial* 3 (October 1842): 201–21.

———. *The Law of God and the Statutes of Men. A Sermon, Preached at the Music Hall, in Boston, on Sunday, June 18, 1854.* Boston: Benjamin B. Mussey and Co., 1854.

———. *A Letter to the People of the United States Touching the Matter of Slavery.* Boston: James Munroe and Co., 1848.

———. *The New Crime Against Humanity. A Sermon, Preached at the Music Hall, in Boston, On Sunday, June 4, 1854.* Boston: Benjamin B. Mussey and Co., 1854.

―――. *A Sermon of the Dangers Which Threaten the Rights of Man in America; Preached at the Music Hall, On Sunday, July 2, 1854.* Boston: Benjamin B. Mussey and Co., 1854.

―――. *Theodore Parker's Experience as a Minister, with Some Account of His Early Life, and Education for the Ministry; Contained in a Letter from Him to the Members of the Twenty-Eighth Congregational Society of Boston.* Boston: Rufus Leighton, Jr., 1859.

―――. *The Three Chief Safeguards of Society, Considered in a Sermon at the Melodeon, On Sunday, July 6, 1851.* Boston: Wm. Crosby and H. P. Nichols, 1851.

―――. *Two Sermons Preached Before the Twenty Eighth Congregational Society of Boston, on the 14th and 21st of November, 1852. . . .* Boston: Benjamin B. Mussey and Co., 1853.

―――. *The Trial of Theodore Parker, for the "Misdemeanor" of a Speech in Faneuil Hall Against Kidnapping, before the Circuit Court of the United States at Boston, April 3, 1855, with the Defense.* Boston: Published for the Author, 1855.

"Pic Nic at Dedham." *The Child's Friend; Designed for Families and Sunday Schools.* Edited by Eliza L. Follen. (October 1843) 21–27.

Pickard, Samuel To. *Life and Letters of John Greenleaf Whittier.* 2 vols. Boston: Houghton, Mifflin and Co., 1899.

Pierpont, John. *The Anti-Slavery Poems of John Pierpont.* Boston: Oliver Johnson, 1843.

―――. *A Discourse on the Covenant with Judas, Preached in Hollis-Street Church, Nov. 6, 1842.* Boston: Charles C. Little and James Brown, 1842.

―――. *Moral Rule of Political Action. A Discourse Delivered in Hollis Street Church, Sunday, January 27, 1839.* Boston: James Munroe and Co., 1839.

Pillsbury, Parker. *Acts of the Anti-Slavery Apostles.* Boston: Cupples, Upham, and Co., 1884.

Proceedings of the Controversy Between a Part of the Proprietors and the Pastor of Hollis Street Church, Boston, 1838 and 1839. Boston: S. N. Dickison, n.d.

Reply of the Friends of Rev. John Pierpont, to a Proposal for Dissolving the Pastoral Connexion Between Him, and the Society in Hollis Street. n.p., n.d.

Reply to the Invitation of "The Friends of Unitarian Christianity in Boston to their Brethren in a Common Faith in England and Scotland." n.p., n.d.

Simmons, George F. *Public Spirit and Mobs. Two Sermons Delivered at Springfield, Mass., On Sunday, February 23, 1851, After the Thompson Riot.* Springfield, Mass.: Merriam, Chapin and Co., 1851.

[————]. *Review of the Remarks on Dr. Channing's Slavery, by a Citizen of Massachusetts.* Boston: James Munroe and Co., 1836.

————. *Two Sermons on the Kind Treatment and the Emancipation of Slaves. Preached at Mobile, On Sunday the 10th, and Sunday the 17th of May, 1840.* Boston: William Crosby and Co., 1840.

Sprague, William. *Annals of the American Unitarian Pulpit.* New York: Robert Carter and Bros., 1865.

Still, William. *The Underground Rail Road.* Chicago: Johnson Publishing Co., 1970 (1st ed., 1871).

Stowe, Harriet Beecher. *Men of Our Times; or Leading Patriots of the Day.* Hartford, Conn.: Hartford Publishing Co., 1868.

Tiffany, Nina Moore. *Samuel E. Sewall. A Memoir.* Boston: Houghton, Mifflin and Co., 1898.

Ware, John. *Memoir of the Life of Henry Ware, Jr.* 2 vols. Boston: James Munroe and Co., 1854.

Weiss, John. *Life and Correspondence of Theodore Parker.* 2 vols. New York: D. Appleton and Co., 1864.

[Whitman, Jason]. *Letter to Rev. Jason Whitman, by a Southerner, and Mr. Whitman's Reply. Occasioned by the Protest of Unitarian Ministers Against American Slavery.* no. 18, Tract for the Times. Boston: Office of the Christian World, 1845.

[Willard, Mary, ed.]. *Life of Samuel Willard, D.D., A.A.S. of Deerfield, Mass.* Boston: Geo. H. Ellis, 1892.

Wilson, James Grant, and John Fiske. *Appletons' Cyclopedia of American Biography.* 6 vols. New York: D. Appleton and Co., 1888.

Winsor, Justin, ed. *The Memorial History of Boston, Including Suffolk County, Massachusetts. 1630–1880.* 4 vols. Boston: James R. Osgood, 1882.

Wright, Elizur. "William Lloyd Garrison." *Unity* 3 (16 June 1879): 120–21.

Wyman, Lillie B. Chase. "From Generation to Generation," *Atlantic Monthly* 64 (August 1889) 164–77.

Young, Edward James. *Tribute to Octavius Brooks Frothingham*. Cambridge, Mass.: John Wilson and Son, 1895.

E. SECONDARY WORKS

Adams, Alice Dana. *The Neglected Period of Anti-Slavery in America (1808–1831)*. Radcliffe College Monographs, no. 14. Gloucester, Mass.: Peter Smith, 1964 (1st ed., 1908).

Atkinson, Minnie. *A History of the First Religious Society in Newburyport, Massachusetts*. Newburyport, Mass.: The News Publishing Co., 1933.

Baer, Helene G. *The Heart is Like Heaven*. Philadelphia: University of Pennsylvania Press, 1964.

Barnes, Gilbert Hobbs. *The Antislavery Impulse 1830–1844*. New York: Harcourt, Brace and World, 1964 (1st ed., 1933).

Bartlett, Irving H. *Wendell Phillips*. Boston: Beacon Press, 1961.

Bolster, Arthur S. *James Freeman Clarke: Disciple to Advancing Truth*. Boston: The Beacon Press, 1954.

Brock, Peter. *Radical Pacifists in Antebellum America*. Princeton, N.J.: Princeton University Press, 1968.

Brooks, Arthur A. *The History of Unitarianism in the Southern Churches*. Boston: American Unitarian Association, n.d.

Brown, Arthur W. *Always Young for Liberty: A Biography of William Ellery Channing*. Syracuse, N.Y.: Syracuse University Press, 1956.

Brown, Marion E. " 'To Smoking Clergymen,' "*Books at Brown* 13 (April 1951): 1–5.

Burbank, Leonard Freeman. *History of the First Unitarian Society in Dunstable New Nashua 1826–1926*. Nashua, N.H.: F. E. Cole and Co., n.d.

Burtis, Mary Elizabeth. *Moncure Conway 1832–1907*. New Brunswick, N. J.: Rutgers University Press, 1952.

Carpenter, J. Estlin. *James Martineau. Theologian and Teacher: A Study of his Life and Thought*. London: Philip Green, 1905.

Chadwick, John W. "Samuel May of Leicester." *New England Magazine* 20 (April 1899): 201–14.

———. *Theodore Parker: Preacher and Reformer*. Boston: Houghton Mifflin and Co., 1901.

———. *William Ellery Channing*. Boston: Houghton, Mifflin and Co., 1903.

Chapman, John Jay. *Memories and Milestones*. New York: Moffat, Yard and Co., 1915.

———. *William Lloyd Garrison*. New York: Moffat, Yard and Co., 1913.

Cirker, Hayward; and Blanche Cirker, eds. *Dictionary of American Portraits*. New York: Dover Publications, 1967.

Commager, Henry Steele. *Theodore Parker*. Boston: Beacon Press, 1967.

Cooke, George Willis. *Unitarianism in America*. Boston: Reprinted from the *New England Magazine*, May 1900.

Cunz, Dieter. "Karl Follen: In Commemoration of the Hundredth Anniversary of His Death." *American-German Review* 7 (October 1940): 25–27, 32.

Davis, David Brion. "The Emergence of Immediatism in British and American Antislavery Thought." *Mississippi Valley Historical Review* 49 (September 1962): 209–30.

DeLong, Henry C. "John Pierpont." *Medford Historical Register*, 6 (October 1903): 75–89.

Dodge, Benjamin; A.B.R. Sprague, and E.E. Thompson, "Samuel May." *Proceedings of the Worcester Society of Antiquity, for the Year 1900*. Worcester, Mass.: Published by the Society, 1901.

Donald, David. *Lincoln Reconsidered*. New York: Vintage Books, 1956.

Drummond, James. *The Life and Letters of James Martineau, LL.D., S.T.D., Etc.* 2 vols. New York: Dodd, Mead and Co., 1902.

Duberman, Martin, ed. *The Antislavery Vanguard: New Essays on the Abolitionists*. Princeton, N. J.: Princeton University Press, 1965.

Dumond, Dwight Lowell. *Antislavery: The Crusade for Freedom in America*. New York: W. W. Norton and Co., 1966.

————. *Antislavery Origins of the Civil War in the United States*. Ann Arbor, Mich.: The University of Michigan Press, 1960 (1st ed., 1939).

Edelstein, Tilden G. *Strange Enthusiasm: A Life of Thomas Wentworth Higginson*. New Haven, Conn.: Yale University Press, 1968.

Edgell, David P. *William Ellery Channing: An Intellectual Portrait*. Boston: The Beacon Press, 1955.

Elkins, Stanley M. *Slavery: A Problem in American Institutional and Intellectual Life*. New York: Grosset and Dunlap, 1963.

Ellsworth, Clayton Sumner. "The American Churches and the Mexican War." *American Historical Review* 14 (January 1940): 301–26.

Filler, Louis. *The Crusade Against Slavery 1830–1860*. New York: Harper Torchbooks, Harper and Row, 1960.

Fredrickson, George M., ed. *William Lloyd Garrison*. Englewood Cliffs, N. J.: Prentice-Hall, 1968.

Furnas, J. C. *Goodbye to Uncle Tom*. New York: Macmillan Co., 1956.

Galpin, W. Freeman. "Samuel Joseph May. 'God's Chore Boy.' " *New York History* 21 (April 1940): 139–50.

Gara, Larry. *The Liberty Line: The Legend of the Underground Railroad*. Lexington, Ky.: University of Kentucky Press, 1967.

Gatell, Frank Otto. "Doctor Palfrey Frees His Slaves." *New England Quarterly* 34 (March 1961): 74–86.

————. *John Gorham Palfrey and the New England Conscience*. Cambridge, Mass.: Harvard University Press, 1963.

————. "Letters of a Salem Conscience Whig: Stephen C. Phillips to John Gorham Palfrey." *Essex Institute Historical Collections* 95 (January 1959): 52–66.

————. "Palfrey's Vote, the Conscience Whigs, and their Election of Speaker Winthrop." *New England Quarterly* 31 (June 1958): 218–31.

Geffen, Elizabeth M. *Philadelphia Unitarianism 1796–1861*. Philadelphia: University of Pennsylvania Press, 1961.

———. "William Henry Furness, Philadelphia Antislavery Preacher." *The Pennsylvania Magazine of History and Biography* 82 (July 1958): 259–91.

Gohdes, Clarence. "Some Notes on the Unitarian Church in the Ante-Bellum South: A Contribution to the History of Southern Liberalism." *American Studies in Honor of William Kenneth Boyd*, edited by David K. Jackson. Durham, N. C., 1940.

Hart, Albert Bushnell. *Slavery and Abolition, 1831–1841*. New York: Harper and Brothers, 1906.

Harwood, Thomas F. "Prejudice and Antislavery: The Colloquy between William Ellery Channing and Edward Strutt Abdy, 1834." *American Quarterly* 18 (Winter 1966): 697–700.

Haupt, Herman. "Follenbriefe." *Deutsch-Amerikanische Geschichtsblaetter* 14 (1914): 7–83.

Hicks, Granville. "Dr. Channing and the Creole Case." *American Historical Review* 37 (1931–32): 516–25.

Higginson, Mary Thacher. *Thomas Wentworth Higginson: The Story of His Life*. Boston: Houghton Mifflin Co., 1914.

Holinger, Cora. "Charles Follen, A Sketch of His Life in New England." *American-German Review* 14 (June 1948): 20–22.

Holloway, Jean. *Edward Everett Hale: A Biography*. Austin, Tex.: University of Texas, 1956.

Horton, John T. "Millard Fillmore and the Things of God and Caesar." *Niagara Frontier* 2 (Spring-Summer 1955): 1–7, 39–41, 45–48.

Howe, Daniel Walker. *The Unitarian Conscience. Harvard Unitarian Philosophy, 1805–1861*. Cambridge, Mass.: Harvard University Press, 1970.

Johnson, Allen; and Dumas Malone, eds., *Dictionary of American Biography*. 27 vols. New York: Charles Scribner's Sons, 1928–1958.

Kraditor, Aileen S. *Means and Ends in American Abolitionism:*

Garrison and His Critics on Strategy and Tactics, 1834–1850. New York: Pantheon Books, 1969.

Lader, Lawrence. *The Bold Brahmins. New England's War Against Slavery: 1831–1863.* New York: E. P. Dutton and Co., 1961.

Ladu, Arthur I. "The Political Ideas of Theodore Parker." *Studies in Philology* 38 (January 1941): 106–23.

Levy, Leonard W. "The 'Abolition Riot': Boston's First Slave Rescue." *New England Quarterly* 25 (March 1952): 85–92.

———. "Sims' Case: The Fugitive Slave Law in Boston in 1851." *Journal of Negro History* 35 (1950): 39–74.

Litwack, Leon F. "The Abolitionist Dilemma: The Antislavery Movement and the Northern Negro." *New England Quarterly* 34 (March 1961): 50–73.

———. *North of Slavery: The Negro in the Free States, 1790–1860.* Chicago: University of Chicago Press, 1969.

Locke, Henry Dyer. *Ancient Parish. An Historical Summary of the First Parish, Watertown, Masstts.* Boston: Stetson Press, 1930.

Loveland, Anne C. "Evangelicalism and 'Immediate Emancipation' in American Antislavery Thought." *Journal of Southern History* 32 (May 1966): 172–88.

Lutz, Alma. *Crusade for Freedom: Women in the Antislavery Movement.* Boston: Beacon Press, 1968.

Lyttle, Charles H. *Freedom Moves West: A History of the Western Unitarian Conference, 1852–1952.* Boston: Beacon Press, 1952.

Mabee, Carleton. *Black Freedom: The Nonviolent Abolitionists from 1830 Through the Civil War.* [New York:] Macmillan Co., 1970.

McPherson, James M. *The Struggle for Equality: Abolitionists and the Negro in the Civil War and Reconstruction.* Princeton, N.J.: Princeton University Press, 1964.

Mathews, Donald G. "The Abolitionists on Slavery: The Critique Behind the Social Movement." *Journal of Southern History* 33 (May 1967): 163–82.

The May Memorial Church. An Account of its Dedication, together with a Brief Sketch of the Origin and Progress of the Unitarian Congregational Society of Syracuse. n.p.: Columbia Press, n.d.

Mead, David. "Theodore Parker in Ohio." *Northwest Ohio Quarterly* 21 (Winter 1948–1949): 18–23.

Meltzer, Milton. *Tongue of Flame: The Life of Lydia Maria Child.* New York: Thomas Y. Crowell Co., 1965.

Meyer, Howard N. *Colonel of the Black Regiment: The Life of Thomas Wentworth Higginson.* New York: W. W. Norton and Co., 1967.

Mood, Fulmer; and Granville Hicks, eds., "Letters to Dr. Channing on Slavery and the Annexation of Texas, 1837," *New England Quarterly* 5 (July 1932): 587–601.

Moody, Marjory M. "The Evolution of Emerson as an Abolitionist." *American Literature* 17 (March 1945): 1–21.

Munsterberg, Margaret. "The Weston Sisters and 'The Boston Controversy.'" *Boston Public Library Quarterly* 10 (January 1958): 38–50.

————. "The Weston Sisters and the 'Boston Mob.'" *Boston Public Library Quarterly* 9 (October 1957): 183–94.

Murdock, Charles A. *Horatio Stebbins: His Ministry and His Personality.* Boston: Houghton Mifflin Co., 1921.

Nelson, Truman, ed. *Documents of Upheaval: Selections from William Lloyd Garrison's The Liberator, 1831–1865.* New York: Hill and Wang, 1969.

Oates, Stephen B. *To Purge This Land with Blood: A Biography of John Brown.* New York: Harper and Row, 1970.

Pearson, Henry Greenleaf. *The Life of John A. Andrew: Governor of Massachusetts, 1861–1865.* 2 vols. Boston: Houghton, Mifflin and Co., 1904.

Pease, William H.; and Jane H. Pease, eds., *The Antislavery Argument.* Indianapolis Md.: The Bobbs-Merrill Co., 1965.

————. "Freedom and Peace: A Nineteenth Century Dilemma." *Midwest Quarterly* 9 (1967): 23–40.

————. "The Role of Women in the Antislavery Movement." *Canadian Historical Association. Historical Papers Presented at the Annual Meeting held at Ottawa, June 7–10, 1967.* Pp. 167–183.

Pope, Charles Henry; and Katherine Peabody Loring. *Loring Genealogy.* Cambridge, Mass.: Murray and Emery Co., 1917.

Pregizer, Richard. *Die Politischen Ideen des Karl Follen.* Tuebingen: I. C. B. Mohr, 1912.

Quarles, Benjamin. *Black Abolitionists.* New York: Oxford University Press, 1970.

Ravitz, Abe C. "John Pierpont, Abolitionist." *Boston Public Library Quarterly* 8 (October 1956): 195–200.

———. "John Pierpont and the Federalist Muse in Essex County." *Essex Institute Historical Collections* 96 (April 1960): 140–48.

———. "John Pierpont and the Slaves' Christmas." *Phylon* 21 (Winter 1960): 383–86.

Reinhardt, John E. "The Evolution of William Ellery Channing's Sociopolitical Ideas." *American Literature* 26 (May 1954): 154–65.

Richards, Leonard L. *Gentlemen of Property and Standing": Anti-Abolition Mobs in Jacksonian America.* New York: Oxford University Press, 1970.

Rockwood, George I. "George Barrell Cheever. Protagonist of Abolition: Religious Emotionalism the Underlying Factor in the Causes of the Civil War." *Proceedings of the American Antiquarian Society at the Semi-Annual Meeting Held in Boston, April 15, 1936.* n.s. 46 (1936).

Ruchames, Louis, ed. *The Abolitionists: A Collection of Their Writings.* New York: G. P. Putnam's Sons, 1963.

Schlesinger, Elizabeth Bancroft. "Two Early Harvard Wives: Eliza Ward Farrar and Eliza Follen." *New England Quarterly* 38 (June 1965): 147–67.

Schneider, Heinrich. "Karl Follen: A Re-Appraisal and Some New Biographical Materials." *Society for the History of the Germans in Maryland* 38 (1959): 73–86.

Schwartz, Harold. "Fugitive Slave Days in Boston." *New England Quarterly* 27 (June 1954): 191–212.

Sewell, Richard H. *John P. Hale and the Politics of Abolition.* Cambridge, Mass.: Harvard University Press, 1965.

Shapiro, Samuel. The Rendition of Anthony Burns." *Journal of Negro History* 44 (January 1959): 34–51.

Sherwin, Oscar. "The Armory of God." *New England Quarterly* 18 (March 1945): 70–82.

Shippen, Rush R. "Early Days of the Western Unitarian Conference." *Unity* 49 (22 May 1902): 182–84.

Sillen, Samuel. *Women Against Slavery*. New York: Masses and Mainstream, 1955.

Silver, Rollo G. "Emerson as Abolitionist." *New England Quarterly* 6 (March 1933): 154–58.

Slater, William M. "Emerson's Views of Society and Reform." *International Journal of Ethics* 13 (July 1903): 414–21.

Small, Edwin W.; and Miriam R. Small. "Prudence Crandall: Champion of Negro Education." *New England Quarterly* 17 (December 1944): 506–29.

Spindler, George Washington. *Karl Follen: A Biographical Study*. Chicago: University of Chicago Press, 1917.

Stampp, Kenneth M. *And the War Came: The North and the Secession Crisis, 1860–1861*. Chicago: University of Chicago Press, 1968.

Stanton, William. *The Leopard's Spots: Scientific Attitudes Toward Race in America 1815–59*. Chicago: The University of Chicago Press, 1966.

Stanton, George A. *The First Parish in Waltham, An Historical Sketch*. Boston, 1914.

Studley, Marian H. "An 'August First' in 1844." *New England Quarterly* 16 (December 1943): 567–77.

Sykes, Richard E. "The Changing Class Structure of Unitarian Parishes in Massachusetts, 1780–1880." *Review of Religious Research* 12 (Fall 1970): 25–34.

Taylor, Jr., Lloyd C. " 'Reader, I Beseech You' A study of Lydia Maria Child's 'Appeal.' " *Negro History Bulletin* 20 (December 1956): 53–55.

Thomas, John L. *The Liberator: William Lloyd Garrison*. Boston: Little, Brown and Co., 1963.

———. "Romantic Reform in America, 1815–1865." *American Quarterly* 17 (Winter 1965): 656–81.

———. *Slavery Attacked: The Abolitionist Crusade*. Englewood Cliffs, N.J.: Prentice-Hall, 1965.

Thomas, John Wesley, ed. *The Letters of James Freeman Clarke to Margaret Fuller.* vol. 2. Britannica et Americana. Hamburg: Cram, de Gruyter and Co., 1957.

Thompson, Ralph. "The Liberty Bell and Other Anti-Slavery Gift Books." *New England Quarterly* 7 (March 1934): 154–68.

Treasures New and Old: A Memorial to James Freeman Clarke. Boston: American Unitarian Association, [1910?].

Van Tassel, David D. "Gentlemen of Property and Standing: Compromise Sentiment in Boston in 1850." *New England Quarterly* 23 (September 1950): 307–19.

Ware, Ethel K. "Lydia Maria Child and Anti-Slavery." *Boston Public Library Quarterly* 3 (October 1951): 251–75; 4 (January 1952): 34–49.

Wells, Anna Mary. *Dear Preceptor: The Life and Times of Thomas Wentworth Higginson.* Boston: Houghton Mifflin Co., 1963.

Wilbur, Earl Morse. *A Historical Sketch of the Independent Congregational Church, Meadville, Pennsylvania, 1825–1900.* Meadville, Pa., 1902.

Williams, George Huntston. *The Harvard Divinity School: Its Place in Harvard University and in American Culture.* Boston: The Beacon Press, 1954.

Wright, Conrad. *The Beginnings of Unitarianism in America.* Boston: Beacon Press, 1966 [1st ed., 1955].

———. *The Liberal Christians: Essays on American Unitarian History.* Boston: Beacon Press, 1970.

Wyatt-Brown, Bertram. "Abolitionism: Its Meaning for Contemporary Reform." *Midwest Quarterly* 8 (October 1966): 41–55.

———. *Lewis Tappan and the Evangelical War Against Slavery.* Cleveland, Ohio: Case Western Reserve University Press, 1969.

Zuck, Lowell H. "The American Anti-slavery Movement in the Churches before the Civil War." *Zeitschrift fuer Religions- und Geistesgeschichte* 17 (1965): 353–64.

F. THESES AND UNPUBLISHED MATERIALS

Brennan, Sister Thomas Catherine. "Thomas Wentworth Higginson: Reformer and Man of Letters." Ph.D. dissertation, Michigan State University, 1958.

Colville, Derek Keith. "James Freeman Clarke: A Practical Transcendentalist and His Writings." Ph.D. dissertation, Washington University, 1953.

Denton, Charles Richard. "American Unitarians, 1830–1865: A Study of Religious Opinion on War, Slavery, and the Union." Ph.D. dissertation, Michigan State University, 1969.

Glick, Wendell. "Thoreau and Radical Abolitionism: A Study of the Native Background of Thoreau's Social Philosophy." Ph.D. dissertation, Northwestern University, 1950.

Harwood, Thomas Franklin. "Great Britain and American Antislavery," Ph.D. dissertation, University of Texas, 1959.

Katz, Seymour. "The Unitarian Ministers of Boston, 1790–1860." Ph.D. dissertation, Harvard University, 1961.

Martin, John H. "The Unitarians and Slavery." B.D. thesis, University of Chicago Divinity School, 1954.

Ohrenstein, Edward W. "Samuel Joseph May: Unitarian Minister and Social Radical." B.D. thesis, Meadville Theological School, 1937.

Perry, Lewis Curtis. "Antislavery and Anarchy: A Study of the Ideas of Abolitionism Before the Civil War." Ph.D. dissertation, Cornell University, 1967.

Ravitz, Abe Carl. "John Pierpont: Portrait of a Nineteenth Century Reformer." Ph.D. dissertation, New York University, 1955.

Weeks, Louis Bonzano, III. "Theodore Parker: The Minister as Revolutionary." Ph.D. dissertation, Duke University, 1970.

Index